Fit f

LIVE
and love
TO BE
100

LIVE *and love* TO BE 100

160 natural ways to reverse the aging process and live a longer, more vital life.

DR. DONALD J. SALLS

Published by

CRANE HILL
PUBLISHERS

2923 Crescent Avenue
Birmingham, Alabama 35209

Published by Crane Hill Publishers
First edition, first printing, May 1995

Library of Congress Cataloging-in-Publication Data

Salls, Donald J., 1919-
    Live and love to be 100 : 160 natural ways to reverse the aging process
    and live a longer, more vital life / Donald J. Salls -- 1st ed..
         p.   cm.
    Includes bibliographical references (p.   ).
    ISBN 1-881548-56-2
    1. Health.   2. Nutrition.   3. Longevity.   I. Title..
RA776.S26   1995
613–dc20   95-12295
                                CIP

Crane Hill Publishers
2923 Crescent Avenue
Birmingham, Alabama 35209

Contents

To my friend,
my most beautiful, most loveable wife,
Diane;

our children,
Donna, Trisha, Cherie Dee, Tracy, and Mark;

and to Sue Vondracek of the *Anniston Star,*
Dr. Margaret Pope of Jacksonville State University,
and Regenia Reaves of Pleasant Valley High School.

Introduction

This book is about personal choices—the choices you make because your life is precious. It contains one hundred sixty natural ways to help you choose to preserve your precious health and live a longer, happier life.

The 1990s have brought about an increased awareness of fitness. Basic to that fitness is your cellular health—particularly your cellular immunity. Proper attitude, proper food, proper exercise, and proper nutrition can help you reach the 50 trillion cells in your body, taking charge of your cellular fitness for superior health and increased life expectancy.

But that is not to say this book is a substitute for your doctor. Always consult your physician before you make substantial changes in your lifestyle. Then use this book to expand your awareness of the long-life potential your body naturally holds by making the daily choices that will unlock your everlasting youth.

Dr. Donald J. Salls

Food

1.

"Let food be thy medicine."
*—Hippocrates, "Father of Medicine,"
450 B.C.*

2.

Lose weight by waiting a few minutes before you reach for a second helping.

3.

"My own remedy is always to eat, just before I step into bed, a hot roasted onion if I have a cold."

—Statement attributed to
George Washington

4.

Eat yogurt to help you sleep better at night.

5.

Count on carrots to help suppress bad cholesterol and raise good cholesterol.

6.

"There is no love sincerer than the love of food."

—*George Bernard Shaw,*
Man and Superman

7.

"To ensure health and longevity, eat a little ginger every day."

—Confucius, 500 B.C.

8.

"Adults and children can safely try ginger to thwart migraines."

—Dr. Krishna C. Srivastava,
Odense University, Denmark

9.

All nutrients work together for your total long-life benefit. If they're all present and accounted for, you'll feel good.

10.

New research underscores the enormous lifesaving power of fat in fish.

11.

Seafood eaters worldwide have less heart disease.

12.

For maximum health and longevity, eat fish two or three times a week.

13.

If you aren't getting enough natural
iodine, you'll know it. Iodine deficiency
can cause depression, an inability to
metabolize foods efficiently, and unex-
plained weight gain. Seaweeds, high in
iodine, can help you overcome these
problems.

14.

Sprouts give you more vitamins and minerals than other foods.

15.

Eat alfalfa sprouts, a super food even supermarkets supply, and your lease on life can be longer because your heart will be hardier.

16.

Sprouts supply a "40-and-feeling-good" substance called aspartic acid that provides a "natural high."

17.

According to Dr. Benjamin Frank, biochemist and rejuvenation expert, a diet based on fermented foods, such as sauerkraut, and nucleic acid foods, such as sardines, can cause "an elderly person to look and feel 10 to 12 years younger."

18.

To improve the fiber level of bread, toast it.

19.

Contrary to popular belief, one does not need meat and dairy products for proper nutrition.

20.

To stay slim, eat a high-fiber (low-sugar) cereal with skim milk.

21.

"Always have color on your plate" is an old wives' saying predating the Christian era. This bit of folk wisdom means eating green, yellow, and red vegetables for health.

22.

Include five or more servings of fruits and vegetables in your diet every day.

23.

Apples and other foods high in soluble fiber, called pectin, can help drive down your cholesterol levels.

24.

Fiber in your diet keeps things moving.

25.

For more fiber, eat whole-grain breads and rolls.

26.

To avoid becoming a victim of heartburn and its attacks, cut down on fatty foods.

27.

The idea that food can stave off asthma is very old. The Ebers Papyrus, an Egyptian medical text dating to 1550 B.C., prescribed grapes, figs, cumin, and sweet beer for asthma. Other foods that may relieve asthma include onions, garlic, fish oil, hot chili peppers, fruits and vegetables rich in vitamin C, and coffee.

28.

Never shop for groceries when you are hungry.

29.

"From many surveys on the island of Crete, I have the impression that centenarians are common among farmers, whose breakfast is often only a wineglass of olive oil."

—Dr. Ancel Keys, renowned epidemiologist

30.

Food is the best source of vitamins and minerals.

31.

Olive oil is the good, heart-safe fat that acts like an antioxidant, protecting healthy cells from "wear and tear." It contains a monounsaturated fat that evidence suggests helps counteract cancer, lower blood pressure, reduce cholesterol, and prevent gallstones.

32.

Frozen or canned fruits and vegetables contain as much fiber as their raw counterparts.

33.

A Slavic treatment for sleeplessness uses a combination of two tablespoons of honey with the juice of a lemon and an orange.

34.

There's no question that adding potassium to the diet can lower blood pressure. Taking it away can raise it.

35.

You are the fat you eat—very quickly after you eat fat, it shows up in the membranes of your cells, where its metabolic fate is determined.

36.

Drink four to eight glasses of water every day.

37.

"Most people can lower cholesterol by eating two-thirds of a cup of oat bran cereal or one cup of beans per day."

—James Anderson, M.D., University of Kentucky School of Medicine

38.

Nuts are rich in fiber and monounsaturated olive oil-type fats, known to counteract heart disease.

39.

Hippocrates prescribed propolis (a resinous substance collected by bees from tree buds) as far back as 400 B.C. to help heal sores, ulcers, and wounds. Known as "nature's wonder drug," propolis is available today as a capsule, tablet, powder, or lozenge.

40.

The best live-longer root vegetables are carrots, potatoes, parsnips, celery, beets, horseradish, radishes, parsley root, celery root, turnips, jicama, garlic, and kohlrabi.

41.

Root vegetables—especially celery and beets—also increase your body's reserve of stay-young nucleic acids. Root vegetables are as high (or higher) in live-longer fiber and life-extension minerals than fruits and grains.

42.

The magic fiber in fruit flushes carcinogens from your body.

43.

Eat tuna, sardines, herring, and mackerel. These are desirable fatty fish.

44.

Choose tuna packed in water and sardines canned without oil, unless it is sardine oil, noted on the label as "sild."

45.

In the county in Georgia where Vidalia onions are grown, the stomach cancer rate is only half that of other Georgia counties, and one-third that of the rest of the United States, according to the National Cancer Institute.

46.

Vegetarians have the lowest rates of cardiovascular disease.

47.

Wheat bran has the best documented reputation as a formidable colon cancer fighter.

48.

According to rejuvenation expert Dr. Benjamin Frank, adding more nucleic acids in your diet should raise your immunity to respiratory problems, including colds and the flu.

49.

Stay-young note: Foods abundant in nucleic acids are a great defense against Father Time. Nucleic acid-rich foods include bran, spinach, asparagus, mushrooms, fish, chicken liver, onions, and oatmeal.

50.

The "right stuff" to keep strokes away is fruits and vegetables.

51.

"You either do or do not have a headache tendency. It is built-in and genetic. What you eat then, can influence that suscepti-bility, triggering headaches."

–Joel Saper, M.D.
   Clinical Professor of Medicine,
   Michigan State University

52.

Foods that can trigger headaches for those with the tendency are ham, bacon, hot dogs, and salami, to name a few.

53.

Trying to shake that blood-pressure-raising salt habit? Start with your salt-shaker, says a group of researchers from Australia. They found that the size and number of the holes in the shaker can have a dramatic effect on the amount of salt sprinkled on food at the table.

54.

Of all the refined foods we eat, perhaps none is so damaging as sugar.

55.

The link between sugar and impaired immune functioning has been established by a number of studies.

56.

Sugar is the Number 1 junk food in America.

57.

"To keep your bones strong, try drinking pineapple juice or eating other foods high in the trace mineral manganese."

–Dr. Jeanne Freeland-Graves,
Professor of Nutrition,
University of Texas at Austin

Exercise

58.

"Those who think they have no time for bodily exercise will sooner or later have to find time for illness."

–Edward Stanley, 15th Earl of Derby

59.

"Walking three miles in an hour helps you develop good muscle tone and it metabolizes a lot of fat."

–F. S. Goulart

60.

Simple as it seems, walking actually involves the synchronization of many of the body's more than 200 bones, over 650 muscles, and some 70,000 miles of circulatory channels.

61.

Walking keeps you slim and trim without pain.

62.

Walking is the least demanding and probably the most rewarding of all the indoor/outdoor activities you can do after 40. And it may be the only one you can keep doing well into your golden years.

63.

Walk every day at a brisk gait, and mile for mile, you can burn as many calories as jogging.

64.

Practice good posture when walking for a more efficient stride. Keep your head high, your back erect, and tuck in your buttocks.

65.

Walking may be the best way to prevent senility.

66.

Regular exercise produces very small charges of electricity that help remineralize bones, making them harder, denser, and more resistant to breaking.

67.

Exercise properly and you will probably look younger than your age.

68.

"A journey of a thousand miles starts with the first step."

−Lao Tsu Te Ching,
Chinese philosopher

69.

Skipping rope reduces tension, raises energy levels, and works like a charm to produce post-30 fitness quickly.

70.

Doctors, coaches, and sufferers agree that
the fastest, surest cure for a cramp is to
stretch the affected muscles.

71.

It pays to develop muscles. They burn
more calories than fat.

72.

Exercise keeps you in "nitrogen balance"
as you age.

73.

The best all-around long-life activity?
Swimming.

74.

"Your older but better brain benefits when you keep your body moving."

–Richard E. Dustman,
Research Psychologist,
Veterans Administration,
Salt Lake City

75.

Exercise reduces depression and anxiety better than drugs.

76.

Being a busy-body slows down middle-age spread by keeping pounds in the right place.

77.

Swimming is advised for people whose joints have stiffened with age or arthritis.

Vitamin A
(Beta-Carotene)

78.

Vitamin A itself has limited antioxidant properties. The more powerful form of vitamin A is beta-carotene, which acts as an antioxidant and is protective against many forms of cancer. Antioxidants are important because they protect your healthy cells from the damage caused by toxic levels of oxygen that damage cells.

79.

"Beta-carotene finds its way into the membranes of all body cells."

–Norman Krinsky, Biochemist,
Tufts University Medical School

80.

Unlike vitamin A, which has limited antioxidant properties, beta-carotene is among the most powerful antioxidant nutrients. As such, it can help guard against the development of cancer cells. Antioxidants protect your cells from many other diseases, too.

81.

Of the 563 carotenoids that give fruits and vegetables their yellow pigment, beta-carotene is the most efficient source of vitamin A.

82.

Our intestinal cells reproduce so rapidly that they are completely replaced about once every three weeks. Vitamin A is absolutely essential for this process to occur correctly; this is true for all the 50 trillion cells in our bodies.

83.

Vitamin A is essential for the development of all tissue, but it is especially critical for the eye tissue.

84.

Good sources of vitamin A and beta-carotene include pumpkin, olive oil, alfalfa, papaya, sweet potato, cantaloupe, butternut squash, apricots, collard greens, carrots, spinach, and broccoli.

85.

What vitamin A does for your eye development, it does for all tissues throughout your life.

Vitamin C

86.

As an antioxidant, vitamin C's primary role is to neutralize free radicals. Free radicals are molecules missing an electron; they occur naturally in your body and in certain foods. Their purpose is to attack foreign bodies but when too many of them are produced, they will attack healthy cells.

87.

Much like the immune system itself, which operates at a cellular level, the hardworking vitamin C reaches every cell of the body.

88.

Vitamin C hastens wound healing. Faced with trauma, the body's stores of vitamin C are rapidly depleted. Possibly as a part of the effort of being mobilized to fight injury, vitamin C goes directly to the site of the injury.

89.

Over the years, many studies have found that vitamin C is an effective anticancer agent.

90.

Lettuce is good for lots of vitamin C, and according to California dermatologist Dr. Harry Daniell: "It is likely that relatively high doses of this antioxidant vitamin can help to slow the aging process in general, including a retardation of skin wrinkling."

91.

If you eat the white inner rind of oranges or grapefruits, you'll be getting extra vitamin C, bioflavonoids, pectin, and potassium.

92.

Lets not knock potatoes. A medium baked spud with its skin has 944 milligrams of potassium (almost half of what adults require), 30 milligrams of vitamin C (half the RDA), and 4 grams of fiber, about a third of what many people get in a day.

93.

The bioflavonoids (sometimes called "vitamin P") strengthen the tiny capillaries throughout the body, making them less permeable.

Vitamin E

94.

The scientists who discovered vitamin E in 1922 named it tocopherol, a Greek word meaning "the ability to reproduce."

95.

We find vitamin E in all cells of the body. In each of our 50 trillion cells, vitamin E is an integral part of the cell membrane.

96.

While it is true that vitamin E aids the reproductive organs—and even helps cells to reproduce themselves correctly—this nutrient has many other talents that deserve recognition.

97.

As an antioxidant, vitamin E can help prevent premature aging, which gets its start at the cellular level.

98.

Vitamin E strengthens both the minor-league capillaries and the major-league deep veins, which in turn tune up whole-body circulation, according to the Shute Foundation in Canada, pioneers in vitamin E therapy.

99.

Vitamin E also keeps arteries clean and clear of the fats and peroxides that promote clots and atherosclerosis.

100.

Vitamin E deficiency is often a cause of varicose veins, a circulatory condition that's likely to cramp your style if you're over 30 and eating from the wrong side of the menu.

101.

To benefit the most, take your vitamin E in the morning and your iron at night. This will prevent the neutralizing effect they may exert on each other.

102.

The only nutritional way to prevent the onset of age spots is with vitamin E, and wheat germ oil happens to be the best natural source of vitamin E.

103.

Cell membranes are the first line of defense against toxic agents, i.e., free radicals and superoxides.

104.

Vitamin E is a protector in our fight against toxic agents. Other good sources of E include sunflower seeds, almonds, peanuts, peanut butter, boiled lobster, broiled salmon steak, corn oil, and pecans.

105.

Vitamin E protects the cell membrane from attack by free radicals and super-oxides.

Vitamin B-Complex

106.

The B-complex vitamins are essential to growth, reproduction, energy, and a healthy immune system.

107.

Do you need a B-vitamin brewer's yeast boost? Take a look at your tongue. If it's blue or white and lacy around the edges, you're deficient in the B vitamins that brewer's yeast is rich in.

108.

In addition to the B vitamins, brewer's yeast also provides trace minerals and amino acids.

109.

A few of the best sources of B-complex are brewer's yeast, wheat germ, organ meats (liver, kidney, heart, etc.), egg yolk, and nuts.

Garlic

110.

Eating garlic regularly can deter artery clogging and, more remarkably, even reverse the damage, helping heal your arteries.

−Arun Bordia, Cardiologist, Tagore Medical College, India

111.

Onions and garlic are good for your health.

112.

Without garlic we'd have no pyramids—
the colossal wonders of the ages were
built by slaves fed with great quantities
of garlic.

113.

Garlic is a champion carrier of antioxidants, containing at least fifteen different
antioxidant chemicals.

114.

Garlic is one of nature's strongest, most complex, broad-spectrum antibacterial agents.

115.

Count on garlic to stimulate immune functioning.

116.

Add a little garlic and/or ginger to your pot of beans or other gaseous vegetables. Both are reputed in folk medicine to be antiflatulents.

Zinc

117.

It takes zinc to think! According to British physician Roy Hullin, M.D., the difference between a sharp mind and a fuzzy one could depend on the amount of zinc in your diet.

118.

The trace mineral zinc operates on many levels to support the immune system.

119.

After selenium, zinc is number two on your life-extending shopping list. Zinc is a constituent of nearly 100 human enzymes involved in all the body's major metabolic processes.

120.

Take zinc-C lozenges when you feel a cold coming on.

121.

Some good natural sources of zinc include raw oysters, cooked chicken heart, cooked calf liver, braised beef liver, lean cooked lamb, tuna in oil, and dark turkey meat.

Magnesium

122.

According to the American Medical Association, 40 percent of all fatal heart attacks may be caused by coronary spasms caused by magnesium deficiency.

123.

Magnesium is essential to energy metabolism after age 30.

124.

Doctors have shown that magnesium may play a key role in the treatment of the potentially dangerous condition of arrhythmia, or irregular heartbeat.

125.

Magnesium also helps prevent kidney stones, gallstones, and calcium deposits.

126.

Stay-young note: One-quarter cup of brown rice supplies 88 milligrams of magnesium, which makes it a healthier magnesium-booster than peanut butter, apricots, or Swiss chard.

127.

Other good sources of magnesium include pineapple juice, bananas, and mangoes.

Calcium

128.

Ninety-nine percent of the calcium in your body is found in your bones and teeth. Maintaining the remaining one percent in other compartments of your body is so important that if there is not enough calcium in your diet, your body will remove calcium from your bones to meet bodily requirements.

129.

Calcium is one of the nutrients most frequently lacking in diets after age 30.

130.

"Yogurt is just about a panacea for women. It boosts immunity, delivers lots of available calcium, and helps prevent vaginitis."

–George Halpern, M.D.,
University of California at Davis

131.

The American Heart Association recommends a daily intake of two or more cups of skim milk or skim milk products.

Outlook

132.

"Have a happy day. Dissatisfaction with life increases your risk of premature death by at least 10 percent."

—Holistic Health Federation

133.

Make friends. They are good for you.

134.

A healthy heart is found in a youthful body. If you've got one, you've got the other.

135.

Chances are, you are as good as you think you are.

136.

What you do this ten years, you will be the next ten years.

137.

Let go. Give your full potential to the world.

138.

Get a dog. "Talking to pets can reduce blood pressure."

> *–Dr. Aron Katcher,*
> *Associate Professor of Psychiatry,*
> *University of Pennsylvania*

139.

Volunteer. Give of yourself and live well with yourself.

140.

Reach out and touch someone; "The death rate is twice as high for men and three times higher for women who have the fewest friends."

–Dr. Leslie Breslau, The New York Times, *October 2, 1984*

141.

Worry less… heal faster.

142.

Your intuition can be your most powerful tool.

143.

Take time out. Find some private time just
for you.

144.

"Aging is a self-fulfilling prophecy, and only you can decide the kind of person you'll become."

–Walter Bortz, M.D.,
Runner's World

145.

You think your best in the morning.

146.

Thought about giving up smoking? Now is a good time.

Odds and Ends

147.

"By the time you are 74, you will have eaten the combined weight of six elephants."

–Boyd's Book of Odd Facts

148.

Married people are more content than single people.

149.

"Eighty percent fullness is good for the health."

–Japanese adage

150.

You can thank your parents for your height, your hair color, and your personality.

151.

If you know what is going on in your cells, you know what is happening to your health.

152.

Uptight? A hot shower that runs on the back of your neck and shoulders will help relax the muscles in that area.

153.

"To avoid or fight colds and flu bugs, eat a bowl of spicy chicken soup every day."

–Dr. Irwin Ziment,
Pulmonary Specialist, UCLA

154.

For a super laxative, try rice bran, a food-stuff long used in Asia and now found in many American food markets and health food stores.

155.

Every time you wash your face, follow with a rinse that removes everything you have put on it.

156.

Your senses are most acute in the late afternoon.

157.

The saying "you are all wet" is correct.
The adult is about 60 percent water.

158.

Colds can hang on for seven to ten days.

159.

You make love best in the morning.

160.

Marriage and a satisfactory sex life may contribute to a longer life.

Dr. Don's Prescription for Life-Prolonging Exercise

Through this daily program of motionless exercises, you can improve your physical fitness and figure without strenuous effort.

This kind of exercise is called isometric. It was developed and first popularized in the 1960s. The term isometric refers to the lack of muscle movement. Muscle is said to contract isometrically when its length doesn't change.

Follow these three simple isometric exercises daily and your muscles will grow stronger and healthier, and so will you.

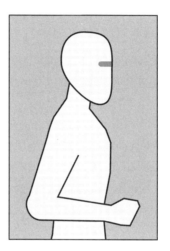

1.

The Six-Second
Waist Reducer

Stand erect with chin horizontal, chest high, and shoulder blades back. Draw in stomach muscles and contract. Try to picture the stomach muscles touching your backbone. Draw in and back as far as you can. Then hold this position for six seconds.

In a 21-day test of this once-a-day, six-second exercise, a solid majority experienced waist decreases ranging from a half-inch to as much as four inches.

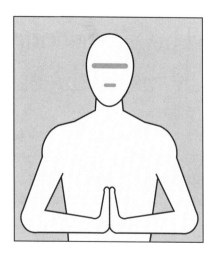

2.
The Six-Second Bust Exercise

Clasp your hands together, palm to palm, fingers interlocked. Keep elbows and hands at same level and forcefully push against each palm. Increase pressure until you feel a slight quiver. Hold this position for six seconds.

In a 21-day test of this once-a-day, six-second exercise, a solid majority experienced bust increases ranging from a quarter of an inch to as much as three inches.

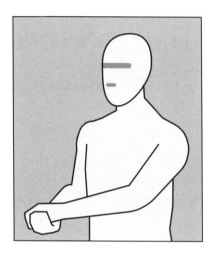

3.
The Six-Second Bicep Exercise

Bend the right arm at the elbow and extend arm with palm up. Use the left hand to press the right hand downward. Resist forcefully both ways until lower right arm and bicep muscles react by quivering lightly. Hold for six seconds. Repeat with the left arm.

In a 21-day test of this once-a-day, six-second exercise, a majority experienced desirable increases in bicep size ranging from one-half to one-and-one-half inches.

Postscript: Total Mind and Body Wellness

It is generally believed that vitamins and minerals and other nutrients can help prevent a wide variety of ailments. Nutrition from food and/or over-the-counter vitamins can help in this daily effort.

This plus a young and inquisitive mind and an attitude for strength and energy through daily activity means a more dynamic and attractive personality.

The fountain of youth is an attitude, every day, for healthful living by way of proper nutrition, exercise, and a joy for living.

Set your mind to live and love to be 100 and chances are good that you will!

Dr. Donald J. Salls

About the Author

Dr. Donald J. Salls is Professor Emeritus at Jacksonville State University in Jacksonville, Alabama, where he has been faculty member since 1946. During his tenure, Dr. Salls has taught health and physical education. He has also served as a football coach and an instructor in the university's college of education.

He is an inductee to the University's Athletic Hall of Fame, the Alabama Sports Hall of Fame, in Birmingham, Alabama, and to the Westchester County, New York, Hall of Fame in Mamaroneck, New York

In the 1960s, Dr. Salls published his *Ten Static Exercises,* and was a pioneer in the distribution of these isometric exercises in the United States and abroad.

Exercise, nutrition, and vitamins have played a major role in Dr. Salls life and his own remarkable vitality. Since his retirement, he has written and spoken widely on these subjects.

Bibliography

Carper, Jean, *Food - Your Miracle Medicine,* Harper Collins, New York, NY, 1993.

Comprehensive Home Medical Encyclopedia, Prevention's Giant Book of Health Facts, Wings Books, New York, NY, and Avenel, NJ, 1991.

Goulart, Frances Sheridan, *Staying Young,* Prentice Hall, Englewood Cliffs, NJ, 1987.

Null, Gary, & Feldman, Martin, *Reverse the Aging Process Naturally,* Villard Books, New York, NY, 1993.

Scala, James, *Eating Right for a Bad Gut,* Penguin Books, New York, NY, 1992.

Scala, James, *Prescription for Longevity,* Penguin Books, New York, NY, 1992.

The editors of the *Prevention* magazine health books:
> *Everyday Health Hints,* Rodale Press Inc., Emmaus, PA, 1985.

> *101 Age Remedies, The Prevention Guide to Reversing the Aging Process,* Rodale Press Inc., Emmaus, PA, 1988.

> *Positive Living,* Rodale Press Inc., Emmaus, PA, 1990.

The Complete Book of Vitamins and Minerals, Wings Books, New York, NY, and Avenel, NJ, 1988.

Glossary

antioxidant A chemical compound or substance that inhibits oxidation. (See *oxidation*.)

atherosclerosis A disease of the coronary arteries in which the arterial opening becomes narrower due to deposits of fat, cholesterol, and other substances on the inner lining of the artery.

beta-carotene A previtamin A compound found in plants. The body converts beta-carotene to vitamin A.

bioflavonoid Any of a group of biologically active substances found in plants and functioning in the maintenance of the walls of small blood vessels in mammals.

brewer's yeast Used as source of B-complex vitamins and also as a ferment in brewing.

bran The outer layers of the grain of cereals, such as wheat, removed during the process of milling and used as a source of dietary fiber.

carcinogen A cancer-causing substance or agent.

carotene   An orange-yellow to red pigment found in animal tissue and certain plants, such as carrots and squash. It is converted to vitamin A in the liver.

carotenoid   Any of a class of yellow to red pigments, including the carotenes and the xanthophylls.

cholesterol   A fatlike substance found in animal tissues and various foods, normally synthesized by the liver and important as a constituent of cell membranes. Its level in the bloodstream can influence certain conditions such as the development of atherosclerotic plaque and coronary artery disease.

fiber   An inert material found in certain foods that adds bulk to the diet and may help prevent colon problems.

free radical   An organic compound in which some of the molecules are missing an electron. Occurs as a normal byproduct of oxidation reactions in the metabolism. Free radicals attack foreign bodies in the human system, but if too many of them are produced, they will attack healthy cells. Antioxidants such as beta-carotene and vitamin C help prevent this.

gallstone A small, hard, pathological concretion, composed chiefly of cholesterol, calcium salts, and bile pigments, formed in the gallbladder or in a bile duct.

holism The theory that living matter is made up of unified wholes that are greater than the sum of their parts.

holistic Emphasizing the importance of the whole and the interdependence of its parts.

kidney stone A hard, small mass in the kidney that forms from deposits chiefly of phosphates and urates.

lipid Any of a group of organic compounds, including the fats, oils, waxes, sterols, and tryglycerides, oily to the touch, and together with carbohydrates and proteins constitute the principal structural material of living cells.

mineral Used to provide hardness to body tissues and to control chemical functions in the body.

nucleic acid Any of a group of complex compounds found in all living cells and viruses.

nutrients　Chemical substances obtained from food during digestion that build and maintain body cells, regulate body processes, and supply energy.

oxidation　Damage caused to healthy body cells by toxic levels of oxygen in the body. This process, similar to the way oxygen causes a car to rust, is triggered by the presence of too many free radicals in the body, and not enough antioxidants.

oxide　A binary compound of an element or a radical with oxygen.

pectin　Carbohydrates of high molecular weight found in ripe fruits and used to jell various foods, drugs, and cosmetics.

plaque　Deposits of fat, cholesterol, and other substances on the inner lining of arteries that cause the arterial opening to become narrower and thus restrict blood flow.

vaginitis　Inflammation of the vagina.

vitamins　Control chemical functions in the body.

xanthophyll A yellow carotenoid pigment found with chlorophyll in green plants.

cold baths don't work

A HISTORY OF MENTAL HEALTH CARE
IN THE HITCHIN AREA

by Mike Clarke

A HITCHIN HISTORICAL SOCIETY PUBLICATION

A HITCHIN HISTORICAL SOCIETY PUBLICATION 2011
http://www.hitchin historical.org.uk

© Hitchin Historical Society and Mike Clarke

ISBN: 978-0-9552411-6-1

Design, layout and photo-enhancing: Barrie Dack and Associates 01462 834640
Printed by: Olive Press, Stotfold, Hitchin, Herts, 01462 733333

Cover illustration:
Picture from Wellcome Library, London [L0003549]. Dated as 1230, but source uncertain. The bath, shower or douche, had many variations and uses for the attendants of the insane in the 18th and 19th centuries, and was in use for centuries before then. Cold baths were seen as helpful in calming the excited or violent patient, and the warm bath for reviving melancholics. Trials were done on pouring cold water on the head while the body was immersed in warm water. Cold water baths were at times used as punishment, but warm baths were used as part of the 'moral treatment' and were comforting for the distressed.

For the nervous and stressed there was the so called 'water cure' as advocated by Sir Edward Bulwer Lytton, preferably taken at Malvern under the care of an esteemed physician. The regime involved frequent baths as well as good intake of water, while avoiding the poisons of alcohol and those prescribed by other doctors, particularly mercury and iodine.

Inside front cover: Map of local area with the three counties provided for by the asylum, with locations of places named in the text

Half title page: Mortar and pestle, doubling as sundial, in the Physic Garden at Hitchin Museum Photo by author.
For more details see
http://www.hitchinhistoricals.org.uk/publications/physic_garden.php

Frontispiece: A corridor, Fairfield Hospital, circa 1985. Author's collection

Inside rear cover: The author's reproduction of a map of Hitchin circa 1900

Rear cover: Mortar and pestle in the Physic Garden at Hitchin Museum Photo by author. Mike Clarke 2011

cold baths don't work

Dedication

This book is dedicated to the memory of Frank Lappin and Bernard Mallett, who knew this corridor in Fairfield Hospital well. Bernard was appointed as Consultant to Fairfield in 1963 and wrote a very good account of the local mental health service soon after. He worked hard to set up the new service at the Lister Hospital. Frank was appointed 10 years later and spent much of his working time humanizing the institution and caring for his many patients. He was particularly interested in the history of Bedford and Three Counties Asylums. They were my close colleagues at the Lister Hospital when I arrived in 1981, and were loved and respected by all. Both contributed to the content of this book but sadly died before it was completed.

Contents

Acknowledgements

Many people have contributed in one way or another to this book. Some with information, some in proof reading, some in questioning and everybody in encouraging me. My thanks to all. Many have commented on the content and also my use of English and punctuation, to an extent that would shame my childhood teachers, but any errors or misinterpretations in the text are entirely my fault.

Particular thanks are due to Wendy Abondolo, Jean Boothby, Caroline Brownlie, Diana Ellis, Alan Fleck, David Heymans, Sukhwinder Kaur, Brian Limbrick MBE, Dana Maciejczak, Kevin Mason, Phil Mollon, Nick Parsons, Michael Ransom, Francis Russell, Andy Smith, Audrey Stewart, Joyce Taylor, Simon Walker, Richard Whitmore, and Diana Parrott of Harpenden & District Local History Society.

So much information is available through archives and I am grateful for both the availability and access to various sources, particularly to David Hodges and Hitchin Museum, Clare Fleck and Henry Cobbold at Knebworth House, James Collett-White and Bedfordshire and Luton Archives and Records Service, Gary Moyle and Hertfordshire Archives and Local Studies, the Hertfordshire Medical & Pharmaceutical Trust, the Royal College of Psychiatrists online archive of journals and to Harperbury Library in the Herts Partnership NHS Foundation Trust.

Illustrations from other sources – the Gardiner-Hill family, Laurie Hughes, Richard and Rosalyn Knight and the Three Counties Website, Terry Knight, Carola Scupham for the mortar and pestle drawing, Charles Whitbread, 'Together' for the portrait of Henry Hawkins, and Wellcome Library London.

Hitchin Historical Society is a wonderful organization and thanks are due for the support it has provided. This includes a stimulating programme and visits, organized by Stephen Bradford-Best, particularly to Southill Park and the Museum of the Royal Pharmaceutical Society.

Jeremy Chase, Bridget Howlett and Derek Wheeler MBE have been diligent and very helpful in reading the whole script and providing various suggestions. Barrie Dack has provided great expertise in the layout and design.

Dr Gerry Tidy has provided me with much material to incorporate, some at a late stage. When I thought that I had completed the necessary reading he turned up on my doorstep with a bag of 19 books, and wondered if that might be useful. I am particularly grateful to him for directing me to the work of William Drage, for writing the foreword and for his kind words.

Scilla Douglas and Pauline Humphries have from the beginning of this been wonderful collaborators. While I have mostly referred to them as the *"witches"* for their ability to exert influence by charms and all the dark secrets that they have accumulated over many years of producing books, their expertise, hard work, and remorseless encouragement have been great. Vicki Lockyer has joined this team during the year and I have valued her help.

As with anybody who has worked in the health service I have had many teachers, and many have been patients. I have worked in various teams and learnt from them all, and was very fortunate to work with the local assertive outreach team over recent years.

Throughout my life in psychiatry Ellie Clarke has supported and encouraged me and provided much needed counselling! That has continued through the various stages of this project and she has been ever helpful as I worked through ideas and chapters. It would not have been possible without her.

Centenary House in Hitchin, once the Quaker Meeting House, became the base for the Community Mental Health Team on 1993, the intention being to provide a local and accessible place where people could come for help. It later accommodated the Assertive Outreach Team where the author worked.

Foreword

Most disorders of the mind lie in the place between sadness and madness. They are with us always and so we can form a natural empathy with those gone before.

Each generation of doctors and administrators seek the understanding and means of controlling mental illness, often scoffing at their forbears as will be done to us. This is still not an exact science and as William Drage wrote *"disease doth oft above medicine climb"*. Dr Mike Clarke is remembered by colleagues and patients with affection and most noticeably for his compassion. He brings this and his professional experience to this book. This broad canvas covers centuries of the condition morphing from madness, lunacy, mental illness, psychiatry and back to mental health without shaking off its stigma. Here we have insight into how this well ordered but sleepy town and its surrounding parishes responded to changing times while occasionally taking centre stage. He recounts the Bulwer Lytton soap opera which was a media frenzy of its day.

Mike also gives us an account of the common folk whose footprints in the sands of time are faint.

Importantly Mike Clarke has given us an invaluable first hand account of the last three decades which saw institutional mental health care give way to care in the community. We all become history in the end but thank goodness for people who write it down for us.

It has been with pleasure and admiration that I have seen this book take shape. Petrarch the Italian scholar (1304 – 1374) wrote *"Books have led some to learning and others to madness."*

This book does both.

Dr Gerry Tidy

June, 2011

Introduction

This book started as an attempt to give an account of what had happened within the mental health services in North Herts (and Stevenage) over the 29 years I had worked in this area as a consultant in 'general psychiatry'. A young colleague had suggested that I give a talk before I retired in January 2010 about the old days, what it was like in 1981 when I started working in North Herts. When I thought about it I decided that while there might be some interest in the recent events and developments, it would be much more interesting to find out what was the history of providing mental health services in this area and to talk about what had happened in the really old days. I hope at the end you will find that it has also provided some further interest to the town of Hitchin and its surrounds.

The title derives in part from the recognition that in the past those that cared for the mentally ill may have had good intentions but the end result was not always beneficial. The methods were, with hindsight, lacking good evidence of being useful. There are still difficulties in finding effective ways of caring for and treating people with mental illness. Listening and learning from those who

The history of Three Counties Asylum was written before it closed in 1999. 'A Place in the Country' gave an account of the building and development in the 19th century and an oral history of various people who lived and worked there in the 20th century [1 – see notes]. Before it closed it provided a service for all of Bedfordshire as well as North Herts. It had once also been the asylum or mental hospital for the whole of Hertfordshire and Huntingdonshire.

Photo from author's collection.

experience such problems and being more critical about the treatments (using an 'evidenced based approach') has been part of the culture in mental health services over the past few decades, and I believe that has had a good effect.

In 1981 my contract stated that I was to spend 4 days each week at the Lister Hospital in Stevenage and one day at Fairfield Hospital in Arlesey (actually listed as in the parish of Stotfold), just over the border in Bedfordshire. The Lister Mental Health Unit was opened in 1973 but Fairfield had been in existence since 1860, then called the Three Counties Asylum (TCA). In 1981 patients, with a sudden onset or deterioration of a psychiatric disorder, were admitted to the Lister, but if they needed long term care or were too aggressive or too difficult to care for safely at the Lister, they were transferred to Fairfield. Before 1973 all patients would have gone to Fairfield, as they had done over the previous 113 years.

But what was happening before 1860? Bedford Asylum closed when TCA opened and had been in existence since 1812. A history of that institution had been written by Bedford surgeon, Bernard Cashman [2], but I was not clear how much that had been used by people from this area. As I read more I wondered how often people with severe mental illness had been cared for elsewhere, were they in the workhouse, or was there any 'community care' and support for them to live at home?

I had read little about the history of psychiatry and mental health care before the autumn of 2009 but then found a vast number of books that had explored the different aspects of asylum care and madhouses, the diagnosis and treatment of mental illness, and the rise of psychiatry or professional management of the mentally ill. What had not been written was what local care of the mentally ill in Hitchin and the surrounding area had been provided.

In writing I am aware of different potential audiences, some will be very familiar with local history but not with the world of asylums and mental health, and some will know all about the latter but not about local history in Hitchin. So, excuse me if I say things which you may find obvious, but I hope you find out things which you were not aware of and which you find as interesting as I have.

My focus is on the services for people with the more severe types of mental illness. I have not tried to unravel what people with anxiety and mild depression might have done in years gone by. I have not tried to address how the *"nicely nervous"*, as people with minor emotional problems in Sheffield were called, or the highly strung of Hitchin might cope. I have also not dealt with the world of counselling and psychotherapy. That is not to say that I do not value these activities. Much of the most valuable part of my training was in psychological therapies and the most interesting part of my 'continuing professional development' was to explore how psychotherapy could be used in daily practice. One of my most valued colleagues was an innovative psychotherapist who worked with the whole range of psychiatric disorders, and I am pleased to be involved in the Hitchin Counselling Service which offers free long term counselling. But I am no expert in these fields and they are not central to this story.

I have focussed more on what services the main body of the population received, what the NHS mainly provides now and what the paupers of the 18th and 19th centuries received. However as this is a local history I have been led astray somewhat by people and places that have local connections. There is a surprisingly rich array of connections for a small town and its surrounds, a 17th century apothecary William Drage, some 19th century reformers, Samuel Whitbread and Samuel Tuke, and Sir Edward Bulwer Lytton of Knebworth House.

Definitions

"The word lunatic, being derived from luna the moon, signifies moon-struck. Now that the theory is abandoned of the moon's having any influence over diseases of the brain, this word is become improper. It is a superstitious expression, which inculcates error, and tends to perpetuate incredulity." Monthly Magazine. 1810 [3].

In writing about what has become a specialist subject I know that terms may be in common usage for some but unfamiliar for others. I have already used various terms which I should define, such as mental illness and asylum. I also need to be careful as words can give offence and can add to stigma. Some of the terms I will use are those that were the technical terms for what was regarded as mental illness in the past but would be offensive now. So *"lunatic"* was a technical term for someone suffering from a severe mental illness or lunacy (lunasie in the 17th century). The Lunacy Laws were the Acts of Parliament governing the treatment of the mentally ill until 1930. The word came from 'lunar', relating to the moon, and refers to the observation that episodes of mental illness occurred on a repeated pattern, that some thought coincided with and were due to the phases of the moon. An alternative term to lunacy was 'phrensie', frenzy being the modern spelling with the same root as frenetic and frantic, and schizophrenia having the same Greek root, 'phren' meaning mind. The Greeks did think the mind was in the heart and 'phren' first meant the midriff or diaphragm. An interchangeable term from the 16th century was 'insane', meaning 'not of sound mind'.

'Mental illness' is the term often used now. Some dispute that this is an appropriate use of the word illness, as some conditions do not have the same link to a physical abnormality of the body that is evident in say cancer or diabetes, and 'mental disorder' is an alternative. All mental disorders can vary from mild to severe in degree and in how they affect a person's everyday functioning. But the term 'severe mental illness' usually refers to schizophrenia and the more severe degrees of bipolar disorder (previously called manic depressive disorder). 'Psychosis' is a term used for severe mental illness, usually signifying that the person experiences symptoms such as hallucinations or false perceptions such as hearing voices (the recently introduced term 'voice hearers' is more user friendly) or delusions, being false beliefs that are held despite rational explanations to disprove them.

Services for the mentally ill are usually called 'mental health services', which does give some positive feel about it. But 200 years ago the severely mentally ill were called either insane or mad, and the services available were the mad-doctors in the madhouses. The term mad-doctor was used, perhaps unkindly, in the days when doctors were an unregulated group of people, known as apothecaries, physicians or surgeons. They would often have had an apprenticeship or training, and colleges evolved for each of these three groups, but the level of training was not agreed between them. Apothecaries had evolved from the traders in spices and peppers, then grocers, 'apotheca' being a shop where wine, spices and herbs were stored, and were the traders in medicinal and pharmaceutical products [4]. They were originally located in Bucklersbury in London. The original street in London where this trade went on was called Bokerelesbury, deriving from the name of a 13th century family who owned property there [5] (there seems to be no known connection with the same street name in Hitchin). The Society of Apothecaries separated from the grocers in 1617, though continued to trade in non perishable goods such as spices, and was granted the right to examine and license doctors in 1815. The Royal College of Physicians was founded in 1518, and in 1774 they were entrusted with the licensing and inspection of mad-houses in the metropolitan area. The regulation or nationwide recognition of whether a person was appropriately qualified to practise as a doctor did not occur until 1858.

The 'mad-doctors', known more respectably as 'alienists' in the 19th century (dealing with an alienated rather than an abolished mind), had a form of apprenticeship and learnt on the job, but they did develop some specialist knowledge of the 'mad'. They probably claimed more insight and knowledge of how to treat such problems than they actually had. When the new hospitals for the mentally ill were established (1751 onwards) they were called 'asylums' and in due course the doctors in them became known as 'asylum doctors'. The first organization of doctors working with the mentally ill (established 1841) was called the 'Association of Medical Officers of Asylums and Hospitals for the Insane' and it produced the Asylum Journal of Mental Science from 1853, dropping the 'Asylum' bit in 1859. The first journal in this field however was the Journal of Psychological Medicine and Mental Pathology in 1848. The asylum doctors joined forces with those working outside the asylums and their organization became the Medico Psychological Association (MPA) in 1865, adding the Royal prefix (RMPA) in 1926. They had arrived!

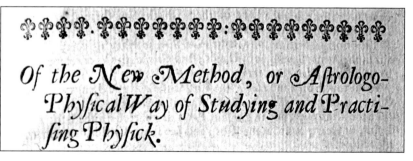

Of the New Method, or Astrologo-Physical Way of Studying and Practising Physick.

Apothecaries dispensed plant extracts to cure diseases. The Hitchin apothecary, William Drage, believed in the influence of the stars in causing those same diseases.
Page heading from Drage's 1664 book. Collection of Dr Gerry Tidy

Psychiatry was first used as a term in 1808 [6] and became the name for this speciality of medicine by the end of the 19th century, and psychiatrists became the name of the practitioners. The Royal College of Psychiatrists replaced the RMPA in 1971 and their publication became the British Journal of Psychiatry. Psychiatrists differ from psychologists in various ways but particularly in being medically qualified and able to prescribe medication. Psychotherapists and counselling psychologists have had special training in one or more of various forms of therapy (including the much recommended cognitive behaviour therapy). Psychoanalysts have undergone the rigorous training and supervision which includes a long period of being analysed themselves.

Other terms which were in use but have become redundant are those applied to people with learning disability. The term commonly used was 'idiocy', meaning a severe learning disability. This was used alongside 'imbecility', a term indicating a lesser degree of disability, but also used at times for people with dementia. The mildest form was called 'feeble mindedness'. These three terms were defined in the Mental Deficiency Act of 1913. 'Mental defect' was replaced by the term 'mental subnormality' in 1959, but the formal diagnoses are still termed 'mental retardation'. Most services for such people have been titled as 'learning disability' services for many years. I have retained the use of such a word as 'idiocy' or 'lunatic' if they were in use at the time I am describing.

Another term I will use is 'patient'. There has been a long running debate about whether people who finish up seeing psychiatrists or being helped by mental health services should be called this. When trying to build community teams with social services there was a strong push to call patients 'clients'. 'Patients' does emphasise the medical nature of the encounter when much of the help may be more appropriately thought of as social, helping dealing with stress, relationships or housing. Another term used is 'service user' and preferred by some, but disliked by others [7]. Overall most people seem not too bothered about which term, it is whether they receive personal and effective care that is more important.

Delving into the past

The books about Bedford and Three Counties Asylums have been very useful about what happened after 1812, but there is little direct information on what was done for people suffering from mental illness before then in the Hitchin area. Much has been written nationally and books by Roy Porter, Andrew Scull and William Llewellyn Parry-Jones and others will be referred to frequently. The website of Andrew Roberts (www. studymore.org.uk) also has a wealth of information. Various archives have also been searched and will be referred to in the Notes. Some of the history is linked to buildings in or near Hitchin, but although some of the linkage is speculative, I hope it is accepted as reasonable. Some of the documents from the distant past have not survived, and some of the documents from the recent past are not accessible, due to rules about the access to patients' notes over the past 100 years. So this is not a complete account but I hope it will be good enough to understand how things have happened over the years.

Mental health care then and now

Patricia Allderidge, the archivist at England's most famous, and infamous, mental hospital Bethlem (once called Bedlam), wrote in 1979 that care has just gone in cycles, or round in circles, and that it has all been done before [8]. There are some traces of such cycles, the 'trade in lunacy' with private mad-houses in the 18th century and the marketing of private rehabilitation units in the recent past (and to avoid any sense of criticism I am sure there were some very good mad-houses in the past!), the call for a half way house between home and the asylum in the 19th century and the suggestions of modern crisis preadmission facilities. What has been true of all ages is that the families and friends of those suffering from some form of mental disorder often provide the most help and for the longest period. This book does not deal with that private and usually undocumented contribution, which cannot be underestimated.

While some aspects of mental illness and its care have moved on, there is still a widespread stigma about the problem and the people who experience it first hand. Various campaigns have and are still being held to reduce such stigma. Increased knowledge about the care and treatment and the stories of various successful people who have suffered from such problems have been extremely useful. I hope that this book does make some sense of the mysterious world of psychiatry, and that the mental health care that is available becomes a little more understandable and less scary.

Mike Clarke   June 2011

Notes

1. Pettigrew, Reynolds and Rouse. 'A Place in the Country. Three Counties Asylum 1860 – 1998'. South Bedfordshire Community Health Care Trust. 1998
2. Cashman, Bernard. 'A Proper House. Bedford Lunatic Asylum : 1812 – 1860'. North Beds Health Authority 1992.
3. 'The Portfolio of a Man of Letters'. Monthly Magazine and British Register. vol 30. Part 2. August 1st 1810. p 434
4. www.apothecaries.org
5. www.british-history.ac.uk/report.aspx?compid=63055#s10
6. Shorter, Edward. . 'A History of Psychiatry'. John Wiley. 1997. p 17
7. Simmons , Peter et al. 'Service user, patient, client, user or survivor: describing recipients of mental health services'. The Psychiatrist, Jan 2010; 34: p 20 – 23
8. British Journal of Psychiatry. 1979. 134. p 321 - 34

Apothecaries, Asylums and the Trade in Lunacy

1

The early history of the care of the mentally ill in England starts with the Priory of St Mary of Bethlehem. This was founded in 1247 and was later known as Bedlam ('bedlam' meaning uproar, deriving from the asylum) but more respectably in modern times as Bethlem Hospital (the names seemed to be used interchangeably at different times and that may be reflected in this text). Many religious houses of that time would set up some care for the infirm. By 1377 this priory cared mostly for the insane, though the reasons for this are unclear. It was located in Bishopsgate in London and probably responded to what was an unmet need, though the number of the insane housed there was less than 10 at the beginning of the 15th century. After the dissolution of the monasteries by Henry VIII the administration was passed by the King to the City of London, and it was from 1557 administered jointly with Bridewell, a house of correction, or prison [1].

By the 18th century Bedlam had become notorious, it was a 'brown sign' site, tourists were welcome and apparently encouraged. Hogarth's famous portrayal of the Rake's progress, really regress, shows him at the end stage of a social decline and eventually committed there. The painting shows society ladies gazing on while the Rake sits amongst the other outcast of society. Bedlam expanded with a move to Moorfields in 1676 and then in 1815 moved to Lambeth, the building now being used as the Imperial War Museum.

Other hospitals at the time looked after the insane. Holy Trinity Hospital in Salisbury had a foundation deed from the 14th century which included the statement *"the mad are kept safe until they are restored to reason"*. It is likely that other religious houses had similar aims for the mentally infirm. Hertfordshire probably had ten medieval hospitals, but little documentation of their activities and responsibilities have survived. There were hospitals at Royston, Stevenage and Little Wymondley but nothing recorded in Hitchin [2,3].

There are no records surviving about any medical care in the religious houses in Hitchin but it is possible that the two priories would have somehow cared for the infirm in the area. The Biggin's history is still being explored and although the

The internal courtyard of the Biggin, in Biggin Lane just across the river from St Mary's Church. It was a Gilbertine priory until the dissolution of the monasteries in 1538. It was then in private hands and was substantially rebuilt in 1585. It became a school in 1635 and then almshouses in 1723 and modernized in 1960.

Postcard Circa 1904

archaeological studies indicate that the building originated in the 14th century, and that the main priory building probably had a number of outbuildings attached, there is no record of what these were used for[4]. It is possible that it had a role in providing health care for local residents, but in the absence of contemporary records this is quite speculative!

There is similarly little known about the use of the Carmelite priory which survives in Bridge Street. The services offered by the religious houses mostly stopped in the 1530s when Henry VIII led the revolt against the Catholic church to help his own marital arrangements. The monasteries were dissolved and sacked and the care system they offered was dismantled. The Biggin and the Priory became private residences. The care available after that outside of the family and friends was still based on the church, now the Church of England, and the parish-based poor law took over. This offered local help for the poor and the infirm, and the lunatics and idiots would have been cared for through that. This is described in chapter 2.

Understanding madness in the 17th century — William Drage, the Hitchin apothecary.

I think it is not unfair or untrue to say that many people now do not understand what mental illness is and that includes those of us who have worked in this field. It is complex and very personal and every 'patient' is different. However, there are certain symptoms or collections of symptoms which become recognizable, *"I recall somebody else saying something like that"*. Knowledge accumulates and in medical disciplines that leads to the identification of diseases and then, by hook or by crook, the discovery of treatments. A bit later we try to work out if there is good evidence if that treatment really does work and if it does so whether it causes any nasty side effects or not.

Someone who tried to make sense of all medical conditions, using the current theories on how disease happened, was an apothecary living in Hitchin, named William Drage [5,6]. He was born in 1636 and moved to Hitchin in 1658. He read widely and wrote about a large number of medical cases that he had seen. He died in 1668 and was buried at St Mary's Church. His achievements and fame are remarkable for one who lived so short a life.

Drage published a medical textbook in 1664 titled 'A Physical Nosonomy or a True Description of the Law of God (called NATURE) in The BODY of MAN' which contained his views on madness and *"lunasie"*. A subsequent edition in 1668, has the title of 'Physical Experiments'. While accepting the old theories about the four humours and the new theories about the astrological causes of disease he emphasised the need for careful observations of patients, and attention to symptoms rather than just the astrological chart.

In the first edition of his book published in 1664 (printed by J Dover) he gives a general view of the causes of diseases in his prologue, the 'Monitory Promium to the Reader':-

> *"It is the casual influence of the Planets... upon our Blood and Humours, and as the quantity and quality of our Blood and Humours, and as our Blood and humours vary, so the stars act variously: for the Agent can do nothing, if the Patient is not fit; and one Planet doth not so powerfully alter one man's body as anothers, because in one it was the Significator at his Nativity, in the other of his Fortune, in another a Significator of his Religion at his Nativity; and so though our Humours and Constitutions are much alike, yet in this respect the Planets vary".*

The four humours, being bodily fluids of blood, phlegm, yellow bile or choler, and black bile, were seen by the ancient Greeks as needing to be in balance to stay healthy. An excess of any one caused disease. Hippocrates (circa 460 – 377 BC) emphasised the need for equilibrium, as was also needed between the four elements of air, fire, earth and water, between the four qualities of hot, dry, cold and wet and the four ages of man, infancy, youth, adulthood and old age. Galen (AD 129 – circa 216) wrote

> P H Y S I C A L
> EXPERIMENTS:
> Being a Plain
> DESCRIPTION
> Of the
> Caufes, Signes, and Cures
> Of moft Difeafes incident to the
> Body of Man.
> To which is added a Difcourfe of Difeafes proceeding from VVitchcraft,
>
> Faithfully Collected from Ancient and Modern Writers, and partly Experimented by WILLIAM DRAGE, Practitioner in Phyfick at Hitchin in Hartford-fhire.
>
> LONDON,
> Printed for Simon Miller at the Star, next the George in Little-Britain, 1668.

Title page of Drage's 1668 edition, from the collection of Reginald Hine in Hertfordshire Archives [7].

prolifically and his name is attached to the system of medicine that was prominent until the 19th century [8]. So melancholy, similar to what we now call depression, was due to an excess of black bile. Mania, a state of excitement, was due to an excess of yellow bile. Keeping these fluids in balance led to the treatments that were then seen as rational, of bleeding and purging and draining the yellow fluid or pus from open wounds which the physicians created. Mania was also seen as the result of hotness, so cooling of the body was advised.

Drage accepted these theories but said that the planets had an effect on the humours, the effect varying depending on where the planets were on your birth date. He explains his understanding of the moon's part in this, with evidence of the timing of deaths caused by plague in Hitchin, and explains the mechanism of the moon's pull on fluids in the body:-

"Concerning the alteration of the Diseases, changing of Symptoms, and of all diseased Parts, dying and growing sick, it is apparently seen in some Diseases by the alteration of the Moon, and divers have told me, That when the Plague did rage in this Town of Hitchin, most fell sick or died at change of the Moon, or full Moon, and four or five were buried then together, and when the moon was at her full state, was the sickness in many in its Crisis or Exaltation: and it is apparent to many intelligent Physicians, that our Bodies are fuller of moisture at full Moon, than other times... Now we know the Moon rules over Moisture much, witness the Ebbing and Flowing of the Sea...".

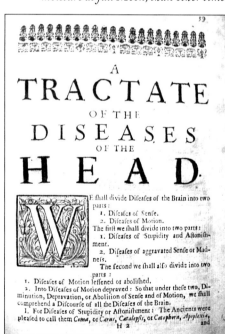

From the 1664 edition of 'A Physical Nosonomy' by William Drage. Collection of Dr Gerry Tidy

The sun has its effect on mad people:-
"Many mad People do chiefly rage when the Sun is in the Tropical point Cancer; and about the Summer Solstice, partly the heat, and partly the quality of the Air, makes divers mad in Summer, that are pretty well all the year beside...".

The planets also cause stress and accidents which upset us:-
"the Planets operate upon our Mindes, not only by moving, increasing and altering the quality of our Humours ... but by raising Contingents and intervening Accidents".

The phases of the moon affect people differently depending on the different properties of water in their brains: *"The Moon ... she signifies water in the head, that may cause palsies, apoplexies, epilepsies, lunasie, convulsions, madness and dullness, as the water is milder or*

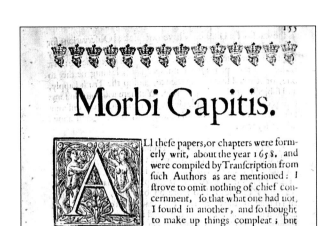

Morbi Capitis.

ALl thefe papers, or chapters were formerly writ, about the year 1658, and were compiled by Tranfcription from fuch Authors as are mentioned: I ftrove to omit nothing of chief concernment, fo that what one had not, I found in another, and fo thought to make up things compleat; but fince I have writ many Obfervations, and read more, fo that I fee the Authors of thofe Practices of Phyfick went conjecturally to work in fome things.

Chapter XII of Morbi Capitis (diseases of the head) concerns 'Headache from Drunkenness'. A unique formula is given to cure this ailment – "To burn Swallows, Feathers and all, in a Crucible, and eat the Ashes of them in a Morning". This has not been tried by the author and is not advised!

From 'A Physical Nosonomy'. Collection of Dr Gerry Tidy

sharper, hotter or colder, more vellicating or narcotical qualitied..."

Having dealt with the causes of disease he sets about classifying them. In the section 'A Tractate of the Diseases of the Head' the diseases of the brain are divided into 'diseases of the sense' and 'diseases of motion'. Diseases of senses are divided further into two parts:-

1. Diseases of Stupidity and Astonishment.
2. Diseases of aggravated Sense of Madness.
We shall treat of the Sickness of the Brain, wherein is an aggravation of Sense, and exaltation of the Spirits, contrary to the other of Stupidity and Drowsiness.
The Ancients, and also the Moderns, call them Phrenitis, Mania, and Melancholia.

He begins to define and describe these conditions:-

Mania, say they, is a fury tiuturne [?corruption of Latin diuturne: longstanding] *with boldness and fierceness, from the fire of the Spirits moved, or yellow Choler burnt; as Etius saith, from putrified blood: …*
Melancholia, say they, is a raging without a Feaver, with Fear and Sadness; without a Feaver from a melancholy humour, which they said was either in the Head it self, or did in vapour steem up thither, as from the Hyperconders and Spleen.

He gives examples of madness as described by others – from Felix Platerus, a Swiss physician and professor in Basel, writing in 'Practice of Physic' –

A Man runs mad by fits, sometimes outrageous, sometimes absurd, from jealousie, he plays divers tricks, carries his child into the field and hides him… from jealousy fell one into melancholy trouble of mind, and desparateness to kill; the other into fury, who killed his wife.

After giving examples of madness and suggesting that some of the things described may be due to the Devil, he mentions that *"some possessed or bewitched, find somewhat rise up in their breast as if they should be choaked"*. This seems to be the same experience labelled as 'globus hystericus', when a panic causes a sense

The mortar and pestle in the William Ransom Physic Garden next to Hitchin Museum. The garden was opened in 1990 by Sir Harold Ellis, an inspiring teacher and surgeon from Westminster Hospital. It contains many plants used in herbal remedies that apothecaries would have used.

The mortar has an inscribed quote of William Drage. The mortar and pestle was produced by Brookbrae Ltd from a design by Dr Gerry Tidy The garden is managed by the Hertfordshire Medical and Pharmaceutical Museum Trust.

Photo by author 2011

of tightening in the throat, incidentally thought by the ancient Greeks to be due to the womb rising and blocking the throat. He then mentions how *"some see the Witch or her Imp, come in form of a Spider or Beetle, and creep in at their mouths, and then they are hoven, and rage and delire, and are convulsive"*. This is a good description of delirium tremens, the phase when heavy drinkers have no alcohol for a few days and begin to have visual hallucinations and brush imaginary spiders off their bedclothes, become quite confused and can have fits (ie. convulsions).

In talking about the outward and inward causes (which is always worth a doctor thinking about, whether illness is due just to an internal chemical problem, or due to some external stress, or both), he continues:

> *"both the inward Cause that is moved by the outward, and the outward cause, being but one and the same, in two parties have different effects; nor is any thing much to be attributed to the colour or consistence of an Humour, but an hidden quality in it: for it is apparent that the same Humour visibly that causeth the Falling-Sicknes in one, causeth Apoplexies in another, and Palsies and Stupor in another…"*.

He then talks about the inward Cause and about physicians who dissected bodies after death and found holes in the membrane around the brain, water in the brain, blood which looked *"flegmatic, raw and wheyish"*, clearly trying to make sense of the body and its fluids or humours -

> *"Certainly the Planets put a Quality upon the Humours, that makes one torpid, another garrulous; one raging, another loving; one at one time stupid, a while after phrenitick: for visibly from one and the same Cause, come divers Effects…"*.

His descriptions of mental disorders are recognizable today, though the diagnoses are different. He talks about womb melancholy, which he defines as:-

> *"a Delirium, and sadness, with perturbation of the Mind and Senses, coming by Intervals, and without a Feaver; made from base exhalations from the Uterus, affected with a Melancholly Humour, dulling the Animal Spirits…"*
> *Signs Diagnostic. There is fearfulness, sadness, unsatisfiedness in every thing,*

> *dejection of mind, and sometime raging, anxiety and weeping, they sleep little. They laugh, dote, talk idley, and are most garrulous at such time that the Menstrua might be expected."* With *"...want of appetite ... sense of choaking ..."*. And the cure is *"Bleeding ... (after an orderly Dyet ...). If blood be more hot and black according to the Galenical Rule, we more freely draw it out ... cordials and Specifics for Melancholy; Borage, Buglois, Dodder of Time, Balm, Rosemary, Archangel, Woodroof, ... Fumitary, Featherfew ... Purge with such as properly purge Melancholy, and are made friendly to the Uterus ... extract of black Hellebore, of Lapiz Lazuli".*

and ends with eternally useful advice:-

> *"Comforters of the Heart, and Cherishers of the Spirits, are continually to be given, and whatever may avert and turn away Melancholy, and make her cheerful."*

And are people moonstruck in Hitchin?

Drage clearly believed that the moon and other planets affected our health, but by 1810 such thoughts were clearly seen to be irrational (see introduction). But, but... this is still a subject being researched. A variety of academic articles on various aspects of human and animal behaviour have failed to kill off the idea, despite many negative findings [9]. Described as the Transylvania effect, the popular belief persists, and may have a rational explanation after all. Research from Kyoto University apparently indicates that the moon causes changes in geomagnetic activity which may affect melatonin production in the body (The Independent newspaper, 9/11/2010). Melatonin is linked to our day/night changes in the body and is useful to counter jet lag. It has been tried with certain forms of depression, particularly if associated with a worse mood in winter (seasonal affective disorder). A recently introduced antidepressant, valdoxon or agomelatine, appears to relieve depression by adjusting melatonin actions in the brain. So maybe some rational link between the moon and mood will eventually be found, but it seems likely that anybody who is moonstruck in Hitchin will be experiencing some earthly and less sinister passion than Dracula, and not suffering from a mental illness.

Witchcraft and Spirits

William Drage is regarded as one of the medical experts on witchcraft, having first written about it in the 1665 edition of his book. In 1668 he published *"Physical Experiments"* to which is added a *"Discourse on Diseases proceeding from Witchcraft"*. He was regarded as more concerned to find cures than to punish witches at a time when witch hunts and execution still happened, and although he considered it legitimate to frighten them with threats, he did not advocate execution [5].

Various descriptions and local examples of witchcraft are given in Simon Walker's book on the subject [10]. The last person in England to be convicted of witchcraft and sentenced to death was Jane Wenham of Walkern (just east of Stevenage) in 1712, though she was later reprieved. She was formally charged with *"conversing with the Devil in the shape of a cat"*. Amongst the various writings about her is the pamphlet by Francis Bragge, son of the Vicar of Hitchin. He believed that she was a witch but other writers argued that witchcraft could not exist and therefore she could not be a witch. One of the commentators was a *"physician in Hertfordshire"*. His view was that the accusations were all nonsense and suggested that one of the accusers who was supposedly bewitched, Ann Thorn, was more amongst the *"maniacks"* than the *"demoniacks"* and describes her as having the fits of an *"epileptick"*. He closes his letter by suggesting that *"if the clergy would be a little more conversant with the History of Diseases and enquire more narrowly into the physical causes of things they would not be so forward to Ascribe these diseases to the Devil"* [11]. Jane was later reported as saying that it was all just due to malice.

Other cases suggest a combination of factors, finding someone to blame when death or misfortune occurred, dislike of others due to strife, personality or simply appearance. Within a society where religious and supernatural beliefs were strong, and rational scientific explanations were lacking, witchcraft quickly became the explanation for anything that had gone wrong. There may also have been misattributions when someone acted strangely due to mental illness and was then thought to be a witch, or with the boot on the other foot, a mentally ill person might have had a false belief or delusion that someone else was a

Two of the pamphlets from many produced about Jane Wenham in 1712. Images from collection of Simon Walker

witch and had special powers, and then convinced others of this. I have been in a home where the two occupants gave a vehement denunciation of such evil, of the person next door shining rays through the walls when one of them was in the bath. Such shared delusions (assuming their account is false - and I am here relying on my limited knowledge of what electronic apparatus is stored in a modest back street of a local town) are called 'folie à deux'. But less sinister in psychiatric terms is the human truth that on the basis of rumours and with a hint of non supernatural malice or misinformation people can believe something that is quite untrue about another.

Drage gave advice on how to protect against witchcraft, noting that the ancients believed that hanging up rosemary, mistletoe and ivy in the house would be effective, but adding that the best way was to pray to God. He then listed various cures, including those used by the ancients who thought that *"hystericks"* arose from demons and spirits and were helped by tying rosemary, rhue, mistletoe and birch around their necks. He also mentioned St John's wort, now effectively used for depression, which was good for *"love-enchantment"* (possibly an early identification of erotomania, a delusional fixation, also called de Clerambault's syndrome).

In 'Daimonomageai' Drage gives descriptions of demon possession, or bewitchment, which seem fictitious but he appears convinced of such a phenomenon in his own encounter with a Mary Hall of Little Gaddesden in Hertfordshire. He was called to see her by two priests and a doctor who believed her to be possessed. Drage describes her having a *"trembling shaking and convulsive motion... like Epileptick"*... then after some *"were heard in her strange noises, like mewing of Cats, barking of Dogs, roaring of Bears &c.... and after this evil Spirit spoke often..., when some came to pray, they would say, You shall not cast us out.... Sometimes they would bid her Mary, choak yourself when she went to eat; and when she went nigh water, Mary drownd your self;..."*. When he talked to her the 'spirits' would answer through her, and then he asked the spirits questions directly [12]. This type of phenomenon has been described in people with 'multiple personality' or 'dissociative identity disorder' [13]. This can be the result of abuse in childhood, when a person has adopted two or more quite separate personalities, as though under stress they have had to become a different person to protect themselves, but are unaware of that change. It is also possible that she was displaying signs of schizophrenia, hearing voices inside her which she responded to, or believing that other people's thoughts were put in her mind, or feeling that others controlled her. Drage's description of Mary Hall also raised the possibility that she suffered from a form of epilepsy, known as temporal lobe where hallucinations occur [14], as he likened her to an *"epileptick"*

He also described how a Hitchin lady, named Elizabeth Day, had an *"imp"* that leaped from her like a mouse, such imps or young spirits being a clear sign of being possessed by spirits.

While his descriptions of natural diseases are easily identified as the sort of illnesses that people suffer from now, his descriptions of witchcraft, bewitchment and supernatural phenomenon appear to be just hearsay and myth.

The laws against witchcraft were repealed in 1736, having been in operation

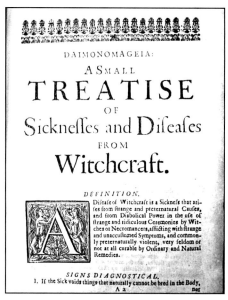

Drage wrote in 1668– "get the witch, put her in prison, her Power then Ceases, Satan leaves her; sometimes she then acquits those she has bewitched, if Satan will give leave; however her bewitching of others is prevented." Hertfordshire Archives [7]

since 1542, though the belief in such dark arts did not die so quickly. It seems likely that Jane Wenham was the victim of a combination of ignorance, malicious behaviour and of simplistic religious beliefs. However the belief in witchcraft and the scapegoating of certain members of society has been described as part of the religious culture. Myths arose which fitted in with the prevailing beliefs. Thomas Szasz has compared the myth of witchcraft with, as he saw it in the 1960s, the myth of mental illness. [15].

Ideas of bewitchment and possession by the devil are ancient, but the idea that people could be possessed remains part of the Christian heritage, with Jesus described as driving out demons in his time, and belief in possession and oppression by evil spirits persisting into modern times. The occasional response of church people to problems that they have blamed on demon possession has led to extreme examples of exorcism. The House of Bishops, within the Church of England, recommends that 'deliverance from evil' be preferred to 'exorcism' in dealing with people who need help with *"evil oppression or possession"* [16]. The Church also recommends that a comprehensive approach should be taken, with diocesan representatives employing prayer and counselling in close collaboration with doctors, psychologists and psychiatrists, recognizing that various psychiatric disorders may confound the picture.

The Trade in Lunacy

At some indefinite time in the late 17th century the care and management of the lunatics became a trade, a development described in great detail in William Llewellyn Parry-Jones's 1972 book 'Trade in Lunacy'[17]. Possibly starting with wealthy families who had responsibility for some unruly relative and hired someone to take the person into their own home and look after them, the 'trade in lunacy' began.

One of the first recorded examples is Edmund Franklin, a Bedfordshire landowner, who was found to be unfit due to lunacy to manage his estate in 1628 [18]. He was taken to London and treated in the home of a Dr Helkiah Crooke at a charge of £200 per year. Crooke was then the physician in charge at Bethlem. This is quoted in another early account of the Reverend John Ashburne and his private madhouse [19]. It appears that in 1656 Ashburne, the vicar of the Norfolk village of Norton, provided care for Edmond Muskett, at a charge of 14 shillings a week with further charges *"for physicke, care, paine & endeavour"*. The man under care was *"troubled with phrensy and distemper in his braine"*. The details came to light much later because the bill was not paid and Ashburne went to court in 1659 to seek recompense and those records were preserved. It is uncertain whether he had medical training. He described himself as a *"Practitioner in Physicke"* as well as a clerk in holy orders, but at the time the local bishop approved or licensed doctors and it is not certain what criteria they may have used to approve his medical skills. It is suggested that the clergy had to seek additional income as the tithing system had broken down after the English Civil War (1642 – 51) which may have been why the vicar was moonlighting. Sadly Ashburne was subsequently murdered by one of his patients in 1661.

Those who undertook the care of one mad person then realised they could look after two or more, and earn more money. By the end of the 17th century small institutions caring for many individuals were developing, particularly in London. Private madhouses would take on the care of both individuals whose families could no longer cope with them and were prepared to pay the fees themselves, and paupers who had become the responsibility of the parishes and could not be contained in the community.

The London madhouses included Hoxton in the north which had been open since at least 1695 [20]. The date from which people from the Hitchin area were sent to Hoxton is unknown as there are no records from the mad-houses to establish that. However some legal records have survived which do give an account of admissions to such institutions. The case of William Hanscombe of Shillington, a Bedfordshire village close to Hitchin, indicates the processes involved [21].

The first record of the parties involved is in a marriage settlement drawn up by Andrew Goodman senior, a maltster of Hertford, for his son, also Andrew, and Sarah Hanscombe on January 22nd 1684, for them to have the use of Brickendonbury Manor near Hertford, probably leasing it as it was then owned by Edward Clarke [22]. Five years later in hearings before the Lords Commissioner the Crown granted custody of Andrew Hanscombe to Andrew Goodman jr, his son in law. By the following year Hanscombe was petitioning to be discharged, saying that he had *"recovered of his indospition of melancholy & requests grant of custody to be discharged"*, having been kept at a madhouse where Goodman would not allow his friends to see him. He had been released from the madhouse and *"had gone to John Goch, an apothecary of Hitchin where he has ever since remained and was now of sound mind and capable of governing himself"* (Goch was possibly related to William Drage, whose wife was Elizabeth Goche). In 1691 the 'grant of custody' was revoked and he was declared to be sane. There are no details of the mad-house but it seems that it was in London.

Apart from the care of members of their family a person had certain responsibilities to their servants. So, in 1661 the Quarter Sessions records state that *"Anthony Gray of Sandon maintain Jeffrey Salmon, his servant, who has become sick and subject to strange fits of lunacy…until the full end & expiration of the length of his said service"* [23]. The said service was usually a contract for one year, so sick leave pay could have been expected for however long the contract had to run. A subsequent record states that *"Anthony Gray be discharged from keeping Jeremiah Salmon, a lunatic, late his servant, as the contract of service between them be discharge by both their consents before the said Salmon "was taken with the lunacy"… and … Salmon of Little Hormead, father, shall pay the overseers of Sandon 12d weekly toward his relief"* [24]

George Radcliffe and the Custody of a Lunatick, 1731.

Ralph Radcliffe lived in the Priory in Bridge Street in the early 18th century, when he had a problem with his brother George. The Delmé Radcliffe archives contain some details of that, revealing the processes of dealing with someone who was mentally ill.

The first sign of a problem was in 1716 when George wrote to his grandfather, Sir Ralph Radcliffe (who died in 1720) [25]. He was working in Aleppo in northern Syria, where the grandsons were sent to become merchants in the Levant trade. In a long and rambling letter trying to defend his reputation, George said that he had been told *"I was drunk or mad and had been so for eight months"*. The next significant letter is in 1729 when George wrote to brother Ralph hinting at disloyalty and the need for secrecy, which indicates that he was slightly paranoid [26]. Ralph was seeking advice in 1731 and received a letter on April 10th

The Priory in Bridge Street, home of the Radcliffe family from 1548, and of Ralph Radcliffe from 1727. The family became Delmé-Radcliffe in 1802 and they owned it until 1965. This was formerly a Carmelite priory founded in 1317 but dissolved in 1538 [27].

Photo in Hitchin Museum [28]

from George Draper, a lawyer who worked in Hitchin and also in Grays Inn Fields. He was one of three George Drapers, probably grandfather, father and son [29], whose firm became Hawkins & Co a century later. He gave a clear explanation of the legal processes necessary for placing a person in care, seemingly with George in mind [30]:-

> *"You was pleased to speak to me yesterday about the person which would be entituled to the Custody of a Lunatick & his Estate. Before I give any answer to that I beg leave to acquaint you with the processes that first must be gone thro before the custody be applied for (Vizt) there must Affidts made of the condition he is in of divers of his acts of Lunacy. These Affidts accompanied by a Petition must be layd before my Ld Chancellor who directs a Comision to some Gentlemen of the Neighbourhood with Power to direct a Jury to be Summoned, & to examine Witnesses on Oath before the Jury touching the condition of the Lunatick, & to take the Verdict of the Jury in relation thereto, & to transmit it to my Lord Chancellr. And in case the Jury find the person a Lunatick they also ascertain the time when he first became so. After that the Relations apply for the Custody of this person & estate, the General Rule is to grant the custody of this person to the nearest Relation that cannot inherit to him..."*.

The next fragment of information (the letter is in a very fragile state) comes in the form of a bill for medicines for George provided by Thomas Leask, an apothecary of Hitchin. This covered the period from June to August 1731 and consisted of *"A Formentation of Spirits, An Emetick draught, A Stomach Tincture and 3 Doses of purging pills or potions"* [31]. This seems to be a summary of how the 'lunatick' would have been treated.

Brother John had written to Ralph on a few occasions in July and August when George was probably staying with Ralph. On July 31st he wrote [32] *"despair with you that George will never Recover..."*; on August 3rd [33] *"I am very sorry for the sad condition George is in, nothing ought to be neglected that's for his service; tho I fear its labour is in vain..."*; and on August 12th [34] *"George's case becomes everyday more deplorable as his senses goe more from him, if Tom will not submit to attend him; a Person whis Qualifications ought to be found out, its taken for granted a Man will expect great Wages for such an attendance, but believe our Mother will be ready to pay it".*

John Shipton, a London doctor, wrote to Ralph in August. Further treatment is suggested –

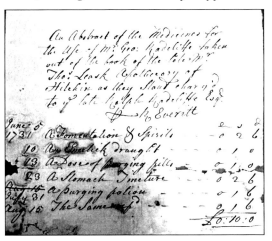

George Radcliffe's medication, specified on the apothecary's bill. A typical combination of purging and an "emetick". Delmé-Radcliffe Archive [31]

"I should be very glad if I cou'd with reason give you any encouragement in Mr George's care; but both (the) nature of his disorder, & the trial Dr Lane has lately made without success, confirm me in the opinion I had before, & wch I related to you, when I saw you last in town. How far cold bathing, I mean in a pond or river, if that may be trusted, at least washing (the) head morning & evening with a large quantity of cold spring water, may be of service to constringe [to bind or tighten] the weakened fibres of (the) brain, I cannot determine" [35].

A few weeks later Shipton wrote again mentioning the cold bathing, but did not hold out hope and was thinking of how else George might be helped –

"Tho I can't promise a great deal in Mr George's case from cold bathing, yet I think, since you have so good convenience, it may be tried, as both rational & a usual practice. After wch if you design to put him under any other care, as will to satisfy (the) world, as to remove him out of your house, I don't know who can better trust him with than with Dr Monro, Physician to Bethlem; who will be by that means both able to administer all that can be done for his recovery, & will take care that he be placed where you shall approve of, & where he will live as comfortably as such unhappy circumstances can admit of." [36]

His mention of the *"good convenience"* may be a reference to the river that runs through the grounds of the Priory, or possibly the 'Cold Bath House' which was certainly in place by 1733. This was sited in the grounds at the end of the park near Charlton [37].

The cold baths did not work and in October 1731 there is a letter from a

The Delmé- Radcliffe Archive was recently bought after a public appeal and is housed in the Hertfordshire Archives. Ralph Radcliffe was at the centre of the communications about his brother George. Brother John provided the most stylish address to him [38].

Michael Duffield, address not given (but someone of that name maintained two private lunatic asylums at Little Chelsea in London [39]), to Ralph stating -

> *"since your brother been under my care he hath been in very good health and hath a very good stomack, the Phisick that Dr Monro order him agrees with him very well, he sleeps better than he did at first coming hear and he hath left off talking to himself".*

Dr Monro was probably James (1680 – 1752), who was appointed as resident physician at Bethlem Asylum in 1728 [40], his family retaining posts there until 1852. George was clearly in some sort of private asylum or madhouse but his date of admission is not known.

It seems likely that he stayed in the asylum until 1733 when brother John wrote to Ralph [41] saying that he had visited George who said he had been *"ill treated and abominably abused"* but appeared to give a rational account and played cards well. John said *"I am altogether for removing him from the Place where he is"*. John later wrote to another brother Arthur in 1741 stating that *"poor George's condition is deplorable"*, George dying in that year [42].

1774 Madhouse Act

There was a steady growth in the madhouses which could be set up by anybody. There was no system of licensing, no inspections, no standards set, no staffing requirements and no rights for patients. Concern grew about what might go on in these places, not for the paupers from the parishes, but for the gentlemen and ladies who might be unjustly incarcerated. Thus in 1774 parliamentary concern led to the passing of the Madhouse Act. This stipulated that madhouses in and around London should be licensed by the doctors of the Royal College of Physicians and should be inspected by them, and elsewhere by two Justices of the Peace and one doctor appointed by the County Quarter Sessions. If someone took on one patient at a time, the 'single lunatic', then no licensing or inspection was needed. Where inspections did occur the inspectors could do nothing if they found malpractice. The Act was not used for pauper patients in madhouses as only the private ladies and gentlemen were of concern, perhaps because they alone had the financial wealth which would be the motive for false incarceration.

Collegium Insanorum

The only Hertfordshire 'madhouse' in the 18th century appears to have been Collegium Insanorum in St Albans, which existed between 1760 and 1788. This was located near where Lower Dagnall Street is, College Street deriving its name from the institution, and was demolished in 1910 [43]. It housed only 6 patients. It was owned and run by a medical man, Nathaniel Cotton (1705 – 1788), who was also a fervent Christian believer. His most famous patient was the poet and hymn writer William Cowper who spent a year and a half there from 1762-3 and was said to have become a Christian under the influence of Dr Cotton. On his death The Gentleman's Magazine said that Cotton was *"Distinguished for his great care, humanity & attention to those unhappy objects to whose cure he had devoted his principal study"* [44]. He was succeeded by his assistant Dr Peller but there is no further trace of the Collegium as a mad-house.

The Asylums

The model of care at Bethlem was probably no more than that of containment, involving restraint if the lunatic was wild or difficult to control. Reginald Hine*, the Hitchin historian (1883 - 1949), wrote that *"those who by medicine or other mischance were driven furiously mad were loaded with chains or hurried off to Bedlam"* [45]. He may have been right, as the Bethlem archivist Patricia Allderidge [46] wrote in 1979 that patients were sent there from as far afield as Bristol. There are isolated examples of people being sent to Bedlam from other areas, for example Hannah Dollomore from St Michael's in St Albans [47]. However whether this was a rare or common event is uncertain. Hine may have just conjectured, and as with some of his other historical writing there is no specified source of his assertion.

Lunatics at the beginning of the 18th century may just have wandered the streets and fields if their family could not contain them. There were no laws regulating the management of pauper lunatics. They first gained a mention in law with the Vagrants Act of 1714 wherein they were specifically excluded from the punishments which could be handed out to others (the rogues, vagabonds, sturdy beggars and vagrants) who could be whipped. Local magistrates (not one alone) could apprehend vagrants who were *"furiously mad and dangerous"*, no doctor was required to assess them, and they could be locked up in a gaol or house of correction. In 1744 another Vagrants Act added little except to mention the possibility of a cure for them, without specifying what this might involve. The Madhouse and Lunacy Acts followed in due course and the Mental Health Acts of the 20th century made the arrangements more fair and robust. However over the past 20 years concern about those who finish up in the wrong system, usually the mentally ill who are sent to prison, has led to court diversion schemes and other provisions for the mentally ill offender.

The first public asylum apart from Bethlehem was in Norwich. A wealthy lady, Mary Chapman, in gratitude for having been spared from a nervous disorder that she had observed in some of her family, bequeathed Bethel Hospital to the local people. This was opened around 1720. In 1721 Thomas Guy founded the hospital which bears his name in London, with one ward for chronic lunatics. By the middle of the century a number of asylums were built in the cities, some being wings of general infirmaries. These were paid for by 'public subscription',

---

Reginald Hine had his own mental health problems – he appeared to suffer from manic depressive disorder (now referred to as a bipolar disorder) with a mood varying from depression to an overactive overexcited state known as mania. In a mild manic state (known as hypomania) people can be very creative and productive, bursting with ideas and energy, but can also be slapdash and irresponsible, being careless in their actions and not bothered about the consequences. Some of these qualities can be useful for an artist or writer, but can be a problem when works are not completed. It is possible that Hine at times dispensed with the research for his writings or just could not be bothered to record the sources from which he obtained information. A full account of his achievements and difficulties, ending with Hine's suicide at Hitchin railway station in April 1949, is recorded in Richard Whitmore's biography [48].}

with the wealthier members of the community contributing to the costs. St Luke's in London (just north of Finsbury Square) was built in 1751, followed by asylums in Manchester (1766), York (1777), Liverpool (1792), Leicester (1794), Exeter and Hereford. Only the London asylums of Bedlam (where Liverpool Street now is) and St Luke's would have been close enough to be used by Hitchin residents. The physician at St Luke's, William Beattie, wrote 'A Treatise on Madness' in 1758, probably the first book to describe and comment on the treatment of mental disorder [49]. He may have been trying to upstage the Monros who were dominant in London as mad-doctors and were in charge at Bethlem. They felt he was personally criticizing them and wrote to defend the usefulness of vomiting and purging as appropriate treatments.

By the end of the century the move to provide special help for lunatics was growing, but in the meantime they were often cared for under whatever provision was made for the poor.

Notes

1. See Bethlem website http://www.bethlemheritage.org.uk
2. Slater, T & Goose, N. 'A County of Small Towns'. University of Hertfordshire Press. 2008 p336-337
3. Griffin, JP. 'Hertfordshire's Medieval Hospitals'. Adverse Drug Reactions & Toxicology Review. 2001. 20(2) p73 - 88
4. Keith Fitzpatrick-Matthews, personal communication.
5. Capp, Bernard J. Oxford Dictionary of National Biography. Oxford University Press. 2004. www.oxforddnb.com
6. Hine, Reginald. 'Hitchin Worthies'. George Allen & Unwin. 1932
7. Hertfordshire Archives and Local Studies. Hine collection /105
8. Porter, Roy. 'The Greatest Benefit to Mankind'. Fontana Press. 1999 p 73-77
9. http://faculty.washington.edu/chudler/moon.html
10. Walker, Simon. 'The Witches of Hertfordshire'. Tempus 2004
11. 'A Full Confutation of Witchcraft' - available on Google Books
12. Drage, William. 'Daimonomageia'. 1668. Hertfordshire Archives and Local Studies/ Hine/105
13. 'Multiple personality disorder' is defined in the International Classification of Diseases, produced by the World Health Organization - ICD F44.8, and 'dissociative identity disorder' in the parallel Diagnostic Statistical Manual of the American Psychiatric association - DSM IV. 300.14
14. For a description see http://priory.com/psych/did.htm
15. Szasz, Thomas. 'The Manufacture of Madness'. Routledge Kegan & Paul. 1971
16. 'A Time to Heal'. Church House Publishing. 2000. Chapter 9, p 167 – 181
17. Parry-Jones, William. 'Trade in Lunacy'. Routledge Kegan & Paul. 1972
18. Bedfordshire and Luton Archives and Records Service FA/FN/1075, quoted in Parry-Jones. p 8
19. Mason, Andrew. History of Psychiatry, v (1994), p 321 – 345
20. Parry-Jones, p 39
21. Bedfordshire and Luton Archives and Records Service H/WS 787 – 797. William Wilshere archives
22. http://www.brickendonbury.co.uk/pages/aboutus.htm
23. Hertfordshire Archives and Local Studies. Hertford County Records. Sessions

Rolls 1581-1698. Compiled by W.J.Hardy (1905). vol 1, p 146
24. Hertfordshire Archives and Local Studies. Hertford County Records. Sessions Rolls. vol VI, p 61.
25. Hertfordshire Archives and Local Studies DE/R/B42/2
26. Hertfordshire Archives and Local Studies DE/R 106/4
27. Howlett, B. 'Hitchin Priory Park'. Hitchin Historical Society. 2004
28. Hitchin Museum. Postcard in Loftus Barham Scrapbook, vol 1, p 7
29. Hine, Reginald. 'Relics of an Un-Common Attorney'. Dent & Sons. 1951. p 47
30. Hertfordshire Archives and Local Studies DE/R/C52/2
31. Hertfordshire Archives and Local Studies DE/R C72/21
32. Hertfordshire Archives and Local Studies DE/R/C107/3
33. Hertfordshire Archives and Local Studies DE/R/C107/4
34. Hertfordshire Archives and Local Studies DE/R/C107/5
35. Hertfordshire Archives and Local Studies D/ER/C 118/1
36. Hertfordshire Archives and Local Studies D/ER C118/2
37. Howlett. p 20
38. Hertfordshire Archives and Local Studies DE/R C107/10
39. http://www.british-history.ac.uk/report.aspx?compid=28720
40. http://studymore.org.uk/mhhtim.htm
41. Hertfordshire Archives and Local Studies DE/R/C107/17
42. quoted in 'The Radcliffes of Hitchin Priory'. Ron Pigram. 1980
43. http://www.hertfordshire-genealogy.co.uk/data/occupations/mad-houses.htm
44. 'The Gentleman's Magazine, Hertfordshire 1731-1800'. Ed Arthur Jones. Hertfordshire Record Publications Publ. 1993
45. Hine, R. 'The History of Hitchin'. George Allen & Unwin. Vol I. 1927. p 264
46. Allderidge, P. 'Hospitals, madhouses and asylums: cycles in the care of the insane'. British Journal of Psychiatry(1979), 134, p 321 – 34
47. Truwert, Eleanor. 'The operation of the Old Poor Law in the Parish of St Michael's, St Albans, 1721 – 1834', in 'Down and out in Hertfordshire. A symposium of the old and new poor law', ed. P. Kingsford & A Jones. Hertfordshire Publications. 1984. p121
48. Whitmore, Richard. 'The Ghosts of Reginald Hine'. Mattingley Press. 2007
49. Morris, Andrew. 'William Battie's Treatise on Madness (1758) and John Monro's Remarks on Dr Battie's Treatise (1758) - 250 years ago'. British Journal of Psychiatry (2008) 192: 257

DRAGE'S TRADE TOKEN

The Poor Law and
the Workhouse.

2

Before 1834

After the dissolution of the monasteries in the 1530s the care of the lame and disabled devolved to the parishes. Various laws directed what should be done and these were consolidated in the Poor Law Act of 1601, during the reign of Queen Elizabeth. The arrangement then was that each parish cared for its own and that this was paid for from the rates – the levy placed on each property owner. Each parish had one or more overseers, who with the churchwardens, administered poor relief. The overseer(s) were appointed by the county magistrates at the Quarter Sessions each Epiphany, Easter, Midsummer and Michaelmas. They provided for the paupers, whether they were able bodied and unemployed or somehow infirm and incapable of working. In their care of the disabled there was no differentiation officially made between those that the parish became responsible for. The lame, the blind, the elderly, the 'idiots' and the 'insane' were lumped together as 'incapable'. It was not until 1714 when a Vagrancy Act was passed that the insane were separately recognized. Those vagrants who were insane were dealt with differently, and were not beaten or otherwise chastised.

Provision for the paupers was made by outdoor and indoor relief. Outdoor relief referred to the help offered to people who stayed in their own homes, whether alone or while being looked after by family and friends. Records from the 17th century indicate that they could be provided for with direct payments or with payment in kind, often bread or other basic foods.

Indoor relief referred to care offered in special residential institutions, the poorhouses or workhouses. It seems that 'poorhouse' was used more often in small towns and villages and indicated that the residents were the incapable poor, whereas 'workhouse' implied that the residents could work but were unemployed, which was more likely to be in the large towns and cities, but the terms were used interchangeably. The provision of such indoor relief started early in the 17th century with the record of a *"workehouse"* in Abingdon in 1631, and in 1652 Exeter recorded *"The said house to bee converted for a workhouse for the poore of this cittye and also a house of correction for the vagrant and disorderly people within this cittye"* [1]. In 1696 Bristol formed a poor relief system incorporating several parishes and designed a large scale workhouse. It was unique at that time in separating off the 'impotent poor' from those competent to work, and placing the lunatic patients in separate wards in St Peter's Hospital, also known as the Mint [2].

The regulation of such places was established by the 1723 Workhouse Act. The Act included the introduction of the workhouse test, intended to cut off outdoor relief, ruling that if people could not cope in the community then they should be in the workhouse [2,3]. By 1732 there may have been 700 parish workhouses established in England and Wales, though many of these probably housed just a small number of elderly paupers [1].

The differences between those who were unable to work and those who could work but were unable to find employment caused many problems, much as welfare benefit issues today cause confusion and resentment. The resentment felt by people in the parish paying for those who did not work could focus on the idea that the poor were just lazy. Different parishes had different arrangements and some experimentation went on. One of the best known schemes, mostly for the problems it caused, was tried at Speenhamland in Berkshire in 1795. The worthy aim was to provide everybody with a working wage, so workers weekly pay was supplemented by the parish so that it reached a minimal subsistence level. Unfortunately this led to employers reducing the wages to below this level, knowing that the parish top-up would provide enough for each household. This gave no incentive for people to work if they received the same whether they laboured or not. Such a scheme increased the idea of the lazy poor and from 1834 there was pressure not to allow outdoor relief and to enforce the 'workhouse test'. While this might have had the desirable effect on the capable poor it did not help those who were incapable and cared for at home with a little support. It also took no account of the available work opportunities.

James Craft. — Collector of Taxes
Agent for the Society for the
Discouragement of Vagrancy.
died 17th march 1859 aged 79

The linkage between vagrancy and mental illness started with the 1714 Vagrancy Act, which identified the lunatics as separate from the usual scroungers and scoundrels, who needed to be punished. James Craft, who died in 1859, had been an 'Agent for the Society for the Discouragement of Vagrancy'. The problem of vagrancy received further attention in the 1960s when it was realised that some of those sleeping on the streets of London had been turned out of the London asylums as they closed wards without any community provision. Subsequent programmes of resettlement were much more carefully designed and reviewed.

Sketch by Samuel Lucas (the elder, 1805-1870). Hitchin Museum [4]

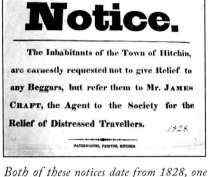

Both of these notices date from 1828, one referring to Mr Craft, and the other being the heading for the notes of a meeting. Civic concerns have changed over the years.
The Society was formed in the previous year "to relieve the necessitous traveller and discourage vagrancy and begging". Craft was paid £10.0.0d in that year, distributing £24.0.1d to 1,302 people. [4]

It took the American Civil War to sort that out. American ports were blockaded, raw cotton could not be exported, the Lancashire cotton mills ground to a halt, the mill workers became unemployed and were pitched into needing poor relief to survive. The lesson was that it was not because of their laziness [5].

The difficult issue of how mental disability could affect a person's ability to work would have been relevant. It has always been easier to identify a physical disability and it would be difficult for an untrained relieving officer to measure the capability of someone with depression or paranoia. Even the doctors of those times had little idea of how to diagnose such disorders, no idea of the implications and certainly no effective treatment, so how would anybody else know what could be expected of them?

Hitchin had a workhouse in the old free school barn from about 1630 in Tylers, later Tilehouse, Street, moving into more substantial premises in the same street about 1688 [6]. In 1725 Hitchin was listed in a national *"Account"* of workhouses and a parliamentary report in 1777 recorded that Hitchin workhouse had 80 residents and that there was a workhouse in Baldock housing 45 residents, 20 in Ippolits, 30 in Offley, 40 in Pirton and more in the other villages [7]. The Baldock site was in Whitehorse Street [8].

In Hitchin the poorhouse was in Tilehouse Street, probably until 1810, where numbers 1 to 3 now stand, opposite to the junction with Sun Street and adjoining the Priory. Dissatisfaction with the state of the building, *"the want of sufficient room as well as the situation"* led to the Hitchin Vestry seeking an alternative in 1803 [9]. They identified the Biggin Orchard as *"the most proper place"* and considered two proposals to build on it. James Wren's tender of £1350 was preferred over one of £1650, but the building did not happen. By 1807 (minutes of 2nd September) they were considering the purchase of Mr Blaxland's late estate in Bancroft which was offered to the Parish for £815. It seems that they must have made a good deal as they sold off part of the land attached to Thomas Wilshere. By December mention was made of the intention to move to the property *"purchased of Sarah Blaxland in Bancroft Street"* within the Article of Agreement for the new workhouse manager[10], and the move probably occurred in 1808, the workhouse being in what is now number 34.

The earliest local surviving workhouse building is in Letchmore Road in Stevenage just south of the old High Street. It was used for this purpose from 1759 until 1835. It was built circa 1550 and had been owned in the 18th century by John Hitchin, a butcher, and was said to have also been a slaughterhouse. In 1773 it was given to the town by Reverend Cholwell [11]. It is now used as a solicitor's office. Photo by author 2010

In 1809 the number residing in the Parish workhouse, often referred to as the 'House of Maintenance for the Poor', was just 30 [9]. What we do not know is how many of the residents of these houses were able bodied but unemployed, how many infirm and how many incapable because of lunacy or idiocy. An 'Article of Agreement', dated

No.34 Bancroft, the Hitchin Workhouse 1808 – 1836. It was then used as the poorhouse for children. It was formerly Blaxland's School (1789 – 1801), and prior to that the home of William Maurice Bogdani, the Lord of the Manor of Hitchin [12]. Photo by author 2011.

November 21st 1800, indicates that lunatics were probably not welcome. The agreement was between the legal vestry in Hitchin (Churchwardens, Thomas Paternoster, Michael Dear and Thomas Topham, and the Overseers of the Poor Thomas Wilshere, Henry Jermyn and David Topham) and a shopkeeper, John Whish. The contract was to pay Whish for the maintenance and support of paupers in the Workhouse. There was an exception clause, *"those afflicted with the smallpox or any other pestilential or contagious disorder or who shall be lunatic or insane"* [13]. The same clause is included in further Articles of Agreement at least until 1807 [10]. Whether a similar exclusion clause existed in other parishes is uncertain. There was no systematic recording of the 'lunatics' in the parishes until a parliamentary act in 1828 which made it mandatory for the county magistrates to collect them. But we do know that in 1828 there were so-called 'lunatics' in the workhouses at Stevenage and Baldock [14].

There may have been other provisions for the pauper 'lunatics'. Hertfordshire Archives contain an example of the provision for an individual, Mary Sam, a *"Lunatick"*. There are three receipts of payment for her care by the 'Churchwardens and Overseers of the Poor' between 1763 and 1773. Three separate people provided this service of maintenance or *"Board & Cloathing"*. One included the bill for *"Boarding & Maintaining Adam's Bastard child"* [15].

After 1834, the Hitchin Poor Law Union

In 1834 a new Poor Law Act was introduced and Hitchin Poor Law Union was established. This consisted of 27 parishes with a total population of over 20,000 (and covered exactly the same area as the North Herts mental health service has covered since 1972). Hitchin then had a population of 5,211 (now more than 30, 000). The Union had a Board of Guardians elected and the first meeting of the Board was on May 16th 1835 [16]. The Board had 35 members and at least one from each parish. The members included William Hainworth (a farmer), Thomas Hailey (who had been an overseer of people from the workhouse who worked on his farm at Highover), Joshua Ransom (miller at Grove Mill), William Lucas junior (owner of Sun Street Brewery and farmer), William Crawley from Ickleford (tenant farmer) and Charles Kingsley from Pirton (possibly a farmer). Revd Frederick Sullivan (of Kimpton) was made chairman and the clerk was Mr Stevens. The minutes of the board meetings, all available on microfiche at Hertfordshire Archives, provide some information about the service provided to the paupers. They agreed to meet every Monday at Hitchin Workhouse and they dealt with all the financial and management business. They also appointed the relieving officers, the workhouse staff and the medical officers. At the first meeting they agreed to appoint two relieving officers, James Coleman and John Smith, at a combined expense of £200 per annum. By June a third relieving officer was in post, John Manning, who was responsible for Hitchin and Walsworth.

The Board divided the union's area into 5 districts for the purpose of appointing one medical officer to each, the *"medical gentlemen"* being expected to visit each workhouse twice each week. It was generally expected that applicants for the medical posts would submit a tender for how much they wanted to be paid for their services and the lowest tender was accepted. The Board identified the medical officers duties as *"due and punctual attendance in all medical and surgical cases, and all medical and surgical requisites, leeches etc and vaccination for all paupers within such district, whether belonging to any parish in such district or not".* They made no mention of care of lunatics however in the Board of Guardian (BG) minutes of July 6th 1835.

In addition, in what must have been a busy meeting, they agreed that seven of them would consult with the Assistant Commissioner on the Poor Law Board, who was at the meeting, to discuss the workhouse accommodation. The Board estimated that accommodation for 400 paupers would be required, and that the current workhouses except Hitchin would be suitable for the aged and infirm. They agreed that they only needed the Hitchin, Offley, Ickleford and Stevenage workhouses for their present needs and would decide in 1836 whether a new workhouse was required. Eventually in 1836 the firm of William Jeeves of Dead (now Queen) Street in Hitchin was contracted to build a new workhouse at Chalkdell on the edge of Hitchin.

In February 1836 there were 198 paupers receiving indoor relief, being the inmates of the various workhouses throughout the area. Their presence in the towns and villages would have been obvious to all as the Board *"Resolved that every article of wearing apparel of the indoor paupers be stamped in a conspicuous manner with H.U. in red paint 4 inches in length (lest they abscond with the clothes)"* (BG January 18th 1836).

The returns to the county magistrates in August 1836 show that 167 were receiving indoor relief (in the workhouse) in the Hitchin Union and 1,082, receiving outdoor relief. For Hitchin town the figures were 59 and 223. The returns do not reveal how many of the Hitchin poor were infirm, but for Baldock out of 99 receiving outdoor relief 66 were able bodied and 33 presumably infirm in some way. There is no division in the official returns between those who were physically infirm and those who had any mental health or development problem, the so-called 'lunatics' or 'idiots'.

The Board minutes reveal little information about those receiving outdoor relief, unless they had appealed against the relief they received or had stopped receiving it. Reasons for granting relief are mostly not given but occasional detail is revealed, for example *"Sarah Brown an illegitimate child her mother in a Lunatic Asylum to be allowed 3/- per week"* (15 pence in new money)(BG 17.08.35). Her mother was in Bethnal Green Asylum, her name amongst a list of people in February 1836 for whom charges to various asylums was noted.

Medical problems have occasional and surprising details offered as on August 10th 1835 in *"Mr Huston's medical return for the week. Hannah Pales of Pauls Walden crippled with disease of hip and knee to be sent to Royal Sea Bathing Infirmary at Margate was acceded to."*

There are better figures available for those lunatics who were receiving asylum care from the county Quarter Sessions records. Since the 1828 Act the magistrates were responsible for collating this information and the Union Boards were expected to provide that [14]. Early in 1836 the Board's minutes state that there were nine 'lunatics' in asylums, 3 from Pauls Walden, 1 from

Kings Walden, Lilley, Kimpton and Letchworth and 2 from Hitchin. Five were in London 'madhouses' (ie. private asylums), 1 at Hoxton and 4 at Bethnal Green, and 4 were in Bedford Asylum (opened in 1812 – see chapter 4). Later in the year at Michaelmas the Quarter Session records show an increase in numbers, 15 were identified including 10 at Bedford (that was the year that Hertfordshire Magistrates made an agreement for Bedford to accommodate the county's lunatics). Five others were then accommodated in London asylums, at Bethlem, St Luke's, Hoxton and Bethnal Green. It is uncertain whether there was a real increase in numbers needing care as the details are not available to judge this. Perhaps the closeness and availability of the places at Bedford made it easier to arrange admission and so the number receiving asylum care increased.

The Quarter Sessions records also show that 4 lunatics were in the workhouse and 11 were *"with friends"*. From later records it is likely that most of these were the so called 'idiots' and not what we would now think of as mentally ill.

There are details from the Board minutes in March 1836 on payment, *"Parish of Pauls Walden. Messrs Warburtons (at Bethnal Green) account for Lunatics amounting to £8.0.0d from 1st of August last allowed"*.

In January 1836 a report from Pauls Walden is given, *"Sarah Dollimore, a dangerous lunatic, relieving officer to take necessary steps to remove her to Bedford Lunatic Asylum"*. An accounts page for the charges due show that the cost to the parish was 12/0d (or 60 pence now) per week, *"not including clothes"*. At the same time Mary Cox from Letchworth was being cared for at Hoxton madhouse at the cheaper rate of 9/6d per week. In July 1836 the minutes reveal the sort of problems that had to be dealt with, *"John Dearman from Hammersmith, Parish*

Money

How much is that? Comparisons between prices then and prices now are difficult to make with accuracy. It depends on what retail or prices index is used. The National Archives have a currency converter (http://www.nationalarchives.gov.uk/currency/) which calculates that £1 in 1840 would be the equivalent of £44 now. However the website http://www.measuringworth.com calculates that according to the retail price index £1 would be worth £71, but in average earnings the comparable amount is £771.

In quoting the sums for care I am stating the amount in old money, when we had 20 shillings in the pound, and 12 pence in the shilling. 50 pence now was 10 shillings (10/0d) then. 9/6d then would be 47 1/2 pence now.

Quoting a cost of 12/0d per week for asylum care in 1836 and using the currency converter indicates that would be £26.40 now, which is clearly an under-estimate. Using an average earnings comparison 12/0d translates to £462 now. The cost of inpatient care for the mentally ill is now estimated by the Personal Social Services Research Unit to vary from £1,505 per week in a long stay unit to £1,624 in an acute unit, rising to £4,228 in a psychiatric intensive care unit. The cost in a local authority staffed hostel for people with a mental health problem is £496 [17]. It seems that much more is being spent on in-patient care now.

of Hitchin, his wife insane, he to remain in the house (ie workhouse), and an order for her admission into a lunatic asylum to be obtained". (It is likely that he was removed from Hammersmith to Hitchin, which was his legal settlement. Such resettlement was used when a person required poor relief in a place that they did not originate from).

The 1834 Poor Law Act had stated *"nothing in this Act contained shall authorise the detention in any workhouse of any dangerous lunatic, insane person, or idiot for any longer period than fourteen days".* The meaning of this was uncertain but it came to be accepted that it was the 'dangerous lunatic' rather than any 'insane person' who was being referred to. 'Dangerous' was not defined and there must have been a temptation to avoid labelling someone as a 'dangerous lunatic' and avoid the responsibility and expense of finding them a place in an asylum. Given that there was no effective treatment available, other than containment or confinement, such a course and attempt to manage such people in the workhouse would have also seemed reasonable. While asylums were seen by many as offering a hope of cure, there were many who disputed this and saw the asylum as a harmful place for the 'madmen' [18].

Hitchin Board of Guardians minutes for 1856 & '57 [19] show that a new county rate had been imposed for the purpose of building a new lunatic asylum. By then Bedford Asylum was being well used and was not large enough. There is an account of an Elizabeth Henchard from Knebworth who had been certified by a George Hill Smith, to whom the payment of one guinea was made for completing a lunacy certificate. There is a later note that a letter had been received from Bedford Asylum (BG December 5th 1856) stating that she was then 'out on trial', a period of 4 weeks then being required before discharge was arranged.

Edith Perry, age 57, *"a lunatic pauper from Baldock"*, was less fortunate. In April 1857 letters had been written to Bedford and Hoxton Asylums requesting a place for her, but by the next week a letter was received saying that there was no place for her, but there might be by the following week. One week later Bedford were writing to say that two other patients, Mary Freshwater of Bygrave and Mary Watson of Willian, had had a two month trial and that their removal was required at the earliest convenience, and that Edith Perry could be received.

At the April 28th meeting the Board were informed that Mary Freshwater and Mary Watson had been removed from Bedford Asylum and placed in the workhouse, the outdoor relief officer had fetched Edith Perry from Hoxton to be removed to Bedford Asylum, but the following week he said he had not done so yet. The clerk to the Board was asked to write to St Luke's Asylum (London) and ask if she could be admitted there, but by May 12th St Luke's had written back to say that pauper patients could no longer be admitted there. The Board met on May 19th and read a letter from Hoxton Asylum to say that Edith Perry had died there, and from Bedford Asylum to say that they now had a bed for a female patient. The last entry on her was in October when it was noted that the cost of her stay at Hoxton had been erroneously charged to Baldock Parish whereas the Union as a whole accepted such charges.

In July 1857 the Lunacy Commission was involved in finding a placement for Mary Howard, *"a wandering pauper lunatic"*. A place was found for her at

Buckinghamshire Lunatic Asylum for 13/0d per week (65 pence now) by 21st July and the Master of the workhouse was ordered to *"remove her there forthwith"*. By August 4th it was reported that she had been removed there and that the cost was due to be paid by Hertford County.

Other entries concerning pauper 'lunatics' were about money, payments to Hoxton and Bedford Asylums for the keep of Hitchin Union patients, and a letter from a Dr R W Philson who wished to be informed of reasons for the Guardians objecting to the payment of lunatic certificate fees for Betty Izzard & Wm Hales. The Board quickly decided that he should be paid.

At each Board meeting a list of those granted outdoor relief were listed. In 1857 it was reported that *"James Bonfield, 46, wife insane"*, and William Hare, 35, of Hitchin is also listed as deserving relief, having five children and *"wife insane"*. Such cases are infrequent amongst many other entries which identify problems as *"he bad leg"*, *"he rheumatism"*, *"he injury"* and *"sons funeral expenses"*. The minutes also record payments to various contractors, usually bakers or flour providers, presumably the payment in kind of provisions for the paupers, rather than cash.

Hitchin Board of Guardians Minutes for 1859 show what must have been the last account to be made for the patients at Bedford Asylum, soon to be replaced by Three Counties Asylum, amounting to £127.13.11d *"for the maintenance of Lunatic Paupers therein from this Union"*. Twenty-three patients are listed, the charge being a quarterly rate of £5.17.0d for the 13 weeks, or 9 shillings per week, with 6 patients from Hitchin. By the end of 1860 the patients had been transferred to Three Counties Asylum in nearby Arlesey. The charges were exactly the same, despite the new building and extensive grounds which must have felt like an upgrade.

At that time the Relieving Officer, William French, reported that a Sophia Hare, who had been out on trial from the Three Counties Asylum had become dangerous and was taken back that Saturday to the asylum.

My next dip into the Board's minutes was for 1886. There is a surprising lack of detail in how money was spent. At a meeting on July 8th 1886, chaired

Photo of a model of the (Chalkdell) Hitchin Union Workhouse, on Union Road (now called Oughtonhead Way), on the outskirts of the town. Made by Alfred Fowler, industrial trainer at the workhouse from 1877 until 1882, and then Master until April 1903. Hitchin Museum.

by William Lucas and attended by nine others including William Ransom, Lawson Thompson and Frederic Seebohm, (all three successful Hitchin Quaker businessmen), an account from the Three Counties Asylum was received. This amounted to £348.7.6d for the maintenance of 65 patients, which worked out at 8/10d per patient per week (44 pence in new money). Also noted are fees of 7/6d and 10/0d for Drs Gilbertson and Shillitoe for Lunatics, presumably for signing certificates for their admission to the asylum.

Workhouse or Asylum?

One of the puzzles that intrigued me was how people would finish up in the asylum, how decisions would be made that they needed to be there and not elsewhere, and, given that the workhouse had a role in supporting, or at least accommodating, the infirm paupers, how many of the insane did remain in the workhouse?

The first entry in *A Return of Lunatics*[14] is for Bishops Stortford and lists 10 people who were *"confined in the workhouse"* at a weekly cost of 2/6d each (12 1/2 pence now). Hitchin Parish had 3 at Bedford Asylum, costing 9/0d each per week, and 5 with friends, at a weekly cost of between 1/6d and 3/0d (7 1/2 – 15 pence now) per week. Other parishes in what became Hitchin Union had people mostly being looked after by friends, a few in Bethnal Green asylum, Sandon had one resident in Bethlem and Yardley had one in St Luke's in London. It seemed from this sample that different parishes had different patterns of caring for their *"lunatics and dangerous idiots"*. The total for Herts was 26 in public asylums, 18 in private licensed houses, 33 in workhouses and 58 with friends or at large.

The cost of care was undoubtedly as much of an issue then as now. National figures for 1845 were that average weekly costs for care were 2/7d for the workhouse and 7/3d for asylums [20]. The implication is clearly that if a 'lunatic' could be accommodated in the workhouse then that was much cheaper than moving them to an asylum.

In 1847 the Hitchin Union had 18 'idiots' listed in the Hitchin Workhouse, 16 'idiots' were at home, and 13 'lunatics' were in Bedford Asylum. The pattern seems clear in that lunatics were not kept at the workhouse, though whether it was only dangerous lunatics who were at the asylum is uncertain, and whether those with mental health problems but who were not dangerous remained in the

A Return of Lunatics and dangerous Idiots in the several parishes in the County of Hertford (not including the Liberty of Saint Albans) with an Account of the weekly cost per head and the places in which they are confined according to the Returns made to the Clerk of the Peace at Michaelmas Session 1836'. [14]

workhouse but were just not referred to as 'lunatic'. That may have been kind, and as there was no active treatment known for such people, the addition of diagnosis would have had no practical benefit. There was also the complication of the confusion in the Lunacy Act as to whether keeping 'lunatics' in the workhouse was allowed.

The Lunacy Commission was trying to monitor the whereabouts of the 'lunatics' for which they clearly felt responsible. From 1847 they produced an annual report on the 'lunatics' in the workhouses and requested that the number of 'lunatics' and 'idiots' be recorded in books by the relieving officers. The reports do not give details of every parish union in every year but in 1856 there is an interesting comparison between Hitchin and two other local unions:-

Lunacy Commission 10th Workhouse Report June 2nd 1856 [21]

Number Insane, Idiots or Imbeciles	Male	Female	Total
St Albans	4	19	23
Hitchin	3	3	6
Biggleswade	9	11	20

The three unions were of similar size and it is strange that the numbers in the workhouses should be so different. The report does not identify how many were insane and how many were 'idiots' and 'imbeciles'. We know from other sources that the Hitchin workhouse did not usually identify any of their residents as 'lunatics'. Perhaps the other two unions did have more 'lunatics' identified by the medical officers. It could be that some medical officers had more experience with such people and could diagnose them better, perhaps others thought it cruel to label someone as a 'lunatic', perhaps the Board of Guardians differed in ensuring that 'lunatics' were transferred to asylums, perhaps St Albans and Biggleswade Guardians refused outdoor relief to 'idiots' and thus had more accommodated in the workhouses. The figures do not mean that the people of these other towns were any less sane than those of Hitchin, whatever prejudices we may hold.

In 1866 Hitchin Workhouse had 3 'idiots' and 2 'lunatics', 17 'idiots' and 5 'lunatics' were with friends and 39 'lunatics' were in Three Counties Asylum. There is insufficient information to know the severity of the problems these people presented. Were they in the asylum or workhouse because their behaviour was difficult, because there was nobody to care for them at home, or because their family or 'friends' who might care for them were ill? We get an idea of where they were, but not why they were there.

Another source of information for the residents at that time is the census returns. From 1871 it was required that 'idiots' or 'lunatics' were identified and included in those with a disability – for the two previous censuses only the blind, the deaf or dumb were required to be recorded. The 1871 census at the Workhouse listed 150 inmates, no 'lunatics' and 6 'idiots'. 1881 listed 207 inmates with no 'lunatics' but 9 'idiots', 4 'imbeciles' and 3 'weakminded' since birth. 1891 listed 140 inmates, no 'lunatics' and 2 'idiots'. However such census data has been described as *"untrustworthy"* [22]. Families were likely to hide information about 'medical disability' and it seems likely that institutions would not have an accurate record of such problems. In 1901 when 'feeble minded' replaced the term 'idiot' on the census form, the numbers recorded as having a mental disability rose markedly.

By 1874 the government made available a 'central grant' of 4/0d per person per week for 'pauper lunatics' to be looked after in asylums. This alleviated the pressure on parish funds, but the grant was then blamed nationally as being the cause of the continuing increase in numbers of people in the asylums. There is no indication from the Hitchin Board minutes that this had any impact on the management of the local workhouse.

The idea that a workhouse infirmary could provide suitable care for any ill person seems unlikely. There might be only one nurse to 30 patients, if there were any at all. However in some areas the workhouses provided a special ward for the lunatics, so that by 1874 104 out of 688 workhouses had lunacy wards [23].

The Local Government Board had visited Hitchin Workhouse in May 1873 and reported –

> *"Infirmary is detached, as also are the wards for infectious cases. Lying in ward is in the body of the house. There is a paid nurse... Workhouse school - 16 boys, 19 girls. 17 dissenters, 2 Roman Catholics. C of E inmates accompanied the Master and attended the Parish churches. Vagrant wards - new wards for 13 males in course of construction - in the meantime vagrants are lodged in the town. Present number - 166, last year 146."* [24]

They made no mention of number of 'lunatics' or 'idiots' in that report.

The care of the physically ill was done with limited resources. Workhouse residents would take on the duties we nowadays think of as a nurse's duties. In July 1885 a committee was set up to *"consider proper efficiency in nursing"* [25] and they applied to the *"association for promotion of trained nursing in workhouse infirmary"* to supply Hitchin Union with a nurse. I was interested in the Hitchin Board of Guardians minutes for 1886 [25] as there had been planning for an extension to the Hitchin Workhouse Infirmary (also on the Chalkdell site and not to be confused with the Hitchin Infirmary built on Bedford Road in 1840) and wondered if there had been any thoughts then about housing the mentally ill. The impression from reading accounts of the movement of lunatics was that it was not until someone became dangerous that the transfer to the asylum took place. People who have a long term illness such as schizophrenia and who do not receive any treatment will often have symptoms and behave erratically for long periods and may only rarely become 'dangerous'. So I would expect that people with that illness would be known and would cause concern long before admission to the asylum became essential. Some intermediate placement such as a workhouse ward would fill that need, but there is no evidence that such a lunatic ward was developed.

Mr Fowler, the Master of the workhouse was summoned to a meeting of the Poor Law Board in October 1886 where *"the defects of the plans for enlargement of the Infirmary would be explained to him"*. No details of the use of the extension

Hitchin Hospital, built as the Workhouse Infirmary before 1870. It probably housed a small group of people with learning difficulties but was not used for people identified as 'lunatics'.
Photo by author 2010

are given in Board minutes, but it was built, presumably after the plans had been modified, in 1887. The builder was Matthew Foster, who submitted a tender of £395 which was accepted over George Jeeves' tender of £432.

Mr Fowler, who arrived at the workhouse in 1877 as schoolmaster and assistant master to Mr Wakenell, became Master in 1882. There is an account from him on his retirement in 1902 of what the workhouse was like when he arrived in 1877 [26]. He said that the workhouse infirmary then accommodated 48 patients and had *"one room completely filled with idiots"*. He also mentioned the problem of the workhouse being inundated with tramps, 250 in one week, 60 – 100 in one night. He thought they were attracted by the good markets nearby and by Mad Lucas's generosity (though James Lucas had died 5 years before Fowler arrived - see chapter 5).

The Lunacy Commission has reports which include a document with details of a national survey that was done in 1883 to discover how many patients in asylums were misplaced. Three Counties Asylum was recorded as having 80 patients who could be elsewhere, 44 in a special lunacy ward in the workhouse and 37 in a workhouse infirmary *"with a paid nurse"* [27]. They did not list which of the three counties such 'misplaced people' were from. The Board of Guardians do not indicate any impact of this concern, there was no discussion about it and so-called 'lunatics' were no more present in 1891 than they were in the 1881 census.

The numbers of people detained in asylums had increased over the years since the 1845 Acts and there was much speculation on the causes of this as well as concern about how these increased numbers could be accommodated. Treatment, such as it was (described in chapter 4) had not yielded cures and asylum care often became long term care. The fact that people may have stayed in the workhouse would not seem to have affected the long term course of their illness, treatment was available in neither place. Looking at modern developments it could even be argued that keeping them at the workhouse with easier movement back to the local community and avoiding the long term care and 'institutionalisation' that happened in the remote and self contained asylum may have been to their ultimate benefit. As in the modern era there is an ongoing debate about how many of the in-patients really need to be in hospital or other care and whether alternative provision would be better and cheaper.

Notes

1. http://www.workhouses.org.uk
2. Jones, Kathleen. 'A History of Mental Health Services'. Routledge Keagan & Paul. 1972. p 20
3. Brundage, Anthony. 'The English Poor Laws 1700 – 1930'. Palgrave. 2002. p 12
4. Hitchin Museum. Lawson Thompson Scrapbook (LTS). Vol 1, p 5
5. Brundage, p 105
6. Foster, A.M. 'Market Town'. Hitchin Historical Society. 1987 p 19-20
7. www.workhouses.org.uk/
8. www.baldockhistory.org.uk/downloads/History-Streets-Womacks-Yard.pdf
9. Hertfordshire Archives and Local Studies. DP/ 53 8/2
10. Hertfordshire Archives and Local Studies DP/53 18/5
11. Ashby, Mgt. Editor. 'Hellard Almshouses and Other Stevenage Charities 1482 – 2005'. Hertfordshire Record Society. p 77
12. Dunnage, William. 'History of Hitchin'. 1815. Hitchin Museum
13. Hitchin Museum Archives
14. Hertfordshire Archives and Local Studies QS/Misc/B/3
15. Hertfordshire Archives and Local Studies DP/53 18/2
16. Hertfordshire Archives and Local Studies BG/HIT 1-3
17. http://www.pssru.ac.uk/pdf/uc/uc2010/uc2010_s02.pdf
18. 'The Asylum's Critics', in Scull, A, 'The Most Solitary of Afflictions'. Yale University Press. 1993. p 138 - 146
19. Hertfordshire Archives and Local Studies BG/HIT 16-18
20. Jones, Kathleen. 'Lunacy Law and Conscience 1744 – 1845'. Routledge Keagan & Paul. 1955. p 167
21. National Archives MH 19/168
22. Higgs, Edward. 'Making Sense of the Census'. Public Record Office. 1989
23. Mellett, D.J. 'Bureaucracy and mental illness: the Commissioners in Lunacy 1845 – 90'. Medical History. 1981. July 25(3). p 239
24. National Archives MH12/4620
25. Hertfordshire Archives and Local Studies. BG/HIT 31
26. Lawson Thompson Scrapbook Workhouse III.25.209
27. National Archives MH19/170

The Movers and the Quakers — Changes at the Beginning of the 19th Century

3

It would be difficult to argue that Hitchin was at the centre of any revolution in the care of the mentally ill, but there are a few associations or connections that we can claim to have with the movers and shakers, or Quakers, in the early 19th century. However any account of this era should probably start with the King, who had no specific connection with this part of the world, though in the film 'The Madness of King George' (1994) his part was played by a local resident, Nigel Hawthorne. His illness changed people's perceptions and probably led to changes in the laws and the care of the insane.

The Madness of King George III

George III, who lived from 1738 until 1820, had bouts of what were seen to be insanity from 1788. He had periods when he was quite sensible and lucid but then became quite deranged, although the total time that he was regarded as unwell only amounted to 6 months before 1810. However this was unprecedented. There was a view that such problems were the result of people's bad behaviour or bad inheritance, but clearly the king was above reproach. Parliament was concerned as the monarch's role in governing the country was much more involved than is currently so. The problems he had were beyond the expertise of the court physicians and so doctors who specialised in mental disorders, the 'mad-doctors', previously regarded as inferior to general physicians and surgeons, were brought in. Dr Francis Willis and his sons were the most prominent of these specialists and did try to cure him by imposing a fearsome regime of therapy. The basic care included restraint in 'strait-waistcoat', isolating him to avoid excitement, inducing vomiting and causing blistering to release the bad humours. Despite, or maybe because of this, the ailment did continue to recur and by 1810 he had become so incapacitated that his son became regent for the ten years until George died.

The nature of his ailment or 'malady' was a mystery but in 1960 two London psychiatrists, the mother and son team of Ida Macalpine and Richard Hunter, investigated the 'malady'. They came to the conclusion that George had suffered primarily from a physical metabolic disease, porphyria, which is caused by the abnormal metabolism of haemoglobin (the important protein in red blood cells) [1]. This leads to episodes of confusion and sickness and discoloured urine which is usually described as being like port wine. The condition is inherited and they traced evidence that other members of the family had similar symptoms starting with King James 1 in 1613 or possibly earlier. It is said that after the publication of this research the royal family were not displeased that the spectre of mental illness in the family had been disproved. However in January 2010 a publication in the History of Psychiatry Journal re-examined the evidence and concluded that George really did have a manic-depressive or bipolar disorder [2].

The importance of his ailment was that it did make insanity somehow more respectable and the status of the doctors who treated this type of

King George III of Great Britain and Ireland, who lived from 1738 until 1820. He became King on 25 October 1760, crowned after the death of his grandfather, George II, who had reigned from 1727. He was succeeded by his son, George IV, who also acted as Regent when he became incapable in 1810.

Portrait by Allan Ramsay, 1762.
http://thepeerage.com

problem improved. In modern jargon the stigma of insanity was reduced. Dr Willis claimed that nine out of ten of his patients were cured by his treatment, which was unproven propaganda, but it was believed at the time. Because George did improve between attacks it bred some optimism that such conditions did not always continue to deteriorate.

Another incident involving George also brought about a change in the perception of insanity. In 1799 James Hadfield had tried to assassinate George and Hadfield's lawyers convinced the court that he was suffering from religious delusions which had caused him to act as he did. The conclusion of the court made the precedent that people could thereafter be found 'not guilty by reason of insanity'.

Whilst the 'treatments' tried on King George were often nothing more than restraint and debilitating and unproven remedies, it did prompt a search for something more effective, and perhaps more humane. One recorded effort involved what must have been the first proper trial of a psychiatric treatment. This was organized by way of a committee which was set up in 1812 by the Dukes of Kent and Sussex to investigate the claims of two men, Lucett and Delahoyde. The latter claimed that their treatment could cure insanity within

40 minutes. Whilst they were initially coy about the treatment it was eventually revealed as a special combination of two treatments which had been long doing the rounds. They immersed the patient's body in warm water while pouring cold water on the head. The treatment did seem to have successful outcomes in some, including the wife of Joseph Lancaster (who established the British Schools, as discussed below). Elizabeth Lancaster developed some form of 'insanity' after childbirth which recurred through much of her life, though reading about their life together it seems she must have experienced enormous stress due to Joseph's erratic ways. She had the treatment of Delahoyde and Lucett which was described as *"a new curative treatment for insanity"* and experienced a remission or period without symptoms afterwards. Whether this remission was the result of treatment or just a temporary separation from her husband and the stress he induced is not known. She was later admitted to the Retreat at York (also discussed later in this chapter).

Samuel Whitbread II of Bedford and Southill.

Samuel Whitbread junior was born in 1764 in Cardington, just south of Bedford, where his father lived and owned land. His father, also Samuel, had become very rich from the development of a brewery business in London. Father had moved to Bedwell Park in Essendon, just south of Hatfield, but later bought the estate of Southill Park, near Old Warden, and Samuel junior inherited that when his father died in 1796 [3]. The estate is still occupied by the family. Samuel joined his father's company in 1786 but had other interests. He was a magistrate, an art collector and a radical politician.

Samuel Whitbread took over his father's seat and became MP for Bedford in 1790 and was very active in the town. He was involved in the founding of the House of Industry in 1794, being the workhouse which later became part of the General Hospital, Bedford Prison which was rebuilt in 1801, of Bedford Infirmary in 1803, and the rebuilding of the main town bridge in 1811 [4]. He was a local magistrate with the reputation of hearing cases on every day of the year. He was a Whig or Liberal politician who followed Charles James Fox until his death in 1806. He introduced Parliamentary bills on various issues including a minimum wage for workers and relief for the poor. One of his radical ideas was to provide support or relief for men before they became destitute. The custom was for people wanting relief to sell off all that they had before any relief could be offered. For a craftsman that meant selling the means for them to earn a living, thus condemning them to giving up their trade and their best means of ever earning again.

A zealous reformer, Samuel campaigned for the abolition of slavery and for a national system of education. Following his father he supported Thomas Clarkson who was the main figure in seeking to abolish the slave trade [5]. He also tried to introduce laws on education of the poor with a proposal to have general system of national education by rate aided voluntary parochial schools, mentioning and praising the Lancasterian system [6]. The 'Parish Schools Bill' of 1807 was introduced by him but was thrown out by the House of Lords.

He had become involved with the Lancasterian Schools, which the British School Museum in Hitchin uniquely commemorates. When Joseph Lancaster, the founder and inspiration of the system which bore his name, had financial problems in 1807 he initially turned to Samuel Whitbread to help him out. Lancaster probably suffered from a manic-depressive disorder and was very careless about money. He could be very excitable, and was incapable of managing his or the schools' finances. However the most damaging issues arose when he was accused of using corporal punishment on boys. This was completely against Lancaster's educational principles and it seems that he was gratifying some personal desire. That and the financial problems led to hearings in 1813

Samuel Whitbread II (1764 – 1815). Portrait as a young man by Thomas Gainsborough in 1788, reputedly as a wedding present for his wife [7].
He went into the family brewery business but pursued an active political career in the Whig party, was active in the life of Bedford and established Bedford Asylum in 1812.
From a portrait in the Whitbread collection.

which Samuel chaired. The result was that the Society was renamed the British and Foreign Schools Society and Joseph became quite alienated from it, moving abroad to try and recreate his success in North and South America [8].

Samuel had met Lancaster in Hitchin in 1807, and had business connections with William Wilshere, a Hitchin solicitor (who took over the firm once owned by the Drapers from Richard Tristram, which was later taken over by John Hawkins). Wilshere founded the Hitchin Lancasterian School in 1810, owning the building and adjoining house in which it operated. On his death in 1824 He bequeathed the school and property to support it to Lord Dacre [9]. Wilshere was described as a country attorney and small landowner who bought from Samuel one tenth of his share in the brewery business, which made him a wealthy man [10]. There is an extensive archive of letters between the two men in the Bedfordshire Archives, mostly about legal and land matters, but nothing about British Schools or the mentally ill, although it is recorded that Wilshere was involved in the setting up of Bedford Asylum, which we will come to.

In the period between 1808 and 1815 Samuel was the most frequent

British Schools in Queen Street, Hitchin, built in 1835 after a fire destroyed the original school rooms. Now an active museum which draws school parties to re-enact a day in a Victorian classroom, and houses a unique archive of early school books and other educational material.

Photo by author 2011

contributor to debates in the House of Commons and from 1810 was additionally organizing the rebuilding of Drury Lane Theatre. A busy man. Sadly he was also becoming depressed. It has been suggested that he developed a hormone disorder, Cushing's syndrome, because his physical appearance changed significantly [11]. He then had a crisis in 1815. He had been an advocate of Napoleon's reforms in France and was seen as a Francophile. Unfortunately England was at war with the French. When Napoleon was defeated at Waterloo in June 1815, Whitbread became frightened that the mob would come after him. A Hitchin mob had at that time burnt effigies of those who had not celebrated the victory, usually Quakers who opposed all war [12]. In his depressed state Samuel then cut his throat and died on July 6th 1815.

An Act for the better Care and Maintenance of Lunatics (1808)

There is no account of how Samuel Whitbread first became involved with the care of lunatics but he was on the Parliamentary Select Committee which formulated the first laws specifically for the pauper lunatics. The committee was formed at the instigation of Charles Wynn (a Welsh MP) and included William Wilberforce [13]. The committee met in 1807 and tried to gather evidence on which to decide what laws were required. However there was no system of care at that time, no agreed definitions of who were lunatics or insane, and hardly anybody who could be regarded as specialists. A bit like stone age men trying to write a highway code.

They tried to find out how many pauper lunatics were in each county. The requests for information went to each county's Quarter Sessions. There was no obligation before then for any authority to collect such information. The Quarter Sessions may have been aware of such people in their area because of the problems they caused and the occasional need to have them transported to an asylum, which they would authorize. Since 1774 Quarter Sessions courts had been responsible for licensing and inspection of madhouses. While some counties had some grasp of the numbers which might roughly fall into this category, it appears that Hertfordshire and Bedfordshire were not amongst them. They both reported that there were no pauper lunatics in their county.

Lunatics may have stayed at home if there was someone to look after them and they were not troublesome, but otherwise they may have been in the poorhouses. There was no requirement to report on inmates to any other authority. The parishes may have put dangerous lunatics in madhouses, which were only required to record the private patients they housed, or they may have been in houses of industry or correction (or bridewells, now called prisons). Onesiphorus Paul (a Gloucester MP) advised on a plan to remove lunatics from prisons and workhouses, for asylums to be established and for parishes to pay for the care when families could not [14].

Probably due to the recognition that they had no records of lunatics in the bridewells there was a survey mounted in 1810 whereby each county's Quarter Sessions was asked to report how many pauper lunatics they had placed in custody in the previous 10 years. The response from the Hitchin bridewell was that there had only been one, and he had escaped. The return was made by Henry Bentley, the keeper of the bridewell, on September 7th 1810, who reported that John Wye, a criminal lunatic, had been committed to the bridewell on May 5th 1810 but made his escape on August 6th. He said there had been no others confined since 1800 [15].

It seems remarkable that the Justices of the Peace happened to ask the keeper just a month after his only inmate in 10 years had been confined there, and it seems very likely that the thought of identifying the inmates as lunatics had not previously occurred to him.

Meanwhile parliament did recognize that there was a need to organize some care for the pauper lunatics and the 1808 Act approved, but did not require, that counties could build their own asylums and could raise money for building them from the rates paid by property owners.

Samuel Whitbread set to work to establish an asylum in Bedford [16]. At the first meeting in October 1808, which was a General Quarter Sessions and at which William Wilshere was present, he ordered the Clerk of the Peace to obtain from all the towns , hamlets and places in Bedfordshire a return of all *"Lunatic Insane Persons and Dangerous Idiots therein"* [17]. He identified 147 pauper lunatics in the county and concluded that an asylum with 100 places for lunatics would be needed. The economics led to his plans being trimmed so that when the asylum was built and opened in 1812 it was designed to hold just 40 patients. Wilshere had attended most of the meetings leading up to the opening when they discussed many of the details, with advice from St Luke's Asylum in London on the furnishings, fittings and the staffing necessary.

This was the second county asylum to be built, only Northamptonshire preceding it, and only 12 were built in England before such provision became mandatory in 1845. The asylum was later used for Hertfordshire people, from 1820 until it closed in1860, but more of that later.

Samuel Tuke and the Retreat at York

The third strand at the end of the 18th century which led to widespread change was the founding of the Retreat, a Quaker institution at York, by the Tuke family. A young member of the Quaker meeting had been admitted to the York Asylum in 1791 and died two weeks later in what were described as dubious circumstances. The asylum seems to have operated with a cruel regime of restraint and little care.

The Retreat opened in 1796. William and Henry Tuke, father and son, were tea and coffee traders with no experience of mental illness and its care. They believed that the Quaker people should have access to a better sort of care and so set up the Retreat, originally just for Quakers, but open to all from 1818 when there was a need to subsidize poorer Quaker inmates with higher fees from the affluent non-Quakers [18]. The Retreat has continued to function and is today a specialist private hospital for people with long term mental illness requiring rehabilitation.

Henry's son Samuel had a spell of medical training but never qualified as a doctor and went into the family business. However he was involved with the Retreat and in 1813 published an account of its methods of managing the insane. He described the regime that was adopted as *"moral treatment"*. Some of this was not new but he described a total environment with a consistent approach by the staff which included useful activities, exercise, a good diet, reduced and careful use of restraint when patients were violent, encouragement in religious instruction and measures to improve reasoning and self-esteem. *"The patient feeling himself of some consequence, is induced to support it by the exertion of his reason, and by restraining those dispositions, which if indulged, would lessen the respectful treatment he receives; or lower his character in the eyes of his companions and attendants"* [19]. The prevailing

William Tuke (1732 – 1822) who founded The Retreat at York with his son Henry. His grandson Samuel wrote 'The Description of the Retreat' in 1813. William's daughter, Elizabeth Wheeler, lived in Hitchin, and her house became a second home to her nephew Samuel Tuke [20].

Portrait from Hine's 'History of Hitchin', vol II. p 226, from a painting by H.S.Tuke, R.A.

William Norris, whose case was used to illustrate the inhumanity of mechanical restraints. Norris had been restrained for at least 9 years in an iron cage. He was unable to move more than 2 feet from the iron bar which was fixed along the wall of his cell. The reason given for this was his extreme violence. He was found by Edward Wakefield, a Quaker reformer, who visited Bethlem in 1814, following the scandals at York Asylum. Norris was released from this confinement but died shortly afterwards in 1815. The physician and the apothecary at Bethlem were dismissed after a parliamentary select committee criticized the regime at the asylum [21, 22]. There was an intention to change the laws and improve the care of patients but it took 13 years before that happened. Illustration from Wellcome Library L0010941.

view had been that insanity was a reversion to a primitive and animal like state and would be best managed by restraint, discipline and harsh training, or was due to an imbalance of the fluids or humours in the body (blood and bile) and ridding the body of these by bleeding, vomiting or blistering was appropriate treatment. The Retreat used some of these methods but generally found them ineffective and only applied them carefully. They did advocate the usefulness of a warm bath for the melancholic. At the same time as other asylums were still chaining patients for long periods the Retreat used a strait-waistcoat or specially designed bedding to restrain the patient when occasionally needed. They treated the patients like adults whereas the patients noted that visitors would talk to them like children. Tuke describes the condition of patients as suffering from *"mental alienation"*, rather than the prevailing view that the *"thinking faculty"* had been *"abolished"*. He advised on the need to avoid focussing on the despondent thoughts of the melancholic, but rather find subjects to distract him.

One of the advantages of the Retreat in the beginning was the small size with a good staffing ratio, with one member of staff to 8 patients, compared with up to 1 staff to 22 patients at public asylums, though less than some of the select private asylums [23]. This enabled them to maintain a family like atmosphere. They also had a small number of admissions, only 149 in the first 15 years [24] and no more than 72 residents before 1823 [25]. When the *"treatment"* was adopted in the public asylums there was a dilution of the ingredients, the approach came to be called *"moral management"* and was a more impersonal and rigid institutional regime. This did not bring about the expected cures, but at least the harsher regimes of the 18th century asylums were seen to be inappropriate and were phased out.

One of the immediate outcomes of Tuke's book being published was that the Governors of the nearby York Asylum thought that their own methods of 'care' were being criticized and publicly accused Tuke of defamation. They stirred up a hornet's nest. Tuke and other local activists paid the £20 required to become governors of the York Asylum and investigated the practices there. They found people locked up in cramped, putrid and filthy rooms. While that was happening a fire broke out and a number of patients who were chained up died in the fire [26]. Another group of reformers in London tried to visit Bethlem and after gaining access to the building, which had been in use since 1676, discovered rooms with women chained up and mostly naked, describing them as *"like a dog kennel"*.

The reformers formed a parliamentary select committee in 1814 and prepared a bill to protect the mentally ill, but it was rejected by the House of Lords and new legislation was not passed until 1828.

Philippe Pinel in France had been pioneering reforms and first published his thoughts about this in 1801. He was aware of other reformers in England and Germany and presented a clear case for more careful observation and humane management of the insane, most famously taking the chains off the inmates of Bicêtre, the Paris lunatic asylum. His actions are commemorated by the statue outside the Salpêtrière, the other Paris asylum.

Pinel suggested that the *"surest measure to maintain good health is the rule of mechanical work"*, that *"the reawakening of talent must be grasped in order to promote and accelerate the growth of mental abilities"* and quoted Doctor Haslam from Bethlem that *"it is a most important objective to win the trust of patients and instil feelings of respect and obedience"* [27]. For treatment Pinel suggested that the patient should be isolated from family, fed, encouraged and kept calm when lucid, insomnia be corrected, while reducing physical restraint, cold baths and blood-letting and increasing warm showers, work, reason and relaxation.

Various other treatments were tried but nothing of any lasting benefit was found during the rest of the century. It has been argued by Andrew Scull in 'The Most Solitary of Afflictions' that the apparent ability of medical specialists to understand and treat mental illness was an illusion [28]. They claimed an expertise which society accepted, because nobody had a clue what caused such problems. If the problem behaviour was called an illness it made it seem that doctors would know what to do and could offer advice, if only to say that the problem was incurable. The growth in asylums fitted that way of thinking. The people and problems were confined in one place, the responsibility could be taken on by the doctors and asylum attendants, thus relieving the parishes of the worry, and the staff would be paid and make a living.

At least the 'moral management' was a step in the right direction of not intervening with unproven treatments and possibly making the problem worse. At best it did help the 'insane' feel that they were being valued and treated as humans. So Samuel Tuke was a person to be taken note of, with a reputation that has survived until the 21st century. And he went to school in Hitchin. But more of that later.

The bigger picture — salvation by system?

One of the foremost historians of psychiatry was Roy Porter, a professor at the Wellcome Institute in London. In his book 'Madmen, A Social History of Madhouses, Mad-Doctors & Lunatics' [29], he talks about the changes occurring at the beginning of the 19th century as due to *"salvation by system"* and mentions Jeremy Bentham and Joseph Lancaster's monitorial schools as leading these changes. The fact that Samuel Whitbread was so closely involved with the development of asylums and with the Lancasterian schools raises the question of whether he was a follower of Bentham.

Jeremy Bentham lived from 1748 to 1832 and was known for his inspiration to reformers. He was particularly keen to improve the legal system, but was also quite practical and designed a 'panopticon' as a building which would be suitable for use as a workhouse, prison or mad-house [30]. The panopticon was designed with a central inspector's lodge placed so that the staff could easily keep the inmates under close scrutiny. Whilst he promoted the idea of the greatest happiness for the greatest number, that did include the idea of firmly keeping the miscreants and criminals locked up. He also had no time for religion. Bentham's political ideas took root and were later developed by John Stuart Mill as utilitarianism, briefly expressed as the doctrine that actions should be guided by what gives more pleasure to the majority of people. It was not surprising that when Edward Bulwer Lytton, of Knebworth House (see chapter 6), became an MP for Lincoln in 1831 that he, as a 'radical', was said to be influenced by Bentham and much impressed by one of Bentham's disciples, Robert Owen. Owen was another radical figure of that time who managed the New Lanark cotton mills. He introduced new working practices, reduced children's labour and provided education for the workers. He had some contact with Joseph Lancaster who visited New Lanark in 1812, (Owen's son describing the Quaker visitor as *"a strange mixture of honest, self-sacrificing zeal and imprudent, self-indulgent ostentation"* [31]). Two members of the board of the Lancasterian Society, William Allen and Joseph Fox, as well as Bentham, became involved in his enterprise. Owen did seek an introduction to Whitbread in 1813 but they never met [32].

Whitbread may have been influenced by Bentham, but there is no clear evidence for this and there is no correspondence between them in the Bedford or Southill archives. He was however involved with 26 religious reforming societies, many of them evangelical [33]. His father was regarded as *"conspicuously religious"*, but it is difficult to know how much this influenced Samuel junior [34]. What drove him is not clear, but religious motivation, which inspired William Wilberforce and other lunacy reformers such as Lord Shaftesbury, does seem likely to have been at least as important as the ideas of Bentham.

Scull's view is that the lunacy reformers ranks included leading adherents of both evangelicalism and Benthamism, and the final shape of lunacy legislation in England clearly owes much to the evangelicals' humanitarianism and paternalism, and to the Benthamite emphasis on expertise and efficiency [35].

Notes

1. Macalpine, Ida and Hunter, Richard. 'George III and the Mad-Business'. Penguin Press. 1969
2. Peters, T.J & Beveridge, A. 'The madness of King George III: A psychiatric reassessment'. History of Psychiatry. Vol. 21. No. 1. p 20 – 37
3. Whitbread, Sam. 'Plain Mr Whitbread. 'The Book Castle. 2007
4. Cashman, Bernard. 'A Proper House. Bedford Lunatic Asylum: 1812 – 1860'. North Beds Health Authority 1992. p ix
5. Bell, Patricia. 'Paintings Politics & Porter. S C Whitbread 1995 p 14
6. Dickson, Mora. 'Teacher Extraordinary'. The Book Guild. 1986
7. Deuchar, Stephen. 'Paintings Politics & Porter'. Whitbread & Co. 1984 p 47
8. Taylor, Joyce. 'The Poor Child's Friend'. Campanile Press. 1996. Ch IV
9. Dodwell, Fiona. ' Hitchin British Schools, Schooldays 1810 – 1900'. North Herts District Council. 1993
10. Fulford, Roger. 'A Study in Opposition'. Macmillan. 1967. p 94
11. Rapp, Dean. 'A Social and Political Study'. Garland Publ. 1987. PhD thesis. Bedfordshire and Luton Archives and Records Service. p 488
12. 'Hitchin Quakers Ancient and Modern - a talk given to Hitchin Historical Society by Metford Robson', 2002
13. www.studymore
14. Jones, Kathleen. 'A History of Mental Health Services". Routledge Keagan & Paul 1972. p 55-59
15. Hertfordshire Archives and Local Studies QS Misc .B.11800
16. Cashman. Chapter 2
17. Bedfordshire and Luton Archives and Records Service. Q.G.E.1
18. Digby, Anne.' Moral treatment at the Retreat, 1796 – 1846'. In 'The Anatomy of Madness', Vol II. ed Bynum, Porter and Shepherd. Tavistock Publications. 1985. p 62
19. Tuke, Samuel. 'Description of the Retreat. p 159. Available on http://books.google.co.uk
20. Hine. 'History of Hitchin'. Vol II. George Allen & Unwin. 1929. p 220
21. Arnold, Catherine. 'Bedlam'. Pocket Books. 2009. p 170 – 2
22. Scull, 'The Most Solitary of Afflictions'. Yale University Press. 1993. p 93 -5
23. Digby. p 58
24. Tuke, p 201
25. Digby. p 68
26. Macalpine & Hunter. 1969. chapter 24
27. Pinel, Philippe. 'Medico-Philosophical Treatise on Mental Alienation'. 2nd edition. 1809. Wiley 2008. p 95
28. Scull, Andrew. 1993
29. Porter, Roy. 'Madmen, A Social History of Madhouses, Mad-Doctors & Lunatics'. Tempus, illustrated edn 2004, first publ as 'Mind Forg'd Manacles'. 1987
30. Bentham, Jeremy. 'Panopticon; or, The Inspection House'. 1791. Reprinted Dodo Press. 2008
31. Taylor, p 87
32. Bedfordshire and Luton Archives and Records Service W1/3684-6
33. Rapp. 1987
34. Deuchar, 1984 Introduction
35. Scull, 1993 p 84

The Local Asylums and Madhouses in the 19th Century

4

The House that Sam built

Samuel Whitbread's hopes for creating an asylum in Bedford quickly bore fruit. After an initial meeting in October 1808 a meeting of the magistrates in January 1809 confirmed that they would proceed with the erection of an asylum [1]. By April 1812 they were ready to appoint the staff. Whitbread took the lead on this, sought advice and met some of the candidates before the committee appointed the first governor. He was William Pither, a house painter by trade who had dealt with a lunatic in the course of his work. That, and the amiability of his wife, seemed to decide the issue. His wife Mary became the matron. A surgeon from the Bedford Infirmary, William Leech, was appointed to deal with medical problems. They ordered the leg locks, chains and strait-waistcoats and they were ready for their first patients.

Dr Yeats became Medical Superintendant in the following year but clearly felt unhappy at not having overall control and the authority of Pither was challenged and eventually undermined [2]. John Harris, who had been first appointed to the asylum in 1823, became manager as well as surgeon in 1828 and Mr Pither left. While the struggle for supremacy between the doctor and manager had been a continuing problem, and recurs every time there is some reorganization in the NHS, the first problem that the managing committee had to deal with was the lack of patients.

Payment for lunatics who had been admitted to the asylum was made by their home parish. The parishes were not keen to pay for this and so chose not to send people to the asylum. This was a recurring theme for many decades after. The medical profession claimed an expertise and skill in curing lunatics which had little support, and there seemed little point in transferring incurable lunatics to a more expensive residence at the asylum. However the workhouses could not cope with very disturbed 'lunatics' and those who were very violent or suicidal were transferred. By 1820 people from the Hitchin area were being admitted to the Bedford Asylum, presumably because the nearest alternatives were the London madhouses. In the same year the Marquess of Salisbury offered

Bedford Asylum was built in 1812 on Ampthill Road in Bedford. It closed in 1860 when Three Counties Asylum was built near Arlesey and was later demolished.

Print in Bedfordshire Archives [3]

Hertford Castle for use as a lunatic asylum, but the offer was not accepted by the Quarter Sessions [4].

Patients recorded as being admitted to Bedford Asylum [5] include

John Oakley, age 50, a farmer from Offley who was admitted on April 26th 1821 on the authority of William Wilshere (a local magistrate) and certified by Oswald Foster, a Hitchin doctor (1773 – 1841). {Foster's son, also Oswald, 1808 – 1892, succeeded to his father's medical practice and was medical officer to Hitchin Infirmary in Bedford Road}. Oakley would have been a private patient as paupers did not need to be medically certified at that time.

Edward Ralph, age 34, admitted on April 23rd 1828 on the authority of William Whitbread, certified by Dr Hawkins, also of Hitchin {probably Frederick Hawkins, 1796 - 1864, founder of the Hitchin Dispensary in 1823 and of the Hitchin Infirmary in 1840, which became the North Herts & South Beds Hospital in the 20th century - see Henry Hawkins, chapter 5}. Ralph was 'found lunatic by inquiry' on January 4th 1831, presumably by the Visitors from the County Sessions. He would also have been a private patient.

The asylum would have had formal visitors, including doctors appointed by the county magistrates, who did some form of interview or assessment on private inmates. The Madhouse Act of 1774 stipulated that private patients should have official visitors to ensure that no gentlemen or ladies were wrongly detained in such houses. Visitors to London madhouses were from the Royal College of Physicians. The 1828 Madhouse Act replaced the College of Physicians with

Metropolitan Commissioners in Lunacy who did such visits, while outside London, Justices at Quarter Sessions appointed Visitors (three or more Justices and one or more doctors who had to visit licensed houses four times a year). The 1845 Lunacy Act replaced this arrangement with a national inspectorate, the Lunacy Commission. The Lunacy Commissioners who were employed full time were three doctors and three lawyers. The 1845 Acts were regarded as the outcome of the work of Lord Ashley (Anthony Ashley Cooper), later the 7th Earl of Shaftesbury.

The records of the Lunacy Commission in the National Archives identified how many in each institution had been examined by the visiting Commissioners. In licensed houses and asylums they recorded how many had been 'found lunatic by inquiry'. The examination to determine this would have been done by two Commissioners, one medical and one legal. How they determined that someone was 'lunatic' is not spelt out. Up to half of the residents in the small licensed houses were so examined (and mostly found to be lunatic), whereas it was unusual for any patients amongst the hundreds in the asylums to be examined.

The 1828 County Asylums Act obliged visiting justices to submit annual returns to the Quarter Sessions Clerk of admissions, discharges and deaths. The numbers held at Bedford Asylum became available and in that year, 37 were Bedford paupers, 5 other paupers and 15 private patients [6].

The Bedford Asylum records [7] do not contain much detail about the treatment or the course of people's stay there, except in 1836. It was then noted that

Elizabeth Bigg, age 35 and admitted on December 29th 1835, died on December 14th 1836, Caroline Barker, aged 22, from Hitchin was discharged cured on October 16th , but readmitted on February 20th 1837.

Elizabeth Trolley, aged 57, from Baldock, admitted on October 16th was discharged "relieved" on October 31st.

Sarah Whitney, aged 32, from Hitchin was "removed" on December 23rd.

In 1836 the Hertfordshire magistrates appointed a liaison committee to consider formal arrangement for sending lunatics to Bedford Asylum. From the records it is clear that there followed several admissions from around Hertfordshire and particularly from St Albans. There was initially a limit of 20 patients from Hertfordshire but that was soon exceeded with 36 in 1839. Patients were also admitted from Huntingdonshire, Buckinghamshire, Cambridgeshire and Northamptonshire.

In order to accommodate the influx an agreement was made that the asylum should not receive any private patients. In 1837 the medical officer, John Harris, set up Springfield House in Kempston, just outside Bedford, to take the private patients. This was a licensed house, smaller than those at Hoxton and Bethnal Green in North London where local people had previously been sent.

Local Licensed Houses in the 19th century

While the growth of public and then county asylums would seem likely to have reduced the 'trade in lunacy', there was actually a growth in the first half of the 19th century until the widespread establishment of public asylums in all counties [8].

Most of the asylum growth was for the 'pauper classes' whilst 'respectable' people would have avoided the asylums as much as they would have avoided the dreadful conditions and stigma of the workhouses. After 1774 licensing led madhouses being known by the more respectable title of licensed houses. The records of those licensed houses are very limited with few details available for the Hertfordshire houses, but slightly more from Springfield House. The records of Springfield [9] show that it did take patients from the Hitchin area, but there are no details of the patients admitted to Hadham Palace and Harpenden Hall in Hertfordshire. However they both lead to some interesting diversions.

Hadham Palace

The records for this institution available at Hertfordshire Archives are sparse, mostly consisting of Visitors' reports between 1849 and 1856 and correspondence about renewing the licence [10]. It was located in Much Hadham in south east Herts and had been a home for the Bishops of London [11] and is now a private residence. The first record of it as a licensed house is in the Quarter Sessions records of 1803 when Robert Jacobs was granted a licence (as required under the 1774 Madhouse Act) *"to keep house for reception of lunaticks not exceeding 10"* [12]. Subsequent records show this licence to be renewed each year. In 1822 David Times of Hitchin was named as surety for it while Dr Ord of Hertford was named as visiting physician. In 1826 Mary Munro of Much Hadham was licensed *"to keep a house for the reception of lunaticks not exceeding 10"*. The Munro family were famous in this field – having been the physicians at Bethlem from 1728 (until 1752). Mary had married Thomas, the son of James Monro the first of the Bethlem physicians. When Thomas died she married Robert Jacob who

The Palace at Much Hadham. It was built in the 16th century and was one of the country houses of the Bishops of London until 1746. It ceased to be an asylum in 1882 and was sold by the Ecclesiastical Commissioners in 1888. It is now a private residence. [13]

died in 1825. It seems that she would have continued to run Hadham Palace but she died in 1828. Her daughter Mary went into partnership with James Smith, a *"surgeon, apothecary & accoucheur* (a male obstetrician)*"*, Mary being exempt *"from all personal attendance & exertion"* and *"neither to be engaged in any other lunatic establishment"* [14]. In 1829 the county Quarter Sessions records show that the number of patients allowed increased to 15.

James Smith was also there in 1856 by which time the licence allowed up to 20 patients but in that year just 10 were in residence. The documents in Hertfordshire Archives give no information about the residents or where they came from. There is a record of the visitors that were required to inspect the place in 1849, both the County Visitors, usually magistrates, and the Metropolitan Commission, by then part of the national Lunacy Commission [15]. The magistrates recorded that *"it appears to us...the care of these unfortunate inmates deserves our utmost praise and satisfaction"*. While the Metropolitan visitors, consisting of eight gentlemen and four ladies recorded that *"no one was subject to instrumental coercion"*, presumably a reference to the trend of reducing and abolishing any form of restraint in asylums and licensed houses. These visitors spoke to all three new patients and *"inspected the certificates"*. On March 6 1850 the County Visitors reported *"trifling restraint placed upon 2 of the patients, whose violence requires gloves and a belt to secure them from mischief"*.

When the County Visitors gave a report this was passed on to the Metropolitan Commission, as on May 29 1850 when James Smith copied the report of the visit of May 10th and sent it to a Mr Marchant, Clerk to the Visitors in Lunacy (Metropolitan Commission in Lunacy). N E Campbell and J R Hume visited and recorded that there were seven males and five females.

> *"We found them generally tranquil ...no one was under mechanical restraint or in seclusion... Two females are under occasional restraint at night by means of hand muffs, and it appears by the Register, that one Gentleman is under medical treatment…The patients have the usual means of occupation and amusement... at present one patient is in the habit of going to church on Sundays"*.

Another report describes the patients as, *"each living in separate apartments"*.

James Smith, designated as surgeon, proprietor and resident, is mentioned in the records in the 'Further Report of Commissioners in Lunacy' of 1847 [16]. This was a survey of private licensed houses concerning treatment adopted in 'mania, epilepsy, epilepsy complicated with insanity, paralysis complicated with insanity and melancholia'. The treatments described in the report included local bleeding, although this was condemned by some and general bleeding was not used. Smith was noted to advocate local bleeding from the temporal artery (on the side of the head), saying he used this only occasionally when the patient was highly excited. He also used cupping (then a form of bloodletting*) "on the nape of the neck if the vessels of the scalp or temple are turgid with blood"*. In common with others who were asked to give information he was keen on using purging and encouraged exercise and fresh air. Strangely he still used the warm bath for the body and cold water to the head which had been proven to be ineffective 30 years previously.

Harpenden Hall

John Rumball first had a licensed house for lunatics in St Albans, Herts in 1812. In 1820 he was joined in applying for a licence by James Quilter Rumball and in 1827 the latter moved to Oysterhills in St Albans. Sometime between 1840 and 1847 James moved to The Hall at Harpenden and that continued as a private asylum at least until 1898 [17]. They did take Hertfordshire patients but in the scanty records available there is no one mentioned from the Hitchin area. However the main interest is in the work of James Quilter Rumball. He was known as an advocate of phrenology. Whilst my awareness of this was limited to it being about trying to know somebody's character from the bumps on the head, and the archaic models of skulls with a diagram of the region of each aspect of personality painted on them, phrenology was the first 'science of the brain'. Between the 1820s and 1840s it attracted most of the country's leading psychiatrists. What now seems obviously to have been a misguided theory has been described as having completely reorientated psychiatric thought.

Phrenology emphasised that the brain was where the mind was located, that it consisted of different parts which controlled different aspects of personality and also different sorts of madness. This helped the doctors think more logically and moved them away from believing in the influence of black fluids controlling

Harpenden Hall in Southdown Road, Harpenden. It was let to Dr A H Boys for continued use as a private mental home in 1894 and sold by the Rumballs in 1901. It was subsequently used as a school until 1931 when it became council offices, and is now used as business premises. Hertfordshire Archives [18]

the mind, and away from treating people like disobedient animals. The idea that the skull was shaped by the growth of different parts of the brain was not an important part of the theory [19].

Meanwhile Harpenden Hall continued as a comfortable asylum which *"offers an armchair by his own fireside, horse or carriage exercise … gardening and farming, music and whist".* The Visitors appointed by the County Quarter Sessions attended and passed comments, generally bland and uncritical, and occasionally commented that patients spent too much time alone, or that they should *"join the family table"*, that is to eat with the family.

Springfield House, Kempston, near Bedford

John Harris built and managed Springfield House, initially licensed to have 30 patients in 1837. The official visitors' book shows that in 1845 it had 13 males and 9 female patients [20]. In 1855 it was licensed to receive a further 10 patients. John Harris died in 1861 and his son Henry took over until he died in 1878. It was bought the following year by David Bower, when it was overcrowded with 47 patients and a new wing was added. Bower ran it until 1929 when he died (a 50 year span) and his son took over [22]. Springfield finally closed in 1962 and in 1963 the asylum was demolished to make way for the expansion of Kempston New Town [23].

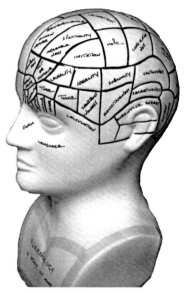

Phrenology skull, with the speculative areas of brain function mapped out. Human nature, benevolence, agreeableness, spirituality, imitation, hope, wit, inquisitiveness, secretiveness, calculation, order, colour and many other functions all find a place. Some alienists based treatment on their understanding of which part of the brain caused which illness, leading to the treatment of applying leeches to the relevant area of the head [21].

From the collection of Dr Gerry Tidy

Springfield took patients from several counties. The register of patients names several from the Hitchin area, but gives no details of their treatment. The notes in the register give the following details [24] -

Henry Blaine Admitted 4.8.1887. Died 21.4.1902. From Hitchin, sent by uncle, certified by F Hawkins and RR Shillitoe. Insane. No known cause.

Elizabeth Vaughan, age 45. Admitted 16.9.1884. Discharged not improved 20.4.1895, farmer's wife from Hitchin. Diagnosis mania. Cause 'drink'. Sent by authority of her father.

Mary Peck. Age 65. Admitted 2.12.87. Discharged relieved 18.11.98. Plumber's widow. Medical certificate completed by Daniel Hack Tuke and W Jenner. Sent by authority of her son. Diagnosis acute melancholia. Cause – family trouble.

Margaret Phillips. Age 33. Address 17 Bancroft, Hitchin. Admitted 12.5.1891. Discharged recovered 3.9.1891. House furnisher's wife. Medical certificate by O H Foster and Shillitoe. Diagnosis puerperal mania (ie. post natal or after childbirth).

Lunacy Commission Visitors came regularly to inspect the premises and at times seeing all of the patients, such as on July 20th 1852 [25]. William Campbell and Samuel Gaskell, a legal and a medical Commissioner, met all the patients and declared them to be *"generally tranquil, no one under mechanical restraint"*. One male patient was reported to require such restraint and wearing cuffs occasionally [26].

	Lunacy Commission 5th report 1850			10th report 1856		
	Private Patients	Pauper Patients	Found lunatic by inquisition	Private	Pauper	Found lunatic by inquisition
Bedford Asylum	0	252	0	0	299	0
Springfield House	17	0	3	23	0	4
Hadham Palace	12	0	3	11	0	3
Harpenden Hall	5	0	2	4	4	1

A summary table of the Lunacy Commission's report on patients in asylums [27]. The number "found lunatic by inquisition" demonstrates the concern felt for private patients who might be falsely detained as insane. The fact that none were found lunatic at Bedford Asylum indicates they did not examine any patients, as there were only paupers there.

Advertisement for Springfield House in Bedford Dated circa 1885 after David Bower had taken over from the original owner, John Harris.

Bedfordshire Archives [28]

The Birth of Three Counties Asylum in Arlesey

The number of patients admitted to Bedford Asylum continued to grow. There had been some debate about who needed admission. The Lunacy Act of 1845 stated that if pauper lunatics were dangerous they should be transferred to the asylum and this should be done within two weeks. In 1849 the Lunacy Commission wrote to the Lord Chancellor to question whether asylums were only for the dangerous insane, as they thought otherwise. They argued that if a person did not have home, family or friends it was not justified to remove that person from the shelter of an asylum [29].

At Bedford Asylum the number of patients continued to grow after the private patients had moved out. By 1847 there were 191 patients (with 9 under restraint) and by 1852 there were 270. There had been talk of a new asylum for Hertfordshire and this led to a protest from certain residents. In 1846 the inhabitants of Sandridge, Watton and Much Hadham sent a petition to the Justices of the County. They requested the delay in the building of a new county asylum, giving their reason that the duration of treatment in provincial licensed houses was two thirds less than in county lunatic asylums [30]. In 1852 Hertfordshire had two fifths of the patients at Bedford and was expected to pay two fifths of the costs of planned improvements to accommodate more patients. But the plans changed and in early 1853 the prospect of building a new asylum arose. The usage of Bedford Asylum by 1856 was noted as part of the accounting of who should pay what each year. Hitchin Union had 8,498 days that patients were 'maintained', ie. 23 in-patients at any time. The total cost for their maintenance was £615.19.9d or just over 10 shillings (50 pence) per week for each patient. Only Bedford town had more patients there, while St Albans had used only 3,965 patient days [31].

There were difficulties in deciding which counties should use the new asylum. Cambridgeshire and the Isle of Ely made a bid to be involved but that was not agreed and a scheme proceeded for Bedfordshire, Hertfordshire and Huntingdonshire (hence the BHH motif which appears on various parts of the building).

When it was decided that the new building should be in the countryside there was some resistance from Bedford, both because of the cost of a new build and also because of the loss of trade from the town.

The first meeting (and most of the subsequent ones) between the three counties to plan the Three Counties Asylum (TCA) was held in Hitchin at the *"Railway Hotel near to Railway Station of Great Northern Railway"* on October 25th 1855 [32]. Marlborough Pryor of Weston was the local representative on the committee and was elected chairman. It was expected to build an asylum according to the 'Lunatic Asylums Act 1853'. They settled on a size for 600 patients on 200 acres of ground and as close as possible to the Great Northern Railway. One site that was examined was Cadwell Farm in Ickleford, just outside Hitchin, then owned by the Delmé Radcliffes, but was found to be too hilly [33]. A good site was found nearby, outside the Bedfordshire village of Arlesey, and the land bought from Major Wilkinson of Stotfold.

The superintendent from the York Asylum, Samuel Hill, advised on the plan

Three Counties Asylum in the Illustrated London News, 1860.
Collection of Frank Lappin

and George Fowler Jones of York was appointed as architect. Hill stressed the importance of 'moral treatment', derived by the Tukes' practice at the Retreat, with the provision of congenial surroundings, good food, fresh air and exercise. The design followed the popular pattern of wards placed along a long corridor, with male wards on the west wing and female on the east. The medical superintendent's dwelling was placed between the two wings. The plans had to be approved by the Lunacy Commission and required some negotiation by Marlborough Pryor before they were accepted. Tenders were received for the building with Jeeves of Hitchin being the only local firm, but theirs was the most expensive at £73,786 and they were not successful. The contract was awarded to William Webster from Boston in Lincolnshire, whose tender of £53,626 was the second lowest. To aid the transport of materials a new station was built on the main Great Northern Railway line, 2 kilometers south of the existing station, and a separate tramway from there into the site of the main asylum building [34]. The building was completed and the first patients admitted in April 1860.

The patients' experience

Four hundred and ninety-four patients were admitted to Three Counties Asylum in the first year. 31 were regarded as recovered and were discharged at the end of the year, 38 had died and 423 remained. Over the next 10 years the annual admissions numbered between 120 and 165, the number recorded as recovered varied from 44 to 64 and those who died from 43 to 80 [35]. By 1870 the total number of patients had grown to 533. There had been optimism that with a proper asylum and careful treatment the numbers should not increase, but there were no effective treatments and while some recovered with time, many did not.

The diagnoses of that time were not the same as those used now, and many conditions were not well understood. The people admitted were not just those with severe mental illness and while many probably suffered from schizophrenia or manic depressive disorder the asylum also accommodated people with learning disability (idiocy or imbecility), people with uncontrolled epilepsy, older people with dementia and some with diseases that are no longer classified as psychiatric but which can have mental symptoms. One of the common problems was called general paralysis of the insane (GPI) and recognized as a disease in 1822. It is a form of advanced syphilis which causes severe damage to the brain and the nerves in the spinal cord causing both physical symptoms, such as paralysis, and confusion, sometimes with fleeting false beliefs or delusions, hence 'insane'. It is caused by a bacteria transmitted sexually but this was not discovered until 1913, and then the fact that it could be transmitted from one person to another was recognized.

Many of the conditions suffered by patients in Three Counties Asylum in the 19th century were not amenable to any known treatment, many were incurable and inevitably deaths occurred. GPI usually caused death within a few years of the person requiring hospital care and many others would have died from a variety of physical illnesses. Other conditions were what we now recognize as severe mental illness. The records of the patients are available at Bedfordshire Archives and I hoped to find descriptions there of the care and efforts to cure. The following are two examples [36]:-

The case of Sophia Olney

The record states that she was the widow of a labourer from Ickleford (near Hitchin), aged 55, admitted Jan 24th 1862. *"Has been under treatment before in the Bedford Asylum about 20 years since. No cause assigned, not epileptic, not suicidal. Her demeanour is very restless, and wild, and she threatens to strike the people around her. She complains of being constantly watched. Nurse ...who is with her, states that she is inclined to be very violent at times and that she is gradually getting worse. Jan 25th 1864. Discharged recovered."*

There is no other account of how she spent her time, what medication or other treatment may have been administered and no account of any changes in her thoughts, mood or behaviour over that 2 years. The fact that her discharge date was just 2 years after her admission suggests that there was an annual review of her condition and then it was realised that she no longer needed to be in hospital.

The case of Eliza Dobbs

More is written about this woman who had been in an asylum 18 years before. She was aged 38, the wife of a labourer, from Ippolyts (St Ippolytts outside Hitchin), and admitted on 27th July 1864.

Patient records at Three Counties Asylum were written in such books, with several patients' notes on each page. Individual patient records with separate files for each person were not introduced until 1912.

Photo by author [36]

*"A moderate sized woman, rather badly nourished. Is pale and weak.
Hair light – head round with low forehead. ...Melancholic...she does not appear to
have any disease of heart or lungs eyes clear tongue white bowels confined. The attack
commenced three weeks ago since which time she has been extremely restless and excited,
has not slept at night and has had various delusions, she has also threatened to kill
some children
When admitted she appeared quiet and in a melancholy state of mind. Would scarcely
answer questions when spoken to. Her memory and understanding appear pretty good
She is not an epileptic and has no symptoms of general paralysis.
She has a child only a few months old which was not weaned until she was brought
to the asylum. The attack appears to have been caused by debility brought on by trying
to suckle her children for a long period. She never had an attack of insanity before."*

The record then contains progress notes in the following months and years:-
*"Aug 2nd. Has been low spirited since she was admitted. Her breasts have been very
much swollen. She has taken some saline medicine and has rubbed her breasts with
Lin: sapon : co (ie. soap)
August 24th. Her breasts are now nearly well. She still continues low spirited and is
very bad tempered at times. Appetite good sleeps at night.
November 25th. Still melancholy in manner and appearance. She has one or two
attacks of menorrhagia which has made her weak and pale. Her appetite is pretty
good and she is quiet at night.
March 3rd 1865. She remains in very much the same state, both in her general health
and mind.
September 1868. Very noisy voice, constantly talking loudly and unintelligently.
Well nourished
May 1869. No change. Chronic mania bordering on dementia.
February 13th 1870. No change physically or mentally.
May 21st 1871 No change.
November 15th No change
April 4th 1872. General health good. Voice squeaky and inharmonious. Very incoherent.
in short she is quite demented
October 4th (?1872) No change.
November 14th 1878. No change.
Aug 8th 1879. No change. Now employs herself usefully. Usually noisy
March 3 1881. No change
December 8th 1882. Has been in feeble health lately. Is often noisy
December 31st 1882 Become gradually worse and died this day
Statement of Death – had post mortem examination and died of valvular disease of
heart age 56."*

So there is not much that can be learnt about her treatment. The terms
melancholy and mania do not necessarily mean what they do today, so she may
have suffered from manic depressive disorder, or not. When the term dementia
was used that seems unlikely to be what we mean. People do not usually improve
after suffering from it unless there has been a specific treatment to correct a
hormone or vitamin deficiency (rare causes which are usually tested for now), and

would not be *"employing herself usefully"* seven years later.

Again there is a frustrating lack of information about her treatment and little to explain the changes that are described. I was curious about the fate of her family and the child she had been breast feeding at the time of her admission but could find no trace of them in the census records of Hitchin or Ippolytts in 1871 or 1881.

Treatment and progress of patients

The general treatment offered to patients was described by the Medical Superintendant of TCA in 1878, *"The treatment of the patients has consisted principally in improving their health by good food, producing sleep in the sleepless and trying to induce them to forget their troubles by employment, amusement, etc. For producing sleep, moderate doses of chloral or hyoscyamine, with bromide of potassium are found the most effective measures we possess"* [37]. Chloral hydrate, hyoscyamine and potassium bromide were all supplied to Three Counties Asylum from Perks and Llewellyn chemist shop in Hitchin [38]. The total cost of medications from Perks, the main supplier to TCA, was £111 in 1879. What seems surprising is that the spending on wines, spirits and porter for the asylum in the same year was £267! [39]

Hyoscyamine is produced from henbane, or hyoscyamus niger, (a relation of belladonna or deadly nightshade) which was grown by Ransom's the local pharmaceutical producer. The active constituents of the plant are hyoscyamine and hyoscine. Hyoscyamine was used as a sedative but could cause hallucinations and confusion. It is now used widely for gut problems such as irritable bowel. Hyoscine is still used by psychiatrists as it alleviates one of the annoying side effects of clozapine, an effective antipsychotic drug, by reducing dribbling or excess saliva (an extract of belladonna is used for the same purpose with anaesthetics).

Three Counties Asylum had its own burial ground. Patients' graves were marked with wooden crosses, staff with metal. In the Burials book of 1904 it reads, 'Burials in the burial ground for the Lunatic Asylum for the Counties of Bedford, Hertford, and Huntingdon, in the parish of Stotfold, in the said County of Bedford, in the year 1904, 2532 book entry No 932, James Bennet Turner, attendant, Of Asylum Road, Stotfold, Baldock, Buried Oct 13th, Age 53 years.'

This marker was found in the grounds of the asylum and its origin traced from records in Bedfordshire and Luton Archives by Rosalyn Knight.

Photo by Rosalyn Knight, collection of Richard Knight

Medicines displayed in the reconstruction of Perks and Llewellyn's chemist shop in Hitchin Museum. The Perks family first opened a pharmacy in the High Street in 1790 and in 1878 Samuel Perks went into partnership with Charles Llewellyn. The shop finally closed in the 1960s.
Hitchin Museum   Photo by author 2011

Ransom's company started in 1846 and may have been direct suppliers to Three Counties Asylum. They continued to grow henbane until about 1975, latterly on their farm at Little Wymondley [40], producing hyoscyamus tincture, which has a continued use for kidney problems and tremors. Hyoscyamine was used for *"quiet restraint in violent and dangerous cases"* [41]. (Henbane has a long association with soothsaying, magic and witchcraft, it has been used as an aphrodisiac and an ingredient of love potions. The Greeks believed that it helped people prophesy and Hamlet's father was killed when some was poured into his ear. [42, 43])

Another of Ransom's products, lavender, has a reputation as a calming herb, being a relaxant and a sedative, but does not seem to have found its way into the asylum pharmacy. Lavender was first produced commercially in Hitchin by the Perks company in the 18th century and then by Ransom's in the 19th century, who refined the medicinal properties to avoid competition with Perks. By the end of the 19th century Hitchin was the most important centre for producing lavender in England [44]. When it was being distilled in Hitchin I wondered if the fumes from it which permeated the town calmed and relaxed the people.

Baths were still being used, an eminent alienist, Dr Harrington Tuke, not apparently related to the Tukes of Hitchin and York, wrote in 1858 [45] –

"I have already described various forms of the douche-bath, properly so called, but their variety is endless, and the object for which they are prescribed in many instances undiscoverable. The effects of "percussion," of surprise, and of frayeur, a favourite French therapeutic effect, seem all invoked in turn. Dr. Willis suspended a bucket on a pivot : this turning unexpectedly sent down a douche upon the patient. At Pirna, in Saxony, the maniac is fastened in a metal-bath sunk in the floor, and buckets of water are poured upon him from a window fourteen feet high, very much the same plan, only still more severe, that I have already quoted from Jacobi. Schneider recommends placing the patient under a continuous stream of water, which is to fall, drop by drop, upon his shaved head."

Having described what seems close to modern methods of torture, he then describes the mechanics of the treatment, the water temperature, the direction of spray of showers, and adds –

"There is no remedy, I believe, more valuable in the treatment of mental diseases than the warm-bath. It will calm the fury of the maniac, or sooth the anguish of the melancholic; under different circumstances it will act either as a tonic or as a depressant, as a sedative or as a stimulant; it is a remedy always at hand, with proper precautions always safe."

He says that Dr John Conolly, an authority on asylums, recommended that in some cases of mania a cold shower be applied to a person who is part immersed in a warm bath. I shiver at the thought. Concern had been raised by the death in 1856 of a patient at the Surrey County Asylum after a prolonged shower-bath [46].

Tuke also describes adding *"oderiforous herbs"* saying that rosemary had been used to induce a reluctant patient to enter the water, and suggesting that lavender water might be used for the same purpose. Henbane had apparently been used with hemlock as part of a 'Bertolini' medicated bath, though for what reason and with what result is not revealed. There is no evidence of any particular regime or additive in the baths used at the local asylums.

Although restraint had been regarded by some as unnecessary there were those who thought otherwise. Dr Bucknill, the editor of the Asylum Journal, superintendent of the Exeter Asylum and a follower of Conolly thought it unnecessary, but Dr Forbes Winslow, editor of the Journal of Psychological Medicine and Mental Pathology and a proprietor of a private licensed house, disagreed [47, 48]. Bucknill advised the use of seclusion or solitary confinement as an alternative, though under strict medical supervision. He also believed in baths or showers to punish patients who had been violent or destructive, using this on 35 patients during 1848 at the Devon Asylum where he was Superintendent [49].

While restraint declined in use there was a revival toward the end of the 19th century, perhaps as the earlier optimism had faded about the effectiveness of moral management. Acceptance of it, albeit in a limited and humane way, was provided in the 1890 Lunacy Act [50].

The treatment that did have wide support was that of moral management, which though humane does not seem to have been effective. The 'moral therapy' had seemed effective at the Retreat in York but had been used there on a small

Various forms of restraint were tried and remained in use despite the opinion that they were unnecessary, if not cruel. Muffs and manacles, short waistcoats and the straitjacket as illustrated here were all used. Strangely this illustration comes from a surgical equipment catalogue from Allen & Hanbury, dated 1957! Whether this was still being bought at that time, and by whom, is not known.

Hitchin Museum

scale and a family atmosphere was created. This was quite different from the large numbers accommodated in the bulging asylums with relatively few staff. Many of the patients in the asylum would have difficulty caring for themselves and the time taken to get the hordes of people fed would alone have occupied staff's time. Those that were able were put to work, the women in domestic duties, the men on the asylum farm. It was not until the 1960s that the effect of putting a large number of mentally unwell people in large hospitals was fully recognized and then it was realised that what had been seen as symptoms of schizophrenia, apathy, social withdrawal and lack of motivation, were just the effects of this sort of warehousing. It was called institutionalisation [51].

Families and 'community care'

While the admission of patients to the asylum may seem like an abandonment by their families, a study by Claire Sewell at the Bedfordshire Archives shows another side of this. The following information is from the Bedfordshire Archives website [52]. Working from a register entitled 'Discharges of Patients to Custody of Friends' for the period 1878 -1897, she noted that many patients discharged into the custody of friends were 'unrecovered'. This suggests that they continued to require care. It was also evident from the case records that patients had often been unwell for some time before admission, with relatives stressing *"the dangerous, suicidal and/ or generally unmanageable nature of their affliction"*. It seems likely that only when there was a severe threat to self or others did admission occur. Also the majority

Each 'discharge to custody of friends' was formally recorded, with a commitment that the person "shall be no longer chargeable to any Union, Parish or County, and shall be properly taken care of, and shall be prevented from doing any injury to her/his self or others". It was signed by a relative and approved by two of the Committee of Visitors. Bedfordshire Archives [53]

of patients admitted in 1871, '81 and '91 were in the asylum for less than a year. Letters in the archive demonstrate that there was regular contact between the asylum and friends or relatives. Sewell concludes *"This strongly indicates that the Three Counties Asylum was used as a space for respite for families who were willing to act as carers when circumstances allowed"*. The Three Counties Asylum and the staff does seem to have fostered a spirit of community care.

The pauper lunatics in the asylum

As discussed in chapter 2, the Lunacy Commission collated the numbers of lunatics and idiots in the workhouses and produced annual reports. The differences between the three Unions of Hitchin, St Albans and Biggleswade have been commented on. In 1856 their usage of Three Counties Asylum show that while St Albans Union had 2,723 patient days (ie. an average of nine patients there every day of the year), Biggleswade had 2,288 and Hitchin 2,097 patient days. Hitchin was making less use of the asylum and might have been expected to have more cared for at home or in the local workhouse. Other factors in operation may have been the size of the local workhouse, family support, family income and the attitudes of each Board of Guardians. Unfortunately from the minutes of the Hitchin Board there are very few details of any discussion about how they managed the insane in their parishes.

The 10th Annual Report of the Lunacy Commission [27] did comment on the *"ability of medical officers to identify lunatics"* and complained generally about the medical officers not completing the returns and of one who said he visited patients when he had only met them on the road. It is quite possible that the varying skills, interest and enthusiasm of the doctors in the different parish unions would have determined who was deemed appropriate for the asylum or workhouse. People may have been left at home if their needs and those of their family were ignored, or the doctor may have provided the support and help which enabled the family to cope with the patient at home. Hitchin Workhouse did not appear to contain the insane, but the recording of the presence of such people may have been unreliable.

Another source of information is from the Quarter Sessions records [54]. The sessions had to collate the numbers of 'lunatics' and 'idiots' in the county and send those to the Lunacy Commission. In 1866 TCA had 39 patients from the Hitchin Union, all 'lunatics'. Two were 'on trial', that is at home but could be recalled to the asylum. In 1870 from the Hitchin Union there were 35 'lunatics' and 2 'idiots' at TCA, 2 'lunatics' at Burntwood Asylum (Stafford), 5 'lunatics' with family, 6 'idiots' and 1 demented person at the workhouse and 18 'idiots' at home.

In May 1873 the Local Government Board, who were overseers of workhouses, visited Hitchin and made no mention of any 'lunatics' or 'idiots' in the Union Workhouse [55]. As discussed in chapter 2 the Master, Alfred Fowler, reported later that in 1877 the infirmary accommodated 48 patients and that it had *"one room filled completely with idiots"*, but said nothing about the 'lunatics'.

So we know that there was a scatter of 'lunatics' and 'idiots' between the asylum, the workhouse and home. It is not clear to me whether these figures are

1870 photograph of Three Counties Asylum, rescued from lying on the basement floor at Fairfield Hospital by James Collett-White, archivist from Bedfordshire and Luton Archives and Record Service. Bedfordshire Archives [56]

in anyway accurate. As still happens it is quite possible that people who were quietly unwell or insane would not have been noticed or recorded as insane. It is possible that once people left the asylum after a period of care they would not have been regarded as 'insane', but might still be experiencing abnormal states of mind, without drawing attention to themselves.

The cost of care

Generally the asylum was reserved for the more difficult and violent 'lunatics', but there was some liberty in how officials applied the rules. There was a financial penalty on those who did send 'pauper lunatics' to the asylum - it cost the parish more.

My calculations from the Hitchin Union Board of Guardians minutes for 1836 [57] indicate that the weekly charges for indoor relief at the workhouse amounted to 2/9 d (quarterly charge of £302 for 167 inmates) and the licensed houses charges varied from 9/6d to 12/0d per person per week (47.5 to 60 pence in new money). The average charges in the workhouses in England in 1845 were 2/7d per week for the workhouse and 7/3d in the asylums (13 and 36.5 pence in new money) [58].

The overcrowded asylums

The effect of putting such large numbers of people in such large institutions and having no effective treatments was that they stayed and stayed, and the numbers grew and grew. Arthur Monk, the Fairfield Hospital Chaplain, who wrote a brief history of the Three Counties Asylum for its centenary in 1960, records that *"after a quarter of a century of work it was reported that since the opening, 4,770 were admitted, of which number 1,801 were restored to their friends, 215 removed and 1,768 had died"* [59]. The total number of patients in the asylum, built for 600, was 680 in 1871, 1000 in 1880, and in both decades extensions were built to accommodate the numbers. By 1894 there were 1099 patients and plans were being made for a new asylum in Hertfordshire. From the early days of the county asylums there had been debates about where the pauper lunatics should be accommodated.

In 1874 the government ordained that there should be a grant paid for all parish paupers who required to be admitted to the asylum, of 4 shillings per week. While this must have been some relief to the parishes it may also have increased the number of admissions to the asylums. In 1882 the Lunacy Commission and the Local Government Board, which oversaw the workhouses, argued about this. The Commission saying that the 4 shillings grant, which was administered by the Board, had contributed to the pressures on the asylums which were *"full or overfull"*. The Board argued that the problem was due to a *"marked increase in lunacy in recent years"*, and to the Commissioners who visited the workhouses and who "always find a few in each workhouse of unsound mind - the Guardians are informed, some are transferred, some examined by the MO and kept at the workhouse" [60].

With the asylums becoming overcrowded, the Government in 1883 conducted a national survey of *"chronic and homeless pauper"* patients misplaced in the asylums [61]. The return for Three Counties Asylum is available and identified 44 patients who were regarded by the asylum staff as suitable to be in a special lunacy ward within the workhouse, 36 who could be in the workhouse infirmary with a paid nurse to attend to them, but none who could have been placed in an ordinary workhouse infirmary ward. There is no information provided as to

The Chapel at Fairfield Hospital, built in 1879. A chaplain was appointed at the time of the asylum's opening when the chapel was in the main building [62]. *With a brewery, a farm and a well most of the needs of the patients could be catered for.*

Photo from author's collection 1985

which of the three counties these 80 people came from. For the whole country 5745 patients were identified as suitable for such workhouse transfer.

The total number of lunatics in England appeared to increase from 20,893 in 1844 to 85,352 in 1890 [63]. The idea that there had been an epidemic of severe mental illness in the 19th century was still being argued in the 20th century with no clear resolution. There has been speculation that while there may just have been the identification of milder cases which had not previously been noted by the authorities, that poor diet or viral infections might have increased the numbers who did suffer from mental illness [64]. Whilst some thought that evolutionary theories should be accompanied by progress in all spheres of life, the awareness that more people were being sent to the asylums indicated otherwise.

An explanation for this increase in insanity was then suggested as being due to the stresses of the life in a more 'mechanical' civilization' [65]. There were also theories that insanity led to increased degeneration with more insanity and idiocy in later generations, and that led to views that some form of control of the breeding of insane people should occur. It was part of Scull's thesis that the apparent growth in the numbers of the insane was all a social phenomenon, that as asylums were built their availability created an increased demand for them, and that families' tolerance reduced when they realised there was a handy local alternative. He also regarded doctors as offering solutions, when in reality they had little expertise, but enjoyed the status and rewards of being regarded as experts. The definitions and diagnoses of these so called experts were so vague that 'normal' people could be redefined as 'insane' and then locked up. So doctors, families and society somehow contrived to detain even more people and the asylums became even more full [66].

Whatever explanation or argument was put forward there was a relentless increase in the numbers in the asylums. Three Counties was bursting at the seams and the Hertfordshire County Council, which had assumed responsibility for the care of the lunatics and idiots after the 1888 Local Government Act, took steps to expand the places available by building a new asylum at Hill End near St Albans.

Hill End Hospital

An account of Hill End, sited just south of St Albans, gives the numbers of the Hertfordshire lunatics in 1901. 347 were at Hill End, 350 at TCA, 56 in the workhouses and 30 residing with friends [67]. In the beginning Hill End admitted patients from the south of the county and Three Counties from the north and east (Bishops Stortford, Buntingford, Royston and Ware) [68]. Although this is a clear demarcation the initial admissions included some from the Hitchin area. 37 were transferred from TCA out of a total of 269 transferred, and a few were transferred from other asylums, presumably because TCA had previously run out of space and patients had been placed elsewhere.

Amongst those transferred to Hill End, and recorded in the Register of patients [69] were –*No. 93. Oswald Folds. Born 1833, admitted to Hill End 1/5/1899, reception order 19/6/1883* (for admission to TCA). *Diagnosis mania - "from sunstroke". Previously in Hitchin Workhouse (in Hitchin Union Workhouse in 1871*

& '*81 census). Had been "strange many years". Removed on May 29 1900.*
No. 257. Fanny Parish, transferred from Beverley Asylum 27/7/00, strawplaiter, age 41, reception order 15/7/1887 (when first placed in an asylum). *Previous abode Baldock, chargeable to Hitchin Union Admitted by authority of W Lucas JP. Diagnosis dementia. Removal or death January 2nd 1913.*
No. 260. Lavinia Sheaf. Kings Walden. Admitted by authority of Delmé Radcliffe JP

The breakdown of patients according to diagnosis indicates the spread of problems managed within the new hospital. In 1904 Hill End had 600 patients, of which 85 were described as mentally deficient, 26 epileptic, 9 had general paralysis of the insane, 29 acute mania, 195 chronic mania, 9 senile mania, 26 acute melancholia, 89 chronic melancholia and 131 dementia. What is uncertain is how much patients were helped by their care. The provision of mental health nursing at Three Counties and Hill End Asylums has been described by Brimblecombe [70]. The care was mostly in the hands of the (male) attendants and (female) nurses. Training for this difficult role had started in 1890, but recruits were often usually untrained. He notes that at that time the image of the asylum nurse was poor, with one report of "*beatings, the use of seclusion in padded rooms and cold baths being given as punishment for even slightly difficult behaviour*" [71]. He noted that in 1903 mechanical restraint and seclusion were not used at Hill End, though the latter was applied more frequently in the years following.

In 1905 Three Counties Asylum decided to buy some of the 'Hertfordshire beds' at TCA and so more patients from Herts had to be accommodated at Hill End, probably those from east of the county, and Hill End built an extension to accommodate them [72]. Thereafter patients from the Hitchin area alone were mostly admitted to Three Counties, though with the weekly charge for patients at Hill End being 12/6d whilst TCA only charged 9/6d (62.5 and 47.5 pence in new money), it must have been tempting for people in the south of the county to go for the cheaper option [73].

Hill End continued as the main hospital for the rest of the county until it closed in 1995. Three Counties closed soon after in 1999. It was not until 2000, after 100 years, when the Hertfordshire Partnership NHS Trust was set up, that the mental health services for the county were again managed as one.

Notes

1. Bedfordshire and Luton Archives and Records Service Q.G.E.1 : http://www.bedfordshire.gov.uk/communityandliving/ archivesandrecordoffice/guidestocollections/hospitalrecordsparttwo.aspx. Cashman, Bernard. 'A Proper House. Bedford Lunatic Asylum (1812 – 1860)'. North Bedfordshire Health Authority. 1992
2. Scull, Andrew. 'The Most Solitary of Afflictions'. Yale University Press. 1981. p 212 – 215
3. Bedfordshire and Luton Archives and Records Service Z54/80b
4. Hertfordshire Archives and Local Studies. 'Hertford County Records. Session Books vol IX, 1799-1833. Ed William le Hardy. p 224
5. Bedfordshire and Luton Archives and Records Service. LB3/10
6. Cashman, p 62
7. Bedfordshire and Luton Archives and Records Service. LB3/10
8. Parry-Jones, William. 'The Trade in Lunacy'. Routledge Keagan & Paul. 1972. p 282

9. Bedfordshire and Luton Archives and Records Service X611/11
10. Hertfordshire Archives and Local Studies QS/MISC/B/8
11. http://www.hertfordshire-genealogy.co.uk/data/places/places-m/much-hadham.htm - quoting Kelly's Directory for 1882
12. Hertfordshire Archives and Local Studies. 'Hertford County Records. Sessions Books Vol IX, 1799 – 1833'. ed William Le Hardy p 47
13. Ruff, Stephen C. 'A Walk Through Much Hadham'. Circa 1983
14. London Metropolitan Archives. ACC 1063/164
15. Hertfordshire Archives and Local Studies, QS/MISC/B/8
16. available on www.books.google. co.uk p 410
17. http://www.hertfordshire-genealogy.co.uk and Hertfordshire Archives and Local Studies QS Misc/B/9-11
18. Hertfordshire Archives and Local Studies QS Misc/B/9
19. for a fuller account see Cootes in 'Madhouses, Mad-Doctors, and Madmen'. Ed Andrew Scull. Athlone Press. 1981
20. Bedfordshire and Luton Archives and Records Service. 611/31
21. Scull et al. 'Masters of Bedlam'. Princeton.1996. p 141
22. Bedfordshire and Luton Archives and Records Service. 611/15
23. http://www.galaxy.bedfordshire.gov.uk/ webingres/bedfordshire/vlib/0. digitised_resources/kempston_springfield_asylum.htm
24. Bedfordshire and Luton Archives and Records Service. 611/7/2
25. Bedfordshire and Luton Archives and Records Service. LSV 3/0
26. Lutt , Nigel, in Cashman 1992. appendix III
27. National Archives MH 12
28. Bedfordshire and Luton Archives and Records Service X611/59/1
29. National Archives, Lunacy Commission files MH19/168, 1840 -1858
30. Hertfordshire Archives and Local Studies. Hertford County Records. Sessions Rolls 1699 – 1850, Vol XI. Ed W J le Hardy. 1905. p 439
31. Bedfordshire and Luton Archives and Records Service. LF 4/5/2,3
32. Bedfordshire and Luton Archives and Records Service. LF 4/5/1
33. Pettigrew, J. Reynolds,R and Rouse,S. 'A Place in the Country. Three Counties Asylum 1860 – 1998'. South Bedfordshire Community Health Care Trust. 1998. chapter 1
34. Pettigrew, p 14
35. Pettigrew, p 60
36. Bedfordshire and Luton Archives and Records Service LF 29/1
37. Monk, Arthur S. 'A Short History of the Hospital 1860 – 1960'. p 12
38. Perks and Llewellyn Day Book, June 1881 – Feb 1882. Hertfordshire Medical and Pharmaceutical Museum Trust
39. Bedfordshire and Luton Archives and Records Service LF 6/5
40. Michael Ransom, personal communication
41. Fennell, Phil. 'Treatment Without Consent'. Routledge. 1996 p 43
42. Savage. 'Hyoscyamine and its uses'. Journal of Mental Science. 1879. 25: 177-184
43. http://www.purplesage.org.uk
44. Festing, Sally. 'The Story of Lavender'. 2009
45. Tuke,Harrington. 'On warm and cold baths in the treatment of insanity'. Journal of Mental Science . 1858. 5 (27). p 102 – 114
46. Scull, 1996. p 193
47. The Journal of Medical Psychology and Mental Pathology was founded in

1848, and was intended not to focus on insanity but to foster a 'discussion of questions in relation to the Human Mind'. Shepherd, Michael. Journal Royal Society of Medicine.79. Nov 1986. p 639 – 45

48. Fennell, chapter 2
49. Scull, 1996, p163
50. Fennell, Ch 4
51. Barton, Russell. 'Institutional Neurosis'. Butterworth. 1959
52. www.bedfordshire.gov.uk/CommunityAndLiving/ArchivesAndRecordOffice/NewsletterArticles/RecordsofFairfieldHospital.aspx
     Original thesis Bedfordshire and Luton Archives and Records Service P 103 STOT
53. Bedfordshire and Luton Archives and Records Service LF 40/1
54. Hertfordshire Archives and Local Studies Qs/Misc/B/3
55. National Archives, MH 12/4620, Hitchin 172, 1873 - May 1874
56. Bedfordshire and Luton Archives and Records Service Z 50/2/18
57. Hertfordshire Archives and Local Studies BG/HIT 3
58. Jones, Kathleen. 'Lunacy Law and Conscience 1744 – 1845'. Routledge Keagan & Paul. 1955. p 167
59. Monk, A. 1960. p 15
60. National Archives, MH 19/170 1867 – 1892
61. National Archives, MH 19/170
62. Pettigrew, 1998. p 48
63. Scull. 1981. p 362
64. Hare, Edward. 'Was Sanity on the Increase?' British Journal of Psychiatry. 1983. 142. 439-455
65. Scull, 1981, p 340 – 1
66. Scull, 1981, p 363 – 70. 'The expanding empire of asylumdom and the growth of lunacy'
67. Anderson, Brian. 'Nearly a Century History of Hill End Hosp, 1899 - 1995'. p 20. Hertfordshire Archives and Local Studies Acc 3959
68. Anderson, p 21
69. Hertfordshire Archives and Local Studies BG/WAR/49
70. 'Asylum Nursing in the UK at the end of the Victorian era: Hill End Hospital'. Journal of Psychiatric & Mental Health Nursing. 12 p 57 – 63. 2005
71. 'The Changing relationships between Mental Health Nurses and Psychiatrists in the United Kingdom'. Journal of Advanced Nursing. 49 (4) p 344 – 53. 2005
72. Anderson p 17
73. Anderson p 21

The initials of Bedfordshire, Hertfordshire and Huntingdonshire, which adorn the main building of the Three Counties Asylum.

Outside the Asylum
and the Workhouse

5

Much of the history written about mental health care focuses on the institutional care; the most visible and well recorded part is associated with the large asylums which arose in the 19th century and are still around us. Many, like Three Counties, are solid and surviving monuments, now converted to pleasant housing estates with imaginative changes to the old structures, with only rumours of ghosts who might have stayed on. Outside the asylums the poor law ordained what relief might be available, from the often harsh regimes in the workhouses and the begrudged help that the relieving officers might provide to the paupers in their own homes. Beyond that various groups tried to correct or complement whatever was being done in the name of help for the insane. Three groups come to mind, though many others then and since have appeared. One local person who stayed outside of the asylum system, despite concern about him, also deserves a mention.

The Alleged Lunatics' Friends Society

This group has no particular connection to Hitchin and North Hertfordshire, it was fairly short lived – from 1845 until 1863 - but it seems to me to have been a wonderful attempt to bring sense to the lunacy system. The main source for this section is an article by Nicholas Hervey [1]. Concern about the possible detention of people (the well off, not the paupers) had started in the 18th century and led to the Madhouse Act of 1774 whereby any private patients admitted to a madhouse should be medically examined. However doctors, who were called apothecaries, physicians or surgeons, did not necessarily have any qualifications or training. There were no standards required to practise until after the registrations of doctors was required by law in 1858, when the General Medical Council was formed.

The 1774 Act also stipulated that madhouses should be licensed and inspected by the Royal College of Physicians if in, or within 7 miles of, London, and outside of that by justices in each county. Despite these provisions there were abuses of the system and further measures were added in later acts of parliament.

By 1830 it might have been thought that abuses would be unlikely, but in 1838, after being confined for almost 6 weeks after a disagreement with his father over money, Richard Paternoster emerged enraged about what had happened. He advertised in The Times for fellow sufferers *"to join him in a campaign to redress abuses in the madhouse system"*. He was joined by a small group including John Perceval, whose father, Spencer Perceval, had been Prime Minister and was assassinated in 1812 at the House of Commons. John's younger brother, Spencer, was briefly a Metropolitan Commissioner involved in the licensing and inspection of asylums from 1830 to 1832.

John had become very religious and involved in a church where Pentecostal happenings such as speaking in tongues, were experienced. In the church his behaviour was regarded as erratic. He then went to Ireland in 1831 and developed some form of sudden mental disorder or acute psychosis. His brother arranged for him to be cared for at a private asylum in Bristol (Brislington House), run by Dr Fox, a Quaker with a good reputation. The following year he was transferred to Ticehurst in Sussex, another licensed house (which is still open), and stayed there until discharged in 1834. He claimed that he was kept in a strait-waistcoat and physically abused. He protested that Fox had not treated him as a gentleman, that his treatment was not discussed with him and when he challenged anything he was punished by the use of solitary confinement, the strait-jacket, or a cold bath. He published an account of his experiences in a book 'A narrative of the treatment experienced by a gentleman during a state of mental derangement' [2].

The group who formed after the appeal, consisting of four ex-patients and one whose two brothers were mentally ill, petitioned the Home Secretaries for reform and suggested changes. They achieved nothing and so formed an organization in 1845 *"to campaign for changes in the lunacy laws, which would reduce the likelihood of illegal incarceration and improve the condition of asylums; to offer help to discharged patients, and to convert the public to an enlarged view of Christian duties and sympathies"*. They had suffered in the process but had learnt what should change and took up the issues. Their ideas for reform are interesting and some remain relevant today. They felt that the admission process should involve a jury trial to ensure its fairness and with more details required in medical certificates before detaining patients. They also wanted an appeal system once people were detained, which is now standard with panels of hospital managers or the national Mental Health Review Tribunal reviewing the need for people to remain in hospital.

They were wary of the Lunacy Commission and decided to highlight issues that the Commission might overlook. The Society believed that much mental illness stemmed from the disappointments and rejections of life, and questioned the medical wisdom that patients had to be isolated from their home associations, desiring practitioners to pay more attention to what the insane were saying [3], wise words that remain relevant. They held a radical view of the seemingly benign 'moral therapy', feeling that patients were treated like children, with the need for re-education and protection being emphasised.

While they were at odds with the Lunacy Commission in some ways, their proposal to have voluntary rather than compulsory admissions was supported by Samuel Gaskell and Bryan Waller Procter [4], medical and legal commissioners who reappear in the next chapter.

The members of the Alleged Lunatics' Friends Society (ALFS) wanted improvements in the private asylums but also tried to improve the situation for paupers in the county asylums.

Hervey argues that the Society was opposed by the Lunacy Commission but it did adopt some of the Society's proposals, while refusing to acknowledge the source of them. The Society also alienated the alienists, often being in the position of accusing the doctors of malpractice. The private asylum owners were known to bend the rules and they would have been upset at this campaigning group exposing dishonest practice and undermining their reputation. The perception of the public that evil deeds took place in the private asylums was later increased by such novels as 'The Woman in White' (by Wilkie Collins), published in 1860 and 'Hard Cash' (by Charles Reade), published in 1863, each portraying abuses of what should have been a care system. How many cases of abuse occurred was uncertain. Lord Shaftesbury, the Chairman of the Lunacy Commission from its inception in 1845 until 1885, accepted they did occur but believed they were few in number.

ALFS received support from various MPs, including Benjamin Bond Cabbell (MP for St Albans) who chaired a meeting where patients from various London asylums made allegations of abuse that they had suffered. Cabbell was a governor of St Luke's Hospital, one of the London asylums. The Society made many suggestions for reform with their loyal MPs trying to introduce these in parliament, but were often unsuccessful. In 1853 they suggested that patients' legal rights be displayed in the wards and that medical reports should record patients protesting about the legality of their detention – ideas which the Mental Health Act Commission, the national inspectorate recently superseded by the Care Quality Commission would have thought excellent practice. They were also known to check the certificates that were used when people were detained. They found in some instances that all of the details had not been completed and challenged the legality of the detention. The careful observation of patients' rights at the end of the 20th century led to the development of various safeguards with mental health units employing specialist administrators to oversee and implement the policies, a move which ALFS would have approved of. The most startling of their suggestions was that patients should be offered a half way house where they could go voluntarily before being admitted and before the compulsory legal detention was enacted. Startling because it makes such good sense and has been on the wish list in many modern services but rarely happened. ALFS also proposed voluntary admission to hospital which was not accepted until the 1930 Mental Treatment Act.

ALFS persistence led to a Select Committee on Lunatics being set up in 1859 at the instigation of Sir William Tite MP. A revision of the lunacy laws was sought to avoid wrongful detention. This led to a discussion at a meeting in February 1859 of the Association of Medical Officers of the Asylums and

Hospitals for the Insane (AMOAHI). At the time the President was Dr John Conolly, an eminent pioneer on reforming the asylums. While chairing the meeting he said -

> *"In mentioning this Society of the Friends of Alleged Lunatics, I know there does exist on the part of some gentlemen, a kind of prejudice against them. Things have happened occasionally, which have been offensive perhaps to particular individuals, without any intention. But I think we are all bound to take specially into consideration that, if gentlemen, whom we allege to be lunatics, consider that they have been ill-treated, whether they have been so or not, it is no use to attempt to put an extinguisher upon their complaints, and it would be unworthy of us to treat them with contempt ; we ought to listen to what they have to say (considering that they have no means open to them except by appealing to the public) and to receive charitably every thing they may do, and to explain where we cannot amend."* [5]

Notorious cases in the previous year had raised the awareness of abuses of the system. Mr Ruck, who was an alcoholic and had been certified and confined, protested that he was seen by the two doctors who assessed him together, while the law required that they see him separately. In court, 6 months after the special AMOAHI meeting, it emerged that one of the doctors, the same Dr John Conolly, had received regular fees from the licensed house where Ruck was detained, a violation of the law which caused damage to Conolly's reputation. Ruck had brought a successful action for false imprisonment against Conolly, who had signed one of the certificates on which Ruck had been confined. Conolly received fees as a consulting physician from the same private asylum but was convinced he had done nothing wrong. In mitigation it has been argued that the law was too vague and it was subsequently changed in 1862 to prohibit such arrangements [6].

Rosina Bulwer Lytton's case (described in the next chapter) occurred at that time but was not publicly brought into the debate for reform. The reforms were not seen through, partly because the Conservative government of Lord Stanley lost power. Lord Palmerston became Prime Minister and it is just possible that he was swayed by the opinion of his step son in law, Lord Shaftesbury, who was generally opposed to modifications of the laws that he had introduced.

While the number of cases where illegal detention was considered by Lord Shaftesbury to be few compared with the numbers who were detained in asylums [7], certain cases showed how the laws could be used badly and needed to be changed. ALFS also brought to court cases where they believed that relatives had patients detained so that they could take over their finances for personal benefit. The sort of problem which occurred was illustrated by the case of Louisa Nottidge. She wanted to give away her inheritance to a religious sect but her relatives intervened and wanted her to be detained under the lunacy laws. In court the judge stated that no person should be confined on the grounds of mental illness unless they were a danger to themselves or others. This simple rule has mostly guided detention under mental health laws, but does not fully cover the problems caused by self neglect or reckless behaviour which can alienate family and friends and also cause financial ruin. ALFS hoped that this ruling would also end the detention of some of the harmless people who languished in asylums such as epileptics and idiots [8].

ALFS had lawyers amongst their members and met with some sympathy from the courts. They tried to influence and educate the magistrates in each county who had the responsibility for appointing Visitors to all the county and private asylums. They were acting as inspectorates have done over recent decades, trying to ensure that all the due processes were followed and that a person's liberties were only restricted when absolutely necessary, and then done with strict observation of the law. It was the first organized group to seek improvements of the lunacy laws, something taken on a few years later by the Lunacy Law Reform Society (founded by a vicar's wife who was confined at his request because of her belief in spiritualism) from 1873 – 1885, the National Society for Lunacy Reform which was founded in 1920, and MIND or the National Association for Mental Health which was formed in 1946 (from the merger of National Council for Mental Hygiene and two other organizations). ALFS was ahead of its time. It faded out in the 1860s when members passed away and perhaps, as Hervey suggests, when *"the appointment of Perceval's nephew as the Lord Chancellor's secretary in 1866, and later as secretary of the Lunacy Commission, finally gave him some peace of mind"* [9].

The Mental Aftercare Association (MACA) and the Reverend Henry Hawkins

Henry Hawkins was born on 25 September 1825 and grew up in Gosmore, a village near Hitchin, the only son of a prominent surgeon who later moved to Hastings. He was ordained in the Anglican church in 1851. In 1867 he became chaplain of Colney Hatch Asylum in North London, later known as Friern Hospital [10].

He married Mary Hawkins, his cousin, whose father Frederick, a doctor, (1796 – 1864), founded the Hitchin Infirmary in Bedford Road, Hitchin, in 1840. His uncle John (1791 – 1877) was a solicitor (in Hawkins & Co of Hitchin). John's son became Sir Henry Hawkins, later Lord Brampton, an eminent barrister and judge.

The first person to have drawn attention to a need for care of people discharged from the asylums was William Ellis, who established charitable funds for patients who had been in Wakefield and Hanwell Asylums in the 1820s and 30s. In 1838 he wrote *"But something further is still wanted. A comfortable place where patients might find food and shelter and a home until they could procure employment would be an invaluable blessing …Many*

The Reverend Henry Hawkins (1825- 1904). He was a son of Francis Hawkins who was a surgeon and later practised in Hastings. MACA has been succeeded by 'Together', which gave permission to use this photo.

patients might thus be eventually restored to society who are now compelled to remain in the asylum in consequence of their retaining some erroneous view on some unimportant matter" [11].

There had been some trials of support outside of the asylums. Dr Bucknill reported in 1858 in a 'Description at the Devon County Asylum, with remarks upon the seaside residence for the insane, which was for a time established at Exmouth' [12]. Henry Hawkins promoted the idea of help outside of the asylum with a paper on the 'Aftercare of Convalescents' at a meeting in June 1879. This was held at the home of Dr John Bucknill, in Wimpole Street in London and was reported in October in the Journal of Mental Science [13]. Included in the small group was Dr Daniel Hack Tuke, who had written a major textbook with Bucknill in 1858. Hawkins presented a paper, which was also published in October [14] with the following description of the problems -

> *"Those who are familiar with the inmates of public asylums will probably be able to call to mind cases of female convalescents whose actual dismissal, though warranted by the state of their health, is delayed - postponed from month to month, because they have no friend who can, or will, undertake their charge, on their first return to the world. Some may be literally friendless, others are estranged from their friends, or so remote from them as to be beyond reach of their assistance. The friends of others are sometimes so poorly lodged as to be unable to receive, even for a limited period, an additional inmate into their rooms…*
> *It is true that the convalescent may be transferred from the asylum to the workhouse. There she would be at liberty to claim her discharge. But the question arises, would her change of abode place her in a more favourable position to start anew in life? In the workhouse it would probably be known that she had been an asylum patient. This would be to her prejudice. No special interest in her case, or trouble on her behalf, could reasonably be expected to be taken; so that, as an inmate of the house she would not find her way to self-maintenance much easier than it had been in the Asylum".*

They envisaged a home where the ex patients would contribute to the work and which would be a base for them *"to seek after employment"*. The running of such a home would be left to women whilst the men would *"supervise financial and general business"*.

Bucknill was elected as President, Hawkins as Secretary and Lord Shaftesbury was subsequently recruited as Patron. Reminiscences of the early years of the Association were recorded by Hawkins. He included the words of Lord Shaftesbury when he was invited to be involved

"Your letter entitled 'After-care' has deeply interested me. The subject has long been on my mind, but, like many other subjects, it has passed without any effectual movement on its behalf. Tell my friend Dr Bucknill that I shall be happy to serve under his presidency in so good a cause" [15].

The Association was first known as 'The After-care Association for Poor and Friendless Female Convalescents on Leaving Asylums for the Insane' and its object was to *"facilitate the readmission of female convalescents from lunatic asylums into social and domestic life"*. In 1894 it extended its brief to help men.

It continued to support discharged patients, taking on the role that social workers later developed and contributed to social work training courses that were developing. It changed its name to the Mental After Care Association in 1940. In the 1950s it began to provide accommodation or residential care, then invaluable as the large asylums began to contract and close. [16]

What Henry Hawkins had started in 1879 had a long life and evolved into 'Together' in 1998, an organization which *"provides care and support to people with mental illness to help them take control of their own lives"*. It provides residential care and resource centres for people to develop new skills and to socialise. It also helps in what is called advocacy, providing special help to those needing mental health services, to have their opinions heard in their dealings with authorities [17]. They have also organized seminars on how people can manage and cope with hearing voices or hallucinations.

The Temperance Movement

Another facet of Victorian life was the demon drink. Beer had been a staple of the diet but the availability of spirits in the 18th century caused problems – *"drunk for a penny, dead drunk for tuppence"*. Hogarth in his paintings portrayed the inhabitants of Beer Street as happy and healthy, nourished by native English ale, whereas those who live in Gin Lane are degraded by addiction to the *"foreign"* spirit of gin [18].

The use of spirits was seen particularly to afflict the working classes. In the USA a temperance movement started in the 1820s to reduce the consumption of spirits and encourage the use of wine or beer. This spread to England in 1830 and within a few years this had changed to a total abstinence goal. It reached its peak between 1870 and 1900 and continued until the 1920s. One of the practical issues in trying to keep the working classes out of the public houses was that they had nowhere else to meet and socialise. Davison describes in the Journal of the Brewery History Society how the 'Built Heritage of the Temperance Movement' led to a variety of alternatives being developed [19]. The buildings started with a simple wooden hut in Garstang in Lancashire erected in 1834, to a complex in Burnley in 1837 which included a large assembly room or lecture theatre, and an educational institute where lessons in arithmetic, book-keeping and other skills were taught, and a library containing a wide range of novels, technical handbooks and temperance tracts. The trend continued with a magnificent Temperance Institute being built in Keighley in 1896 which incorporated a separate hall for meetings. It is now, of course, a Wetherspoon's pub! All sorts of temperance-linked organizations developed including billiard and snooker halls and youth clubs. My mother's only revelation about her youth in the 1920s was that she had belonged to one of the latter.

Hitchin sprouted many temperance organizations. A speaker at the Hitchin Adult Sunday School in December 1869 advocated total abstinence [20]. In 1872 Arthur Latchmore started the Hitchin Blue Cross Brigade, assisted by Theodore Ransom [21]. This was for males only between the ages of 14 and 30, being total abstainers and nominated for membership solely by current members.

Early temperance action? Thomas Shillitoe preaching outside a gin-shop at Smithfield, Dublin, 1811. Shillitoe (1754-1836) was a Quaker preacher, described by Hine as "a man far more beset with hallucinations and nervous prostration than myself" [22]. *In 'Hitchin Worthies' Hine says that Shillitoe trained as a shoe-maker but then suffered episodes of anxiety and "suffered from the delusion that he was a tea-pot and was in terror of moving about or meeting people lest he smashed himself". His health suffered from a meagre diet but he was then put on a diet of beef steak and ale, but became irritable and could not sleep, so dosed himself with laudanum (opium). He was only then helped when "the Heavenly Guide directed my steppings" and he became a vegetarian and abstained from alcohol. He became an itinerant preacher and sought out the crowned heads of Europe to deliver his message. He became President of the British and Foreign Temperance Society. He made a second home in Hitchin from 1830.*

From a drawing by Samuel Lucas in Hine's 'History of Hitchin', Vol II

The Brigade met at the Workman's Hall, which is the gymnasium behind the current Town Hall. In 1889 a new room was opened by James Hack Tuke, to be used for evening classes [21]. There were various branches for cycling, athletics, football and cricket, with teams still in existence until the 1920s and it had a substantial library [23].

In 1882 a Gospel Temperance Mission was held over two days during May, after which a meeting was held in the Town Hall at which it was said that they were determined they would not stop *"until every man, woman and child in Hitchin had on a blue ribbon"* [24]. (The Blue Ribbon movement was started in 1876 by Francis Murphy, an Irishman who had emigrated to the USA, and exported to London in 1877. The 'blue ribbon' came from the Old Testament command of God to Moses, that the people of Israel should wear it on the tassels of their garments to remind them of the commands of God [25]). After the Mission the 'Total Abstinence Society' (TAS) was formed. Alfred Ransom was President of that, retiring in 1884, but remained keenly involved until his death in 1911. He then bequeathed a trust fund to six good causes, including the promotion of temperance in the town [26]. In the notice of his funeral it was mentioned that his son was a supporter of the Blue Cross Temperance Brigade. In 1895 a TAS veterans' benefit tea meeting was held for all who had been abstinent for more than 25 years organized by Miss Jane Ransom, who had been *"dry"* for 25 years. The champion abstainer was Mr Joshua Whiting, who had been abstinent for 57 years [27]. Altogether 45 attended, representing 1477 years of abstinence at an average of over 32 years each. The TAS also held an annual concert in Brand Street, and had a youth's section with 350 members at the end of the century.

An offshoot from TAS appears to have been the 'Total Abstinence Benefit Society' which was formed in 1882. It had insufficient support and a less stringent 'Bond of Union' emerged in 1884, based in Walsworth Road Baptist Chapel. It had a difficult first few years, partly due to the opposition of 'medical men' who thought alcohol was an essential medicine, partly because the payments in sick benefits exceeded receipts, and partly due to hostility of townsfolk (and many must have been employed in the town's breweries, quite apart from those who enjoyed the demon drink). All of this was reported at a meeting in 1905, indicating that they had prevailed [28].

In 1882 a meeting of the Church of England Temperance Society reported that it *"had been in existence some time"*, but no exact date of its founding is given. This society was reported in 1881 to have had a free Saturday night entertainment in St Andrew's Plait Hall (off Hollow Lane) which 90 attended and seven *"signed the pledge"* [24]. Other church based temperance groups included the Church Lads' Brigade, the Band of Hope in the Wesleyan Chapel in Brand Street and the White Ribboners' Club in Walsworth Road Baptist Church [29].

By 1900 every town and most villages had a temperance hall. Inns and public houses had provided the only available accommodation and so it was logical that in 1832 the first temperance hotel should open. Hitchin had a few temperance hotels, but information about them is sparse. In front of the Workman's Hall in Brand Street there was later a Temperance Hotel (in the 1894 Trade Directory), and in 1902 there was Hunt's Temperance Hotel in Bancroft. Mr S. Leete's Temperance Hotel on the corner of Trevor and Walsworth Roads opened in the 1880s and closed in 1953 [30]. 47 Walsworth Road became *"The Acacias Commercial and Temperance Hotel"* early in the 20th century and remained so until 1950 [31].

Not all of the 'hotels' offered accommodation. Some were just coffee houses or restaurants but also provided reading rooms supplied with newspapers, journals and, of course, *"an eating house and coffee rooms… no intoxicating drinks are admitted on the premises"* temperance tracts. The 1875 'Handbook to Hitchin' lists it in front of the Workman's Hall in Brand Street.

The enthusiasm for temperance was fired by the continuing perception of

Kirkland's Temperance Hotel in the Triangle (junction of Queen Street and Bridge Street). This became the Triangle Temperance Hotel which became a regular stopping point for cyclists from north London in the 1920s [32]. *Postcard from Laurie Hughes' collection.*

the damage that alcohol caused. The middle and upper classes of course saw it as something that afflicted and needed to be curbed in the working classes. In 1859 Lord Shaftesbury estimated that half of all patients in the asylums had been made worse by an excess of alcohol [33]. This is not entirely borne out by the diagnoses made by the doctors in an asylum. In Colney Hatch in 1858 only 14 cases out of 157 were said to have been caused by 'intemperance' [34]. Employers became aware of the benefits of reducing the availability of alcohol and where they had a strong moral and religious ethos such as the Cadburys, who built the 'garden village' of Bourneville in Birmingham, the settlement had no public houses. This type of model settlement had a direct effect on the development from 1903 of the first Garden City at Letchworth, which was once a town with no pubs [35].

However, alcohol has continued to be a harmful drug with damage to the liver and brain and hence the scientific, but politically incorrect, conclusion of Professor David Nutt, the recent Chairman of the government's Advisory Council on the Misuse of Drugs, that it is overall more dangerous than cannabis or cocaine [36]. The emphasis on the damage that alcohol can do has focussed recently on the appalling rise of cirrhosis and liver damage and consequent death in the young. The effect in people with severe mental illness is to increase the disabilities and difficulties in recovery, with a third of people with severe schizophrenia and other psychoses also abusing alcohol [37]. Educating people about the units of alcohol in drinks, and talk of raising the price of alcohol are the latest efforts to manage this problem. However the public health aspirations of the temperance movement that the Victorians tried to promote remain unfulfilled.

The Hermit of Redcoats - James Lucas (1813 – 1874).

Turning from some of the organizations which existed outside of the asylums I will briefly mention an individual who stayed outside of the asylums, to his family's despair. The full story of James Lucas, the *"most famous Victorian hermit"*, is well told in Richard Whitmore's book, 'Mad Lucas' [38] and this is a brief summary of that detailed account. For those not familiar with the local geography James lived in Titmore Green, between Stevenage and Hitchin. He was from a family made wealthy by trading in sugar and slaves originally based in Liverpool. They were not of the well known Lucas family of Hitchin.

James Lucas was a difficult child who was very self-willed and difficult to educate. He was once placed with a tutor in Whitwell but was beyond control. At the age of 10 he suffered a severe infection of ringworm of the scalp. The treatment was reported to have been so upsetting that his mother thought it was the turning point of his life. His father died in 1830 when James was 17 years old, and his mother moved with her three children from London to Titmore Green in 1838. James was seen by a Dr Sutherland and a medical certificate was issued to state that he was of unsound mind and that an attendant should be with him night and day. His behaviour was decidedly odd. At times he insisted on

The 'Hermit of Redcoats', in Titmore Green, the pub near the site of James Lucas' home, Elmwood House, which was demolished in 1890. Photo by author 2009

taking his meals in his room and refused to give back the plates which he hoarded for no known reason. When the family became short of plates they simply bought some more. He would refuse to allow his hair to be cut, and then when it was very long would only go out in public with it done up in paper curlers.

When his mother died in 1849 he refused to have her body taken away. After three months local police broke down the front door and removed the body. Thereafter financial affairs became a problem. He believed that the Hanoverians in the shape of Queen Victoria were usurpers of the true Stuart line and refused to sign any document which had Victoria's stamp on it, which was required of most official documents. His solicitor overcame this eventually by the probably illegal but highly sensible device of putting the stamp on later.

Lucas arranged for food and drink to be delivered by local tradesmen and somehow survived. He had some peculiar ways. He never cleaned up or maintained his home. Over the years his living area became piled high with stale and rotten food, ashes and excrement. He eventually wore a ragged blanket and nothing else.

Illustration from "London Society" and used in George Cowley's pamphlet about the hermit, which sold more than 60,000 copies.
Illustration by courtesy of Richard Whitmore

While he seemed to avoid normal society he became a magnet for vagrants. It was said that if they recited a Catholic prayer he would provide them with gin and bread. When Alfred Fowler, the master of Hitchin Workhouse, gave a report of his 25 years in Hitchin he talked about the problem of vagrants when he arrived [39], saying that 250 each week would come to Hitchin and the workhouse might have between 60 and a 100 a night. He gave the reasons as the good markets which existed in Hitchin and the surrounding towns and the attraction of *"mad Lucas"*, who would hand out money. There is a slight discrepancy on dates in that James died in 1874 and Fowler arrived in 1877, but maybe the vagrants were a legacy that James left to the town.

His brother George was concerned that the house and estate were being neglected and tried to have him declared incompetent to manage his affairs. In 1851 George arranged for a hearing with the Lunacy Commission in the hope that James would be declared insane. It appears that the Commission heard evidence from George, three policemen and Mr Hailey, a farmer friend of James [40]. They did not see the man in question or receive a medical report. The records note that Lord Shaftesbury, who was then Chairman of the Lunacy Commission, was involved. He was neither trained as a lawyer or a doctor but was a politician. They concluded that they were not convinced that Lucas was a lunatic and merely suggested that Mr Hailey should use his influence on James to induce him to change his habits.

Despite his neglect of himself and the house James was apparently well able to have an intelligent, if occasionally eccentric, conversation, which must have swayed the Commission. At some other time another person from the Lunacy

Commission saw him. John Forster, who is mentioned in the next chapter, was reported as having seen him by Daniel Hack Tuke and having stated *"that he was struck with his being singularly acute, and without the least trace of aberration of intellect"* [41]. Forster became Secretary of the Lunacy Commission in 1855 and was then appointed as a legal commissioner in 1861, so would not have been involved in the 1851 visit, but was a friend of a near neighbour, Sir Edward Bulwer Lytton.

What the hearing probably achieved was to make James even more suspicious of his brother. He developed rituals to avoid the possibility of his brother poisoning his food, including ordering several loaves of bread at one time but choosing only one to eat. In 1860 he was assaulted by a visitor, the identity of the person and the reason for this is not known. James's behaviour invited attention and ridicule from the respectable society. He was visited also by some soldiers who when unable to rouse him tried to break in. He became alarmed and fired grapeshot, which did no harm but scared them away. He became more reclusive and withdrew more into the safety of his home, boarding up windows and doors so nobody could enter.

Charles Dickens paid a visit in 1861 while staying with Sir Edward Bulwer Lytton at the nearby Knebworth House. He subsequently wrote about James in the 1861 Christmas edition of his weekly 'All the Year Round' under the title of 'Tom Tiddler's Ground'. That seemed to encourage the visitors and Titmore Green was on the tourist map.

James died in 1874 having lived in appalling filth for many years. To clear the house 17 cartloads of the accumulated rubbish had to be taken away.

He was commemorated with pamphlets and china tea sets – the sort of things that only Royal weddings now achieve. Even 30 years later his history was published giving *"A full account of his singular mode of life during twenty-five years of seclusion from society"*.

His death was reported in the Times and the Telegraph, which is some indication of the fame achieved by a hermit.

He was also the subject of a talk by Daniel Hack Tuke, the son of Samuel Tuke, at the annual general meeting of the Medico-Psychological Association, the forerunner of the Royal College of Psychiatrists in 1874 [41,42]. In his talk Tuke described the behaviour and state of James. Tuke tried to interview him through the *"prison-like bars"* of his home, and commented that he seemed to have *"partial insanity – a monomania of suspicion or persecution"* and concluded that he suffered from *"moral insanity… a madness of action rather than of language"*. That was a catch-all phrase which meant nothing more than the person did not apparently suffer from a bodily disease and that he did suffer from some defect of reasoning, emotions or will. He mentioned that treatment of ringworm may have been the cause of his condition, but also said that heredity and a spoilt childhood could have had an influence, *"the unfavourable circumstances of his childhood, acting upon a brain in all probability predisposed to mental disease"*.

In present day terms James might be considered to have suffered from schizophrenia as he appeared to be paranoid - he believed his brother was plotting against him, was frightened of people attacking him in his home and

Elmwood circa 1870, while James was still living there. His fear of intruders led to the barring of the windows. His two bodyguards stand in the foreground; the hut, which was their living quarters, is visible on the right.

Photo and details by courtesy of Richard Whitmore

he neglected himself. There are no reports of him experiencing hallucinations (such as hearing voices) and despite the problem continuing for several years he seemed to retain the ability to converse rationally. He was clearly very odd but not necessarily suffering from schizophrenia.

People had intruded into his life and made fun of him and so his seclusion becomes more understandable, and perhaps not due to delusions or false beliefs in persecution. His accumulation of rubbish can be termed hoarding and while this can be part of the behaviour pattern of somebody with schizophrenia, it may be associated with obsessional disorders. The refusal in his youth to relinquish the dishes on which his food was brought indicates a life-long pattern. If longstanding, such obsessive behaviour can be regarded as a personality disorder, a lifelong, pervasive and often unchangeable disability.

He escaped the confinement that might have been expected when someone's behaviour was so at odds with what society might expect, whose ideas were so strange, and where the relatives requested that something be done about him, but he was harmless and no risk to himself or others. Perhaps amidst the impression that the lunacy authorities could be easily swayed to certify and confine people, there were safeguards which did protect the rights of people and kept them out of the asylums.

Notes

1. Hervey, N. 'Advocacy or Folly: The Alleged Lunatics Friends Society, 1845 – 1863'. Medical History. 1986. 30: p 245-275
2. Perceval, John. Published in 2 vols - 1838 and 1840. Effingham Wilson, London
3. Hervey, p 254
4. Bryan Waller Procter was also an author with the pen name of Barry Cornwall.
5. 'Meeting of AMOAH'. Journal of Mental Science. 1859. 5: p 395
6. McCandless, Peter. 'Madhouses, Med-Doctors, and Madmen'. Ed Andrew Scull. Athlone Press 1981. p 345
7. Hervey p 247
8. Hervey p 262
9. Hervey p 272
10. http://comerfordfamily.blogspot.com/2009_07_01_archive.html
11. quoted in Alexander Walk. Psychiatric Bulletin 1979. 3: p 122-123
12. Journal of Mental Science. 1858. 4: p 317–328
13. Journal of Mental Science. 1879. 25: p 453
14. Journal of Mental Science .1879. 25: p 358-367
15. Journal of Mental Science. 1898. 44: p 299-304
16. Smith, J. 'Forging the 'missing link': the significance of the Mental After Care Association Archive'. History of Psychiatry. viii. 1997. p 407 – 420
17. www.together-uk.org/about-us/history
18. www.quaker.org.uk/TemperanceIntro
19. Davison, Andrew. 'Try the alternative: The Built Heritage of the Temperance Movement'. Brewery History. 123. Summer 2006. p 94 – 109
20. Hitchin Museum. Lawson Thompson Scrapbook, Vol 1b, p 177
21. Lawson Thompson Scrapbook 3a p 120
22. Hine, Reginald. 'Confessions of an Uncommon Attorney'. 4th ed. Dent. 1949. p 187
23. Lawson Thompson Scrapbook 2b p 173
24. Lawson Thompson Scrapbook 2b p 166-7
25. Book of Numbers, Chapter 15, verse 38
26. Lawson Thompson Scrapbook 3a p 164-7
27. Lawson Thompson Scrapbook 2a p 47
28. Hitchin Museum. Loftus Barham Scrapbook, 7, p 1126
29. Pauline Humphries personal communication
30. Taplin, V and Stewart, A. 'Two Minutes to the Station'. Hitchin Historical Society. 2010
31. Taplin, p 19
32. Field, Richard. 'Hitchin. A Pictorial History'. Philimore. 1991. Illustration 15
33. quoted by Hervey. 'A Slavish Bowing Down: the Lunacy Commission and the Psychiatric Profession 1845 – 60', in 'The Anatomy of Madness'. Vol II. Tavistock. 1985. p 104
34. Hunter and Macalpine. 'Psychiatry for the Poor'. Dawsons of Pall Mall. 1974 p 197
35. Davison, p 109
36. Craig, Tom et al. Psychiatric Services. March 2008. 59, p 276-282
37. The Lancet, 6 Nov 2010. Volume 376, Issue 9752, p 1558 - 1565
38. Whitmore, Richard. 'Mad Lucas'. North Hertfordshire District Council. 1983

39. Lawson Thompson Scrapbook. Vol III. 25. 209. Hitchin Museum
40. Whitmore, p 28-9
41. 'The Hermit of Red-coat's Green'. Journal of Mental Science. 1874. 20 (91): p 361-72
42. Daniel Hack Tuke was also involved in MACA. In 1895 Henry Hawkins paid tribute to him after his death:- *"A great loss and sorrow befell the Association in the spring of 1895, when death removed Dr. Hack Tuke, who had been its invaluable supporter and guide from the first. His grave, kindly face was regularly to be seen at committees, where, as chairman, his counsels were of much service. His experience and research in his branch of the medical profession secured for him a wide reputation. A distinguished alienist happily described him as the Historian of his speciality. No doubt his laborious literary occupations overtaxed his constitution. In particular, his editorship of the Dictionary of Psychological Medicine must often have severely strained his mental and physical energies."* Journal of Mental Science 1895. 41: p 556-557

The Dog Inn, which offered good stabling, sandwiched between two temperance establishments. On the right, the Westleyan Chapel, where the Band of Hope met. On the left, a temperance hotel, offering coffee and rooms. Postcard 1905. From collection of Laurie Hughes.

A Victorian Tale: The Lyttons and the Lunacy Laws

6

A few miles south east of Hitchin is Knebworth House, known now more for its pop concerts but in the 19th century it was the home of a famous author of novels and active politician, Sir Edward Bulwer Lytton. He achieved fame for various things, but also some notoriety when he arranged for his wife, Rosina, to be certified and confined under the lunacy laws in 1858. This has been seen as his way of controlling a woman who was oppressed and rebelling against society's unfair rules, as another example of how literary figures seemed to get their own way, and she has been described as *"perfectly sane"*. So how did this happen, were the criticisms of him fair, and how could the medical profession be involved in anything so apparently dreadful?

Edward had lived at Knebworth House from 1811 with his mother, Elizabeth, after the death of her father (her husband General Bulwer had died in 1807). Edward and Rosina met in 1825, possibly introduced and encouraged by Lady Caroline Lamb (wife of a prime minister, Lord Melbourne, and one time lover of Lord Byron) whose home at Brocket Hall, six miles south of Knebworth, was also where they courted [1].

They married in 1827. Elizabeth did not approve of Rosina and ceased supporting Edward after the marriage. He had to earn money and did that by writing and became very successful. His books were as popular as those of his friend Charles Dickens, but his reputation dropped at the beginning of the 20th century. His literary name lives on in the Bulwer Lytton Fiction Prize, an annual contest for the most ludicrous opening line of a novel [2], inspired by the 57 word opening line of his novel 'Paul Clifford'. This also provides the first line of Snoopy's intended novel in the 'Peanuts' cartoons – *"It was a dark and stormy night...."*.

Rosina and Edward had two children but she took little part in their care, seemingly helping Edward with his writing and socializing with him. They had a stormy relationship and there was at least one episode when Edward assaulted her before they separated permanently in 1836. They lived apart but

Knebworth House, built 1563 with four wings, three being demolished by Elizabeth Bulwer Lytton when she inherited it from her father in 1811. He had spent the family fortune and she had to economize. Gothic features were added by Edward Bulwer Lytton in the 1840s. It is now occupied by the Lytton Cobbold family, the 19th generation of Lyttons. Photo by author 2010

Brocket Hall, sited between Lemsford and Wheathampstead, where Edward and Rosina courted, was the home of two Prime Ministers. It was built in 1760 by the father of Lord Melbourne who lived there until his death in 1848. It was then inherited by his sister, Emily Cowper, who had married Lord Palmerston in 1839.

Photo by author 2011

never divorced, the legal process being very difficult and requiring a private bill in parliament until the Marital Causes Act was passed in 1857. Then there had to be evidence of infidelity by the wife or that plus another misdemeanour, either incest, bigamy, cruelty or desertion, by the husband. Edward paid her an annual allowance of £400, which did not increase despite his increasing wealth, and was not enough for her and she accumulated large debts. Rosina would not admit to and Edward could not prove her adultery, which would have been sufficient. Edward had affairs and at least three other families but Rosina did not pursue divorce, perhaps initially preferring to remain as *"Lady Bulwer"* and later to be known as *"Lady Lytton"*.

Portrait of Rosina as a young woman by A.E. Chalon.

Knebworth House Archive

Edward was eventually reconciled with his mother and inherited the house after her death in 1843. Rosina never lived there and may only have visited once. Edward seems to have spent his time between Knebworth and Park Lane in London during 1858.

The death of their daughter, Emily, increased Rosina's resentment of Edward. He had banned the children from seeing their mother from 1838. Emily became ill and probably died of typhus in lodgings in London in 1848. Rosina did find her way to the house where Emily was staying and describes keeping a vigil downstairs from where she lay in bed, without seeing her. Rosina subsequently accused the attending doctor, Dr Marshall Hall, of killing her daughter, and Edward of employing the doctor to do so [3].

Rosina sought whatever means she could to advertise her grievances. She wrote 14 novels which parodied her husband's works with thinly veiled insults and accusations about him. She also wrote volumes of letters. She has been seen as a campaigner for the rights of women (Rosina's mother, Anna Wheeler, was a notable fighter for women's rights, she had married young and separated when Rosina was aged 10), but her main campaign was to embarrass her husband [4]. In 1851 she threatened to appear at the opening night of 'Not as Bad as We Seem' a play written by Edward to help fund the Guild of Literature and Arts, which Edward and Dickens had jointly founded. Charles Dickens and Wilkie Collins were due to act and Queen Victoria and Prince Albert were to attend. Rosina produced a parody of a poster for the event which included –

> *"The New Farce is from the pen of Sir Liar-Coward Bulwer Lytton, that distinguished Embroiderer so celebrated for his Herculean labours in transfer work, unscrupulously selecting whole chapters from contemporary French and German authors, and transferring them to his own pages he, afterwards presents to that concrete ass, "The British Public" as entirely original!!"* [5]

Edward later described in an account dated September 24 1858 how he then submitted some of her writings (which seemed to corroborate the impression that her mind was disordered) to two eminent alienists, Drs Sutherland and Monroe [6]. He reported that they said *"such evidences were conclusive as to a disordered state of intellect... which would probably become worse with time"*. As he felt that *"there might be a doubt that restraint were justifiable, I then took no further proceedings"*. He also consulted medical advisors after she defaced a book, 'Lady Blessington's Diary', with libellous comments on various society figures mentioned therein, and then returned it to the 'circulating library' (that book with her inscriptions is also in the Knebworth House Archive).

October 1857

Rosina, often referred to as Lady L, and Edward lived quite separate lives, she in Llangollen and then Taunton, he in London and Knebworth. She wrote to him on an occasional basis and after a gap of a year wrote on October 3rd 1857 with the envelope addressed

> *"Sir E Bulwer Lytton MP! For The woman Beaumont Alias Laura Deacon Strumpet and Spy To That Loathsome and Ruffian Old Ruffian Sir Liar Coward Bulwer Lytton Knebworth Park Stevenage Herts"* [7].

Laura Deacon was one of his mistresses. Soon after, on October 7th, he wrote to his long term friend John Forster (also advisor on many issues, particularly literary, and a close friend of Charles Dickens) who had been Clerk to the Lunacy Commission since 1855 -

> *"should I adventure..to place Lady L under some restraint or surveillance.. does your experience in Lunacy Law suggest any ...quick mode of doing so?"* [8].

Forster replied on the same day –

> *"Pray, pray be very careful in what you do so as in the matter you mention. There is no middle way between leaving such a case altogether alone, and treating it, out & out, as a case of insanity. I have long been convinced that she is insane - but it is a case belonging exactly to the class which it is most difficult to get medical men to certify."* [9].

He went on however to give details of the certificates which should be obtained by two medical men and the order of admission which was usually issued by the nearest kin, and continued –

> *"On the other hand, if thought more advisable not to place the person in a licensed house – but to have her in a house by herself under medical treatment – which is the course most likely to be thought of in the present case – the best plan would be to go to such a man as Sutherland, or Munro, or Winslow* [prominent psychiatrists doing private practice] *and he would provide a lodging kept by someone in his confidence – to which the order of admission would have to be directed. But the medical certificate, authorizing the restraint and signed by two medical men independently, are still required.*
>
> *You, I think, ought in no case to sign the order. It ought to be signed by someone who has been in the position of knowing her, and the character of her life etc, for the last few months or years. If there is such a person, altogether unconnected & uninfluenced by you"*

Edward appears then to have arranged for a Henry Trenchard to do some scouting. Trenchard wrote to him on November 19th 1857 with various observations [10]. He commented that she spent most of her time in her hotel rooms, he ascertained her spending and that her purchase of wine and spirits was *"not immoderate and certainly not excessive"*, that her state of mind was generally quiet, *"though she is liable to violent fits of passion when provoked"*. He commented on the possibility that she was not of sound mind, saying *"her general behaviour in the hotel does not of itself justify such a conclusion"*.

Edward appeared to do nothing after that, perhaps heeding Forster's note of caution and Trenchard's comments.

February – April 1858

Edward had been an MP from 1831 to 1832 for St Ives in Huntingdonshire and then Lincoln from 1832 until 1841. He left politics for a while but returned in 1852 to become MP for Hertford. By February 1858 the seesawing of national politics led to Edward Smith-Stanley, the Earl of Derby, a Conservative, becoming Prime Minister. Edward was close to the heart of the party and was a long term friend of Benjamin Disraeli, who became Leader of the House of Commons. Edward was offered the government post of Colonial Secretary. This led to Rosina writing to Derby in February using various terms of abuse. The first letter started –

> *"Every one is aware that it is a matter of very little import whether the manure on the political Dunghill be labelled "Whig" or "Tory" "Conservative": or "Radical" as the one thing needful – the amount of corruption is sure to be the same. – The dear Whigs once had a ministry nick-named "All the Talents" yours just formed is far more appropriately named "All the Blackguards" …I remain, My Lord with every species of contempt for you, and your gang your Colonial Secretaries Hunted, and starving Legal Victim Rosina Bulwer Lytton alas!"* [11]

Edward did not become Colonial Secretary at that time. There was some miscommunication following Edward's request that he join the government as a lord. He was uncertain whether he would be re-elected as MP for Hertford, which was the usual protocol when appointed to government, due to a fear that he would be defeated by the Liberals [12]. That led to Rosina's second letter, which started -

> *"My Lord It is much to your credit that you would not sit in the same cabinet with such revolting incarnation of every pollution as Sir Liar Coward Bulwer Lytton."* [13]

There is something manic in the flow of this, all of her rage flowing without a sense of how others might see it, and dismiss her vitriolic flow as somehow mad.

Soon after this Edward engaged the help of Robert Gardiner Hill in dealing with his wife. Hill was a well known asylum doctor who pioneered the abolition of restraint for patients in Lincoln Asylum where he worked from 1835 to 1840 (and may have met Edward when he was MP for Lincoln). Edward wrote to Hill on March 28th with practical instructions on what should be done to her effects *"in removing the patient"*, how to deal with her landlady (Mrs Clarke at Clarke's Castle Hotel in Taunton), and anticipating questions that might be raised by the *"Commissioners"* over a statement that she had been insane for many years but without certification being required before then [14].

Correspondence over the next month shows Hill exploring various details of preparation for having Rosina certified. He first approached Dr John Bucknill from the Devon Asylum (who later became eminent as President of the 19th century forerunner of the Royal College of Psychiatrists), asking if he would assess her. Bucknill was cautious and wanted direct authority from Edward to do so [15]. That led to Dr Charles Hood getting involved to arrange for Edward to give his written authority. Hood was the medical superintendent of the Bethlem Hospital (previously known as Bedlam) and regarded as a reformer [16] and became Edward's close advisor and supporter over the next year.

From Taunton, Hill gave Edward an account of Rosina's circumstances, that she had not been out of her room for six months, that she had changed her solicitor and what her local debts were. He had also spied out her residence at the Castle Hotel and had practical knowledge of the layout and a strategy for dealing with Mrs Clarke, the landlady, if there was any objection to people entering the hotel to certify Rosina [17]. The plans somehow fizzled out but they were continuing to plan for some action in the future, as Hill wrote on April 20th -

> *"I still think that all we require is a man of courage and tact to visit Lady Lytton and as we cannot ask first one person and then another and say that unless you can certify as to her Ladyship's insanity, you must not act – it would be as well if you would leave that matter in my hands. I would find the person without implicating anyone or even mentioning names and after I had done so would ask you for the authority. I would then place the evidences before him and give him benefit of my experience."* [18]

Hill was expecting that Rosina would be placed in his care after being certified and anticipated no problem from the authorities.

Edward was scheming, quite what he had in mind is not revealed in any detail, but he was talking to his solicitor, William Loaden. There was a little bit of blame swapping with Hill denying that the lack of success (ie. certifying and confining) was his fault.

Hood was meanwhile revelling in his involvement and in response to receiving a check(que) from Edward wrote on April 30th -

> *"I felt very much the kind and flattering tone of your letter and altho' the fee you enclosed was larger than in any case I should have desired I was pained to receive it. I had hoped that as I had accomplished so little towards the object which obtained for me your acquaintance – the little time I had devoted to the subject might have been without remuneration. You have removed any supposed obligation and I now ask as a favour that you will allow me to return the check and that I may consider the personal introduction I have been privileged with to one admired in his writings from my youth; the confidence you have placed in me, and the sympathy you have permitted me to express in your sorrows as a far richer reward than any gold or silver, and more in accordance with my wishes than a fee"* [19].

June 8th 1858 - The Hertford Episode

Meanwhile, back in parliament, Edward was offered the post of Colonial Secretary again. He accepted and had to stand for re-election in Hertford. His Liberal candidate withdrew just before polling. The hustings were held at Hertford on June 8th.

Rosina was still in Taunton. She owed money to Mrs Clarke but still persuaded her to provide the funds for them both to go to Hertford, saying that it was only by confronting Sir Edward that the debts she owed Mrs Clarke could be paid off [20]. She had posters prepared for distribution at the hustings, as she had the previous year, which parodied his political views – *"I am many sided. Great minds always are."* It was signed from *"A MAN OF CONSEQUENCE"*, his address being given as *"TAUNT-ON"* [21].

Unfortunately after the long journey Rosina and Mrs Clarke arrived at the scene too late and missed the election process, but Edward was still there - *"their cowardly brute of a county member on the hustings"*. Rosina describes how she addressed the crowd - *"Men Of Herts, if you have the hearts of men, hear me"*, and regaled the assembled citizens of Hertford with a devastating account of her husband's behaviour [22]. She said that the Times' reporter had been bundled off. She was then cheered from the rooftops by the local residents as she returned to the station and took the train back to Taunton. As with other parts of this oft repeated story it is mainly based on her own account, and may understandably contain exaggerations and distortions. However the idea of the press being excluded finds resonance in the diary of William Lucas of Hitchin, a quiet Quaker otherwise not greatly interested in political events. He seems to have only one reference to Sir Edward, when he recorded the re-election, Rosina's intervention and Edward's rapid departure from the scene. He then adds *"Singularly enough no notice of this extraordinary circumstance has been taken in any of the papers, they contained long accounts of the election. Such influence has a great celebrity over the tadpoles of the press"*. [23]

The next day, June 9th, John Forster (who as Clerk to the Lunacy Commission worked closely with Lord Shaftesbury, the great reformer, and Chairman of the Lunacy Commission from 1845 - 85) wrote to Edward -

> *"I have just heard from Lord Shaftesbury a mention of what took place yesterday after you left – and which I think you ought to know. His son Evelyn Ashley – heard it from Henry Cowper [24]. It seems that she addressed the crowd in a most violent & excited way – conveying exactly the impression which it was most desirable she should make, to be thoroughly serviceable to you, the words reported by Mr Cowper to young Ashley were those of utter insanity.*
> *Lord Shaftesbury knows I am writing this to you, and desires me to tell you that there could be only one impression as to the wretched exhibition made by this unhappy person. A full justification of yourself in any measure you may now think it right to take. "It is very fortunate" – are Lord Shaftesbury's words – "it puts him quite right"'* [25].

First assessment - June 12th 1858

Four days after the hustings Edward's solicitor, William Loaden, arrived at Clarke's Hotel with Dr Woodford from Fairwater, the local asylum in Taunton,

Sir Edward Bulwer Lytton (1803 – 1873). Portrait circa 1860, the year following his departure from government when Lord Stanley was defeated by Lord Palmerston. He was eventually made Lord Lytton, Baron of Knebworth, in 1866, receiving much praise from Dr Charles Hood.
Knebworth House Archive

and Frederick Hale Thomson, a medical practitioner from London. They were accompanied by a female attendant from the local asylum – described by Rosina as *"a Patagonian woman of six feet high, who was a keeper from the Madhouse at Fairwater"* [26]. Loaden wrote –

"Dr Woodford had no hesitation in giving the Certificate - Mr Hale Thomson had doubts as to the extent of the unsoundness of her Ladyship's mind and in consequence of these doubts returned to London with Mr Loaden without giving a Certificate." [27]

Rosina's report is that Dr Woodford concluded - *"Well, I don't know. I think I never saw any one in sounder mind or body"*, and that the *"giantess"* said *"I do think this is one of the cruellest outrages I ever witnessed or heard of"*.

The doctors withdrew after Hale Thomson asked Rosina to state the terms she would accept from Sir Edward for her never to expose him as she did at Hertford. She *replied "if he will pay me £500 a year I will not again publicly expose him"* [28]. She maintained that Thomson promised to write to her within four days to report the outcome of that request. When she did not hear from him she wrote two long letters on June 20th & 22nd. The first started in typical fashion –

> *"Hoggishly, and brutally ill bred, as Englishmen of all classes, for the most part are; common decency - & common policy, - should have made you answer at least one of the 3 letters, I addressed to you last week, after the brutal, and ruffianly outrage you were made the creditable! Tool of. – But as you do not think fit to do so, your infamous Employer, My Lord Derby's rotton old dregs of Sodom, and Babylon, converted into a Colonial Secretary…".*

followed by a stream of raging consciousness, mostly vitriolic and repeating accusations about Edward's plagiarism, causing the death of his daughter, his mistress and political corruption [29].

Certification at Piccadilly — June 23rd

Rosina then travelled to London with Mrs Clarke and went to Hale Thomson's house in Clarges Street, Piccadilly on Wednesday June 23rd at noon, talked with Mr Thomson and agreed to return at 6pm. Hale Thomson informed Sir Edward of the letters and said she should be placed under restraint. Sir Edward, with his son Robert and Loaden, went to Dr Gardiner Hill's home at Inverness Lodge in Brentford and arranged for him to be at Clarges Street at 5 o'clock [30].

When Rosina returned to Clarges Street, with Mrs Clarke and her cousin, Rebecca Ryves, she found a number of people in the house. By her account separate assessments by the two medical men, as required under the Lunacy Laws, were not held, as they saw her together. Whereas she described a seven hour assessment being held at Taunton two weeks previously, she said there was no proper assessment. The two medical men had to complete certificates [31] detailing their findings. They both recorded that she was *"of unsound mind"*, rather than describing her as a 'lunatic'. In the section of the document titled 'Facts indicating Insanity observed by myself', Hale Thomson, who described himself as a surgeon and a Fellow of the Royal College of Surgeons, wrote –

"She stated that the government employs her husband because he has habitually committed sodomy with Mr Disraeli and Dr Marshall Hall was hired by her husband to murder her daughter and succeeded in doing so, assisted by a General Practitioner at Fulham."

George Ross, who described himself as a surgeon with the qualification of MRCS (Member of the Royal College of Surgeons), wrote:

"She states that if she had been taken into Custody at Taunton the Yeomanry would have turned out to protect her, that her husband paid the Times Newspaper Two Thousand pounds to suppress a report of the Proceedings at the late election for Hertfordshire, she indulges in most violent language in connexion with numerous persons…"

Neither of these men were specialists in mental disorders - that was not required at the time. Ross emerged later as a friend of Hill, but Hale Thomson seems to have had no connection with any of the parties involved.

Thomson's certificate states that she said that her husband and Disraeli were in a

A copy of the certificate completed by Frederick Hale Thomson, declaring that Rosina was a person of "unsound mind", rather than a "lunatic". Knebworth House Archive [32]

sodomist relationship and for that reason Sir Edward had obtained his place in the government. Was that true? There seems to be no public information on whether the two men had a homosexual relationship. They had been close associates, they were in the same social circles, they were both known as dandies at a time when such a fashion was not associated with any sexual preference. A recent book explored the issue of whether Disraeli was gay and concluded *"maybe he was and maybe he wasn't"* [33]. Hibbert's biography of Disraeli quotes Sarah Bradford that *"the latent homosexual element in Disraeli's friendship with younger men cannot be ignored in the case of Lennox, even if the relationship was almost certainly not physical"*, but he does not suggest that the relationship with Edward Bulwer Lytton, while being affectionate, was sexual [34]. In the absence of any corroborative evidence or accepted public opinion the allegation could be regarded as a delusion or false belief. If there was any truth in her allegation then her utterances could be regarded as disinhibited, for in her situation it would have been more sensible to keep quiet rather than be seen to be making wild and unevidenced accusations.

The full certification included a document signed by Edward Bulwer Lytton – an 'Order for the Reception of a Private Patient' for her to be sent to Dr Robert Gardiner Hill at Inverness Lodge in Brentford. Edward stated *"There has been much unsoundness of mind for more than 20 years but it has become worse during the last 12 years & is now still more violent in its character"* [31]. She went there immediately, the transfer being assisted by two policemen.

The question is then whether they described Rosina's mental state in a way that met the existing concept of insanity and justified her being certified and confined. It seems that there was no agreed definition of lunacy or mental disorder in the 19th century and no clear guideline as to when confinement under the lunacy laws would be appropriate.

Edward completed the required certificate for 'The Reception of a Private Patient'. This is similar to the 'Application' which is part of the process of detention under the current Mental Health Act, but is now usually completed by the Approved Social Worker (a profession unheard of in 1858).

Knebworth House Archive [31]

June 23rd - July 17th 1858
— Confinement at Inverness Lodge in Brentford

By Rosina's account she was housed with Gardiner Hill's family, albeit in a room which was locked for some of the day and night. The grounds of his home were used by inmates of Wyke's House, the private asylum part-owned by Hill, which was nearby. On June 28th Gardiner Hill completed and sent to the Commissioners in Lunacy the 'Notice of Admission', being part of the same certificate that Edward had sent to him on June 23rd. Hill confirmed that he had seen and examined her and noted that she was *"evidently under the influence of delusions"*, but gives no more details [31].

There is a day to day account of her in Gardiner Hill's diary which is in the Knebworth archives [35]. It gives details of her mental state – sometimes calm but sometimes very emotional – understandable as she was clearly very angry about being confined. Edward gave the appearance of being concerned in writing to Gardiner Hill,

> *"Let me know how your Patient gets on. I wish particularly to call your attention to her physical state, ascertain as soon as you kindly can, if there be any uterine or other disease which may account for insanity & have the heart sounded & tested"*,

but was clearly wanting to control events –

> *"Let no one see her that may excite her more, & of course no letters to or from her"* [36].

Rosina commented on the allegations about Edward's relationship with Disraeli in a letter to Rebecca Ryves on July 1st –

> *"it would appear that the tack these wretches are on, is something I said of Disraeli! – years ago (!) which was something as told me by Sir Liar himself – but never taken hold of till now that the latter being a jack in office."* [37]

Despite denying that she had made any recent proclamation on this subject she is recorded in Hill's diary as talking about it on June 24, and on July 2nd to the Lunacy Commissioners. On July 11th Hill reported to Edward that she had *"repeated the accusation against yourself and Mr Disraeli"* [38]. Hill recorded on July 12th that she had seen Dr Forbes Winslow and *"Denied that she had ever made the statement that Sir Edward had had or ever had told her that had had unnatural relations with Mr Disraeli"*.

She seems to have repeated some of her wilder accusations to medical visitors, to Dr Hood [39], Dr John Conolly [40] and the Lunacy Commissioners, Dr Samuel Gaskell and Bryan Waller Procter (pen name Barry Cornwall) a lawyer and poet [41]. She told the Commissioners that she believed Queen Victoria had been involved in a murder plot. Even the alienist, Forbes Winslow, who examined her at the request of her barrister, Edwin James, wrote to the Observer on July 16th partly defending Sir Edward's actions –

> *"I think it but justice to Sir Edward B. Lytton to state that, upon the facts which I have ascertained were submitted to him, and upon the certificates of the medical men whom he was advised to consult, the course which he has pursued throughout these painful proceedings cannot be considered as harsh or unjustifiable."* [42]

(In 1863 Winslow became the subject of criticism by the Daily Telegraph for daring to divide the mad from the sane, a task *"dangerous and deplorable under the present state of our knowledge"*. However it was a job that someone had to do, and society ultimately gave the alienists the power to do so [43]).

Rosina believed that there was a conspiracy by Edward's literary friends, including Dickens and the editor of the Times, to keep things hushed up. She seemed to trust the two Commissioners initially although they had strong literary connections, saying of Procter *"by far the best, and most gentleman like of them – and who listened to my statement with marked attention"* [44]. Wilkie Collins' book 'The Woman in White' and William Thackeray's 'Vanity Fair' were dedicated to Cornwall. On July 8th Rosina expressed her doubts about Barry Cornwall (that is Procter), the *"literary gent"* [45]. Gaskell's sister-in-law was the novelist Elizabeth Gaskell, who wrote for Dickens' periodicals. Rosina loathed John Forster, describing him as an *"unprincipled wretch"* [46], and may have been alarmed to know that Forster, Procter and Gaskell were close, forming a clique within the Lunacy Commission [47].

The literary connections have been explored in a book by John Sutherland, 'Victorian Fiction', in which he suggests that Thackeray, Dickens and Lytton all used the Lunacy Laws to deal with their difficult wives. Thackeray's and Dickens' wives appeared to have mental health problems after childbirth but neither was certified. Sutherland suggests that a veiled threat made by Dickens to his wife, when he wanted a separation agreement, was helped by advice from John Forster and Dr John Conolly. He also suggests that Conolly was behind the conspiracy to confine Rosina, but there is no real evidence of that in the archives. Some of the confusion probably arises from Rosina's varying accounts of who saw her when, and it seems that her memory for events became slightly jumbled. She wrote an account of the events and sent that to Charles Reade when his book 'Hard Cash' was published, as he asked in the preface for other examples of wrongful imprisonment in lunatic asylums to be sent to him. His book was a satire on the lunacy trade with a recognizable lampoon of John Conolly [48].

The editor of the Times, John Thadeus Delane, may have been sympathetic to Edward as his own wife was for many years confined in a private asylum. The evidence is that he was a devoted and loving husband and his wife had not been put away for his convenience [49]. There is no evidence that he was bribed and at one point Edward was very concerned that Delane might join the Daily Telegraph and write against him [50].

The Lunacy Commission were the policemen who ensured that the 1845 Lunacy Act was properly observed. In their regular visitors' reports to Asylums they examined up to half of the private patients and recorded their findings under the heading 'Found lunatic by inquisition', and would have instituted proceedings to release patients if they were not insane. Pauper lunatics were not included in these assessments. In 1858 there was a heightened awareness of abuses with two cases attracting national publicity when the patients claimed they had been certified but were sane. One involved Mrs Turner of York and was reported in the Hertfordshire Mercury at that time. The other case, of Mr

Ruck [51], was mentioned by Charles Hood when writing from Paris in August 1858. Hood said that he did not think much of it, adding that Edwin James, Rosina's barrister, was involved in it.

While Shaftesbury's good name was not brought into question, a letter to the Daily Telegraph on July 15th questioned whether Cornwall and Forster were friends of Lord Lytton, the implication being that the Commission may not have been objective as they might have been.

By July 11th Mr Hyde, Rosina's solicitor, was trying to negotiate terms of a settlement. This sent her into a rage causing *"complete uproar"* in the house [38]. But perhaps she heeded Mr Hyde's advice and when seen again by Forbes Winslow on July 12th she denied that she had ever said that Edward and Disraeli had ever had *"unnatural relations"* [52]. Winslow pronounced her improved and the Chairman of the Lunacy Commission declared that the reunion with her son had calmed her greatly [53]. Rosina thought that pressure was put on Edward because of the bad publicity from the prime minister and Queen Victoria, though later commented on her *"for our little selfish, sensuous, inane and carnal queen would not care if all her subjects were equally distributed in Madhouses, or pounded into mortar"*, and blamed her for not sacking Edward from the government [54].

A settlement was quickly reached, Edward offered to pay her debts and increase her allowance to £500 per year. She had some long discussions with her son Robert, though they had not seen each other for several years. Mr Hyde, her solicitor, and Edwin James, a barrister, also saw her on July 16th and she was released on July 17th and travelled to the continent with her son Robert and Miss Ryves. At the same time letters concerning the arrangements were published in the Observer, with Winslow confirming that her state of mind *"is such to justify her liberation from restraint"* [42].

According to Gardiner Hill's diary, she was *"removed, not improved"* [55].

The Media Storm

Rosina's friend, Rebecca Ryves, wrote to the papers and the story was taken up around the country, particularly in Taunton and Hertfordshire, and nationally by the Daily Telegraph (a liberal paper at that time). Edward became frustrated that the case was becoming *"notorious"* despite the Lunacy Commission and all the experts saying it was appropriate that she was certified and confined.

Some residents of Taunton met on July 6th and established a committee with the purpose to express public alarm and to form a committee to *"watch the results of the extraordinary measures to have been adopted"* [56]. They stated that such confinement should only be possible after a public inquiry, likening this to a gaol sentence after a court trial. They doubted that she was insane, let alone *"dangerously insane"*. They were not immune to some of the less likeable aspects of her personality, saying that she was known for her *"haughtiness"*, and that she had ridiculed in her writings another lady of Taunton. But they had seen no sign of her insanity and thought it utterly wrong that she could be taken to a madhouse on the words of two medical men, noting that such places where *"if not already insane, they are placed in circumstances calculated to destroy reason and*

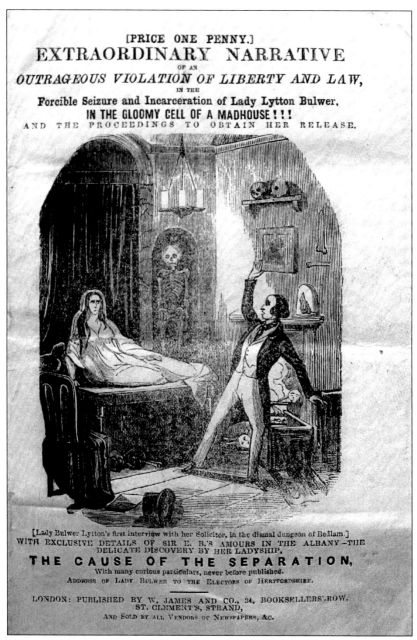

Cover of the pamphlet produced by the Taunton committee protesting about Rosina's confinement.
Knebworth House Archive [56]

produce insanity". Their words mirror those of the Alleged Lunatics' Friends Society. The pamphlet had an evocative cover!

George Ross wrote to Edward on July 28th saying he was taking legal advice about comments in the Daily Telegraph which damaged his reputation [57]. Gardiner Hill wrote to the Telegraph (July 19th) saying *"the mis-statements in your paper are calculated to do me great injury"*, and contradicting their assertions that Lady Lytton was *"feloniously deprived of her liberty and consigned to a notorious madhouse at Brentford, the keeper of which is named Hill"*… *"buried in the depths of a lunatic Bastille"*, or *"left alone with individuals in a ghastly state of lunacy"*, or that she was ever restrained by bolts or bars [58].

W.Pollard of the Hertfordshire Guardian had been corresponding with Edward, as it was the Conservatives' paper and he acted as an agent for Edward. He mentioned printing some handbills for distribution in Luton and Hitchin (which was the town nearest to Knebworth House, and of which he said later *"Hitchin is the place that wants seeing after most"*) to *"set the question in a fair light"*. By August 3rd he wrote that 1000 bills had been posted and including Royston, Stevenage & Welwyn, & intermediate villages, Stortford, Hatfield, Hemel Hempstead & St Albans.

However,

> *"The fact seems to be that the people here, who saw poor Lady Lytton have made up their mind on the matter require little or no convincing. At Hitchin where they have had only hearsay, they seem to have very strong & very false impressions".*

He later added, somewhat unhelpfully -

> *"It is too late now even to mention it, but I had determined to bring Mr (Robert) Lytton and Lady Lytton into contact the afternoon of the Election day, feeling assured that he only could control her. I hurried back after securing the London reporters but Lady Lytton had then left. Had I been in time I believe all this could have been avoided."* [59].

The Hertfordshire Mercury had caused Mr Pollard *"exasperation"* and reported the case in full. However the most surprising letter was that of Rebecca Ryves to the Hertfordshire Mercury on July 23rd, from Paris -

> *"I am the Miss Ryves, whose name has been prominently brought forward in an article of the Somerset Gazette. It suffices to say, that I as the principal witness, there recorded, state that article to be thoroughly inaccurate & exaggerated, & tending to produce the most unjust impressions – Lady Lytton was not for one moment in a Lunatic Asylum.*
>
> *I grant, that in ignorance of the motives & reasons which had led to a step, which occasioned me the most painful surprise, & having been previously reduced to entertain the strongest prejudice against Sir E Lytton, & being under the influence of strong emotions & a deep & true affection for Lady Lytton, it was I, who in the first instance gave way to an anger, which has led to the publicity & misinterpretation I since deprecated & now regret.*
>
> *It is well to know both sides of a question, & without entering into details, which no one wd respect, I am bound to say, that I believe Sir E Lytton,*

acting from impressions conveyed by some acts of violent feeling & writings, which were the result of great excitement of feeling, was led to consult medical authorities on the subject & to act upon their opinions – since acting, however, upon them, I must freely admit, that there has been no secrecy or harshness, but every desire to effect arrangements most conducive to Lady Lytton's happiness & future peace of mind & to free her at once from every restraint, on being fairly & properly appealed to, & quietly convinced of her state of mind by her friends. Therefore it is that publicity is deprecated by her friends, & therefore it is, that justice is due to Sir Edward Lytton." [60]

So she defends Edward's action while saying that Rosina's state of mind was alright. She and Edward then formed some alliance, on August 24th he wrote to her in Paris

"I am glad that the notes & cheque that I sent you are received by you in the spirit in which they were meant. Lady Lytton & myself are no longer young, – we have a son, whose nature is sensitive, whose constitution is delicate & about whose health, as affected by the mind & painful emotions, I entertain the most serious & anxious uneasiness. For the sake of that son, if for no other reason, let there be peace between his parents from this time forth to the end of their days & let that peace be loyally, steadfastly, honourably maintained by Lady L. Let Lady L henceforth respect my good name & honour & I will seek to forget all in her except the mother who loves & proves that she loves my son." [61]

Rebecca continued to write to Edward reporting on Rosina's state, but at some time Rosina felt betrayed by her and correspondence between them ceased (in 1857 she had written 105 letters to Rebecca, with few to anybody else, but Rosina later referred to her as *"that vile wretch"* [62]).

With Rosina abroad the kerfuffle subsided. Dr Hood travelled to Paris to keep an eye on things. Soon afterwards Robert left Rosina and returned to England, disappearing one night over a matter he never revealed. Rosina returned to Taunton by October 23rd, which Rebecca reported faithfully to Edward. Robert and Rosina became eternally alienated. Letters he had written were edited and circulated by her – *"unscrupulously perverted, & unsparingly used, to give effect to the most ruthless vituperation"* [63]. Her affection for him never returned, even referring him years later in her will as a *"contemptible monster"*, and adding a poem there about him –

> *"Too weak to love, too false to hate*
> *Hypocrisy's his normal state*
> *Half Joseph Surface, half Tartufe*
> *Self is his warp, – deceit his woof*
> *The velvet word and fiendish deed*
> *Prove him the true foul Lytton breed!"* [64].

(Joseph Surface is a double dealing character who pretends to be honourable in Sheridan's play 'The School for Scandal' (1777), and Tartufe is a play by Moliere, subtitled 'The Imposter – a hypocrite' (1664)).

Post Script, 1859

Meanwhile back in the government Edward was struggling. By December he wanted to resign and Forster composed a draft resignation letter for him [65], but he was persuaded to stay on. He seemingly worked hard at his job and the naming of British Columbia in Canada, where the town of Lytton was named after him, and the establishment of Queensland in Australia were credited to his efforts.

That might have been the end of the story but for a letter that Robert Gardiner Hill wrote the following March, the result of which led to the whole affair being played out again in private, leaving a rich archive of letters and Hill's own diary which may otherwise not have been preserved.

Hill put 'the cat amongst the pigeons' by writing to Forster at the Lunacy Commission over an unrelated case.

> *"I called upon you this morning to request that if Mrs Burkitt was to be removed from my house she might be removed at once… She is the most treacherous, deceitful and heartless patient I ever had under my care...*
>
> *I consider the steps taken by the Commissioners as very injurious to myself because if the Commissioners place no confidence in me... what support can I look for from the profession and the public…*
>
> *It is strange that if my house be not a "suitable abode" for Mrs Burkitt that it should have been considered suitable for Lady Lytton. I have written evidence to show that Lady Lytton was placed in confinement by your advice and the Commissioners long before the Certificates of Lunacy were signed. I should not have alluded to this matter if I did not feel that there was a prejudice against me."* [66]

With Mrs Burkitt as a thorn in his side, he bemoaned his work with the sad words - *"I begin to think that a man had better break stones than have the care of lunatics"*, but he was about to experience even more stress. He had questioned the integrity of the Commission and reopened the debate on whether Edward had acted with propriety.

Dr Robert Gardiner Hill (1811 – 1878), who trained at Guy's and St Thomas's Hospitals and was Medical Superintendant at Lincoln Lunatic Asylum from 1835 to 1840. He pioneered non-restraint at the Asylum in 1836 but was overshadowed in this by John Conolly whose writings about it were better known. Conolly also wrote extensively about the design and workings of asylums. [67]

Photo courtesy and copyright of the Gardiner-Hill Family

There followed a letter to him from Lord Shaftesbury who *"requests the attendance of Mr Hill at the Board next Wednesday, and requests also that he will bring with him "the written evidence" which, he stated, is in his possession"*[68]. Forster went into panic mode, Hill's letter was quite damning, given that the Lunacy Commission was supposed to be independent and not favouring either side in any dispute over a person's confinement.

The archive contains almost fifty letters over the next two months between the various parties. Hood acted as intermediary, trying to comfort, then persuade and cajole Hill to reveal his evidence, which was the letter written to Edward by Forster on June 9th 1858. When Hood was not succeeding he put pressure on George Ross to help persuade Hill. When that was unsuccessful legal threats were made. Shaftesbury would not allow Hill's letter to be withdrawn, as it had been received by the Commission and was now official, and had to be dealt with properly. Hill tried to defend his actions, only to be told by Loaden, Edward's solicitor, that he clearly had not taken into consideration the Lunacy Acts which would apply in such a case.

Edward and Forster had some disagreement. Forster wrote on March 12th appearing to try and exonerate himself from any type of blame for encouraging Edward and wrote on March 14th –

> *"I fear, from the tone of your letter, that you hardly see the monstrous nature of the charge brought by this man. If it were possible, that "long before the Certificates were obtained," not only the Secretary of the Lunacy Commission, but the Lunacy Commissioners themselves, had advised that the person should be confined – it would indeed be a scandal for inquiry, a matter to be mooted at the Committee or elsewhere, and sifted to the bottom"* [69].

Hill's diary stops at the end of April and one year later it went into Edward's custody, with various letters, including the copy of the letter by Forster on June 9th 1858. The agreement was that Edward would keep them safe, but make them available to Hill if he were ever to be taken to court over the case of Rosina.

The story of Rosina's confinement stopped there, though her hostility with Edward persisted.

Was Rosina mentally ill?

Her behaviour had been very unusual for a Victorian lady, but was she just a rebel who was trying to right the wrongs of society, was some of her behaviour due to an abnormal or disturbed personality, or was she suffering from a mental disorder? A modern assessment includes all three aspects, social circumstances, personality and mental state.

Her social circumstances have been well described by Mulvey Roberts in her Introduction to 'A Blighted Life' and Leslie Mitchell in his biography of Edward, and there was clearly much in society and in the marriage which would be unacceptable to any woman [70]. David Lytton Cobbold articulates this in 'A Blighted Marriage' but also says *"Cheated she was and obsessed she became and as she grew older her obsession lost its reason and all humour"* [71]. Andrew Scull, an eminent historian, though somewhat cynical about Victorian psychiatrists, declared that she was *"perfectly sane"* [72].

Her own description of her life indicates distrust as she *"had never served* *anyone"*who *"had not repaid me by the basest ingratitude, treachery, and injury"* [73]. Rosina said: *"The first mistake I made was being born at all"*. Whilst Edward's behaviour was often awful she did seem to be quite paranoid and expected people, particularly him, to plot against her. Mitchell says her *"behaviour became odder and odder, no doubt assisted by a heavy intake of alcohol"* [74]. Excess alcohol can certainly exaggerate unpleasant personality traits and lead to angry outbursts which may have happened, though this did not apparently occur to the doctors who saw her in 1858, and her purchase of alcohol in 1857 was not regarded by Trenchard as excessive. Her pattern of behaviour does suggest a personality problem. She was isolated, suspicious and distrustful, but this would not fully explain the development of certain beliefs about Edward.

The assessment of her mental state started in Taunton in June 1858. That was inconclusive as Hale Thomson was not convinced that she was of unsound mind, but he changed his mind two weeks later. The report given by Hale Thomson seems credible. He travelled to Taunton but thought there was not enough evidence to certify her, but two weeks later recorded clear observations which supported certification. How he became involved in the case is not revealed but there is no correspondence which suggests connivance by him. He had received letters from her and may have formed the entirely appropriate judgement that she was mentally unwell, that her behaviour was unpredictable and certification was appropriate. The fact that this did suit Edward's desire to remove her from free society does not negate the validity of Thomson's decision. George Ross did not present the reasons in good enough detail on his certificate to be sure what her mental state was on that day, and being a friend of Hill and without specialist knowledge his decision to certify is open to question.

What does seem quite plausible is that she did have a mental disorder, probably a manic illness (known as hypomanic if it is less severe), which manifested itself as having periods of overactivity, pressure of speech (basically unstoppable), irritability and disinhibited behaviour. This can be associated with delusions or false beliefs about being persecuted. Such episodes normally last at least one week. Her allegations about her husband arranging the murder of their daughter and of only getting a government post because of a sodomist relationship with Disraeli are unsubstantiated and on the face of it seemingly false. Was she deluded, disinhibited due to hypomania, or merely throwing out wild accusations because she wanted to embarrass and distress Edward, or perhaps behaving under the influence of all three? She repeated both accusations to different doctors, but denied the sodomist allegation to Forbes Winslow on their second interview and minimized it when writing to Rebecca Ryves.

The testimonies of Gardiner Hill and Charles Hood seem more compromised. Hill was sure of the need to certify her before ever seeing her and stood to gain financially from accommodating her at Inverness Lodge. But his diary does not seem to contain exaggerations which may have served the purpose of providing more evidence of her madness, if he was trying to distort the evidence. During her confinement he often reported on her behaviour being quite normal, alongside episodes when she was making the allegations about sodomy and murder.

Hood was clearly overawed by Edward and keen to do everything in his power to ingratiate himself. But he was well regarded by the Commission and for his work at Bedlam and did seem to take the time to assess Rosina and made a reasoned statement about her. While the relationship between Edward and Hill seemed strained in 1858, when Edward did not seem to trust Hill's judgement, there was a complete breakdown between them in 1859. Hood meanwhile became ever closer and ever more useful to Edward.

Trying to interpret her behaviour and diagnose any abnormal mental state at this distance of time is extremely difficult. Apart from the opinions of the contemporary doctors there is little objective description of her state of mind before the certification and confinement. If Gardiner Hill's information from April 1858 is accurate, and she had not been out of her room for six months, she may have been depressed. The pattern of her communication in the previous year is interesting, writing 105 letters to Rebecca Ryves, varying from 1 in February, 3 in March and 2 in May to 21 in August and 16 in October. Many of her letters have the same feeling of unstoppable flow of consciousness with ideas bouncing around with minimal logical coherence. It could be argued that this is the unstoppable rage of an abused woman, but such mood swings may be a form of a manic depressive illness and the increased number of letters in some months may be due to being manic at those times.

If she had a manic depressive (now called a bipolar) disorder then it may have been triggered by the stress she experienced, the limited finances, the mean and hostile husband, and the prevailing laws which were so unfair to women. While that may explain what precipitated the problem, it does not remove the impression that she did suffer from a mental illness.

Frustratingly someone with a mild manic disorder may control their behaviour when being observed or assessed, as they have sufficient insight to know when they must behave better. It seems likely that Forster was aware of such dilemmas when he warned Edward in October 1857 that medical men may differ in their opinions in such cases.

Was certification and confinement appropriate?

It seems probable that she suffered from a mental disorder, but was it necessary or useful to have her removed for care or treatment? In 1858 there was no effective treatment for such disorders. There was a belief held by asylum doctors that removal from the stress of people's usual surroundings could be curative, but no plan of treatment other than confinement was mentioned. Edward seemed to want to find some cause and hence cure for her behaviour to be found, but that seems to be a veneer over the greater desire to stop her harassing and embarrassing him and Hill in his diary did not identify any treatment plan.

The legal requirements to confine were fulfilled by the certification. The question of whether Ross and Thomson saw her separately as required by law was never fully answered. There is a question over what was required to fulfil the intentions of the law. Today the doctors need to identify the risks involved in not detaining somebody under the mental health laws. At that time there was no need for that. That issue had been raised by the case of a Miss Nottidge in 1849. She had been certified and confined from 1846 until 1848. When she later challenged that in court the judge pronounced that *"no person should be confined in a lunatic asylum unless he was suicidal or dangerous to others"*. This was regarded as wrong by the Commissioners in Lunacy and by Dr John Conolly, then a leading medical expert on such matters, and that criteria did not become incorporated into practice [75].

The Lunacy Commission did assess her and there is no clear evidence that Samuel Gaskell and Bryan Waller Procter, the medical and legal Lunacy Commissioners, who saw her eleven days after she was certified, colluded in any misuse of the Lunacy Laws. It is possible that their close association with Forster may have led to them compromising their standards. But the concern generated by two other well known cases at that time, of Mr Ruck and Mrs Turner, would if anything have pushed them to ensure that the Lunacy Laws were being complied with and to ensure that justice was done and the integrity of the Commission preserved. The evidence does suggest that Rosina displayed signs of mental disorder in the early days of her confinement and their objective opinion that she was in some way insane seems understandable.

She was released probably due to the publicity and public embarrassment that she caused, but did she improve while in Dr Hill's care and was the confinement helpful? His final comment was that she was *"not improved"*, though there seems to have been some improvement in her self control. She was able to keep silent before she left Mr Hill's care – but whether this was because she had improved and had more control, or whether she decided to hide her true thoughts is uncertain. Her solicitor negotiated an improvement in her finances – which she claimed was the main aim of her actions and no doubt gained great satisfaction and some relief from that stress. She must have been delighted with the national interest and publicity for her cause, particularly the embarrassment that Edward suffered and the damage to his career (a political biographer, Charles Snyder, commented that his *"troubles with Rosina undermined his mental and physical well-being and impaired his ability to serve effectively as Colonial Secretary"* [76]) and Mitchell said that the incident made him ever fearful of such a scene again, so neutering his political career [77]. The question of whether confinement was justified by any improvement seems unproven.

Conclusion

The story of the relationship between Edward and Rosina is sad, with both suffering from the fall out over several decades. Rosina seemed to suffer from both a suspicious and perhaps paranoid personality with at least one episode when she was regarded as insane by various alienists, and in retrospect would probably have been diagnosed by psychiatrists today as manic. However she probably experienced mild and transient symptoms and if she did have other episodes of instability did not appear to attract public concern after then. The certification was, as Forster predicted in 1857, contentious, and the reasons for it were more to save Edward's reputation than safeguard her safety or anybody else's. The latter was not required for certification to be accepted as appropriate by the Lunacy Commission, but only that two doctors should decide that she was insane.

There was a remarkable involvement of literary figures in the processes with Forster, Cornwall and Gaskell involved, and the suspicions of Rosina about a conspiracy are understandable, even if the Commissioners did act with due regard to the laws.

Rosina has been seen as having had a literary talent, and her letters at least do have a wonderful flare for ridiculing others, and she was remarkable in being prepared to flout conventions in challenging Edward. Her uniqueness in that may have been due to the effects of the mental illness. Henry Maudsley, John Conolly's son-in-law, who became a leading psychiatrist (the Hospital is named after him) expounded on the theme in an article on delusions in 1863 - saying

"he who possesses great judgement and has his feelings completely under the control of his reason is not likely to be a great reformer in his lifetime... the extreme earnestness and sincerity of a little insanity are almost essential to move a man [or woman] to the unhopeful and laborious task of combating the heavy opposition of the existing state of things", and, *"For it can scarce be questioned that some who exhibit what is called genius only just miss madness, and, on the other hand, that some who become insane lack but a little of having genius."* [78]

Even the great reformer, Lord Shaftesbury, had a degree of instability which led one contemporary in 1820 to comment that he *"seems to me quite unintelligible and can only be accounted for by a dash of madness,"* and Florence Nightingale remarked *"had he not devoted himself to reforming lunatic asylums, he would have been in one himself"* [79].

Rosina did not actually stay in a lunatic asylum, but was certified and stayed in the home of the psychiatrist for three weeks. The justification for that is weak and it did not achieve what Edward had hoped for. It did gain Rosina an improved income but a less dramatic mediation may have served them both better. Edward died in 1873 and Rosina in 1882. They were never reconciled. Her grave, at Shirley in Surrey, was left unmarked. She had wanted a quotation on her tombstone from the Book of Isaiah, chapter 14, verse 3 - *"The Lord shall give thee rest from thy sorrow, and from thy fear, and from the hard bondage wherein thou wast made to serve".* The Cobbold family granted her wish in 1995 when they placed a stone on her grave with that inscription [80].

Edward's crest on his envelopes – bittern and heraldic tiger. The bittern on the left has its place probably because its name rhymed with Lytton!
Motto *'This is the work of virtue' (or valour). The exact meaning is uncertain, Rosina would have disagreed with both. Origins of motto and crest at least from the 16th century* [81]*. Envelope from Hertfordshire Archives* [82]

Notes

1. Preston, Jane. 'That Odd Rich Old Woman – the Story of Elizabeth Bulwer Lytton'. Plush Publishing. 1998
2. www.bulwer-lytton.com
3. Stated by Hale Thomson on the Certificate of 23/06/1858. Knebworth House Archive
4. Lytton, Rosina. 'A Blighted Life. Thoemmes Press. 1994. Reprint of 1880 Edition, see Introduction by Marie Mulvey Roberts, and 'A Blighted Marriage'. David Lytton Cobbold. Knebworth House Education and Preservation Trust. 1999
5. Knebworth House Archive box 42
6. Knebworth House Archive 42/75
7. Roberts, Marie Mulvey. Ed. 'Collected Letters of Rosina Bulwer Lytton' Pickering & Chatto. 2008 vol 2, p 378
8. Hertfordshire Archive and Library Service DE/K C27
9. Hertfordshire Archives and Local Studies DE/K C23
10. Knebworth House Archive 42/81
11. Roberts. Vol 3. p 23
12. Snyder, Charles. 'Liberty and Morality, A Political Biography of Edward Bulwer-Lytton'. Peter Lang. 1995 p 157
13. Roberts. Vol 3. p 25-26
14. Hertfordshire Archives and Local Studies DE/K C23 72/4
15. Hertfordshire Archives and Local Studies DE/K C22 115/1
16. Arnold, Catherine. 'Bedlam'. Pocket Books. 2009
17. Hertfordshire Archives and Local Studies DE/K C23/72/1
18. Hertfordshire Archives and Local Studies DE/K C23/72/9
19. Hertfordshire Archives and Local Studies DE/K C10
20. Lytton, R. p 27
21. Knebworth House Archive 42/44
22. Lytton, R, p 28 – 29
23. Lucas, William. 'A Quaker Journal, Being the Diary and Reminiscences of William Lucas of Hitchin (1804 – 1861)'. Hutchinson & Co. 1933. Vol II. p 518.
24. Henry Cowper became MP for Hertford in 1865. He was a nephew of Emily Cowper, wife of Earl Cowper of Panshanger, who married Lord Palmerston after Cowper's death. Emily was a sister of Lord Melbourne. Her daughter, also Emily, was married to Lord Shaftesbury. Rosina mentioned *"Mr W- C-"* *as being with Edward on that day, describing him as Edward's "bottle holder",* *an "intensely vulgar-looking personage", and as "Lord and Lady Palmerston's* *bastard"* [Blighted Life. p 28]. This W-.C-. must be William Cowper (1811 – 1888), usually regarded as the legitimate son of the 5th Earl Cowper. Emily junior was more widely regarded as the fruit of her mother's premarital liaison with Lord Palmerston.
25. Hertfordshire Archives and Local Studies DE/K C23 72/13
26. Lytton, R, p 30
27. Knebworth House Archive 42/96
28. Lytton, R, p 31
29. Roberts. Vol 3, p 85-87
30. Knebworth House Archive 42/96
31. Knebworth House Archive box 41

32. Knebworth House Archive box 42
33. 'All fine and dandy?'. William Kuhn. Free Press. 2006, review by Virginia Rounding, Sunday Times June 11, 2006
34. Hibbert, Christopher. 'Disraeli. A Personal History'. Harper Collins 2004
35. Knebworth House Archive Box 41
36. Hertfordshire Archives and Local Studies DE/K C23 72/13
37. Roberts, vol 3. p 94
38. Hertfordshire Archives and Local Studies D/EK C23 72/22 letter Hill to EB Lytton
39. Knebworth House Archive Box 41. Hill's diary, visitor's note 29/06/58
40. Hertfordshire Archives and Local Studies DE/K C 22/115/10 letter to EBL 10/08/58
41. Knebworth House Archive. Box 41. Hill's diary 2/07/58
42. Lytton, R. p 96
43. Quoted by Peter McCandless, 'Liberty and Lunacy', in Scull, A. Editor. 'Madhouses, Mad-doctors, and Madmen'. Athlone Press. 1981. p 357.
44. Lytton, R. p 39-40
45. Roberts, Vol 3. p 102
46. Roberts, Vol 3. p 106. letter to Ryves 10.07.58
47. Hervey, N. 'The Lunacy commission and the Psychiatric Profession 1845- 60'. In 'The Anatomy of Madness', vol II, Tavistock Publications. 1985. p 107
48. Sutherland, J. 'Victorian Fiction: Writers, Publishers, Readers'. Palgrave Macmillan; 2nd Revised edition 2005
49. Hamilton, Geoffrey. 'Delane, John Thadeus (1817–1879)', Oxford Dictionary of National Biography, Oxford University Press, 2004; online edn, Jan 2008 [http://www.oxforddnb.com/view/article/7440]
50. Hertfordshire Archives and Local Studies DE/K C14 EBL to Forster July 1858
51. McCandless, Peter. in 'Madhouses, Mad-Doctors, and Madmen'. Ed Andrew Scull. Athlone Press 1981. p 345
52. Knebworth House Archive. Box 41. Hill's diary 12/07/58
53. Hertfordshire Archives and Local Studies DE/K O22/117/2
54. Lytton, R. p 42
55. Knebworth House Archive. Box 41 Hill's' diary p 40-41
56. Knebworth House Archive 42/29
57. Hertfordshire Archives and Local Studies DE/K C25/38/1
58. Hertfordshire Archives and Local Studies DE/K C23 72/18
59. Hertfordshire Archives and Local Studies DE/K C25/3,5,6,15
60. Hertfordshire Archives and Local Studies DE/K C23/72
61. Hertfordshire Archives and Local Studies DE/K C25/15
62. Lytton, R. p 62
63. Knebworth House Archive 42/4
64. Knebworth House Archive box 42
65. Hertfordshire Archives and Local Studies DE/K C27
66. Knebworth House Archive. Box 41. copy in Hill's Diary
67. Obituary. Journal of Mental Science 1878 v. 24, p 327-328
68. Hertfordshire Archives and Local Studies DE/K C23 72/33
69. Hertfordshire Archives and Local Studies DE/K C23
70. Mitchell, Leslie. 'Bulwer Lytton. The Rise and Fall of a Victorian Man of Letters'. Hambleton and London. 2003

71. Knebworth House Education and Preservation Trust. 1999
72. Scull, Andrew. ' Madhouses, mad-doctors and madmen. The social history of psychiatry in the Victorian era'. Athlone Press.1981. p 319
73. Lytton, R. p 20
74. Mitchell, p 61
75. Parry-Jones, William L. 'The Trade in Lunacy'. Routledge Keagan & Paul. p 236
76. Snyder, C. p 160
77. Mitchell, p 64
78. Journal of Mental Science. 1863 9: p 1-24
79. Hervey, N. 'The Anatomy of Madness', vol II. p105 & 122 (note 46)
80. Cobbold, David Lytton. 'A Blighted Marriage'. Knebworth House education and Preservation Trust. 1995
81. Clare Fleck, Knebworth House Archivist, personal communication
82. Hertfordshire Archives and Local Studies DE/K C25

The title of the new Farce is to be

EVEN WORSE THAN WE SEEM ;

OR

THE REAL SIDE OF OUR CHARACTERS!

DRAMATIS PERSONÆ.

Sir Plagiary Puff, *a philanthropic (!) literary gentleman (?) who has literally translated his poor young Daughter into Heaven, and nobly leaves his wife to live on public charity,*

SIR E. BULWER LYTTON, *a Gentleman (?) with a gutta percha rental of* £10,000 *for his acquaintance, which conveniently shrinks into as many hundreds whenever he is applied to to give his wife enough to live on.*

St. Giles's grafted on St. James's, } MR. CHARLES DICKENS, *who to act with the more life, has a dead child in one pocket, and a dead father in the other.*

Jack Gin-Bibber, *Jack-all to Sir Plagiary ; a Gent. of limited capacity, and unlimited audacity* } MR. JOHN FORSTER.

Scaramouche Kick-Mother, *the Wit of the Gang,* - MR. DOUGLAS JERROLD.

Meanwell, *a really worthy, but strangely be-nighted Elderly Gentleman,* MR. CHARLES KNIGHT.

Cornucopia Humbug - MR. R. H. HORNE.

British Charity, - A— STONE.

Rosina produced this spoof flyer for the opening of Edward's play, 'Not as Bad as We Seem', in 1851. Knebworth House Archive

The 20th Century

7

There is a limit to what can be written in a short book. I have not been comprehensive in covering all of the various facets of the care and treatment of the mentally ill and I have not covered the complex developments in the recognition of symptoms, syndromes and diagnoses, or been able to do more than skim over some of the complex social, institutional and legal developments that have moulded the care systems. What I have been most interested in is the local care of those who were severely ill and poor, and who relied on whatever the parishes, asylums and their modern replacements could offer. Unfortunately their history is often the least documented, though the desire for secrecy for the better-off, with the lack of legal obligations, has led to their records in the private licensed establishments also being hard to find.

In the 19th century the professions of psychiatrists and psychiatric nurses emerged and began to identify helpful ways of working with the mentally ill. The Mental After Care Association began to provide what, in a more limited way, the outdoor relieving officers had previously offered, and began a pattern of support from which emerged psychiatric and other specialist social workers. MACA is one of many organisations which have developed to work alongside the hospitals and other providers.

There seems to have been little change in services in the early years of the 20th century. The asylums remained as large depositories for people who had disabling disorders. Some recovered with time but many stayed as in-patients for decades, living a life cut off from the local towns and amenities.

The Casebooks from Three Counties Asylum give glimpses of the lives of patients and the care arrangements [1]. William Oakley, age 70, was transferred from Hitchin Workhouse where the Master, Mr Knight, said he was beyond control. He frequently escaped, *and is not to be trusted with young women or children, for fear of taking liberties with them*. He was diagnosed as having senile dementia. He was transferred on to Hill End Asylum on March 3rd 1909, but no reason for this was given.

Samuel James, an *"epileptic idiot"*, was admitted by Dr A H Foster on February 14th 1906. His father, a maltster of Century Terrace in Highbury, Hitchin was *"now not fit to look after son"*, who was described as *"practically helpless"*.

Frank Pates, age 47, admitted on March 19th 1906 from Hitchin Union Workhouse, also by Dr A H Foster, was a farm worker and pauper. Details were taken from Charles Cousins, a *"lunatic attendant"*, but it is unclear if this was a formal role at the workhouse. He described the inmate as *"continually walks about, threatens to hang himself ... got holden of poker & knife & hid them under his bed... thinks that someone is coming to accuse him of stealing & he will be hung. Continually walks about at night"*. He was diagnosed as having melancholia. Nine months later it was noted that he was still hearing voices. He died in July 1907 from heart failure.

The treatment of the most severe mental illness remained unchanged before the 1930s, except for general paralysis of the insane (GPI), or neurosyphilis. The bacterial cause of this was discovered in 1913 and the first treatment to be successful was pioneered in 1917. Julius Wagner-Jauregg had been experimenting with fever therapy and discovered that injecting someone who had GPI with blood from somebody who had malaria brought about a cure. For this he was awarded the Nobel Prize in 1927 [2]. Active treatment consisted of infecting people with malaria using mosquitoes, a treatment which continued to be used at Three Counties Hospital until the 1940s when penicillin was introduced [3].

Meanwhile the efforts to understand and identify mental illness had moved on. The term dementia praecox was first used for what we now call schizophrenia in the 1860s, and by the 1890s the careful observations of Emile Kraepelin in Germany had differentiated this from manic depressive disorder. He took less notice of current symptoms and on speculation about cause, eg. 'masturbatory insanity', but focussed on the course and outcomes [4]. Eugen Bleuler, a Swiss psychiatrist, who was interested in psychoanalysis, coined the term 'schizophrenia' in 1911. He emphasised how the different functions of the mind were split from each other, in part and simplistically that mood is not consistent with thoughts, but expressed as a splitting of 'psychic functions'.

In the 1920s Three Counties Asylum began providing some outpatient clinics. At the same time the daily activities of patients in the asylum were being organized with more purpose as the profession of occupational therapy developed. In 1927 the asylum became Three Counties Hospital (TCH) and in 1960 'Three Counties' became Fairfield Hospital.

The asylum was a total institution. The bottle bearing the Three Counties name was produced circa 1911 when the Asylum's water supply was believed to be causing typhoid. Water was bottled in Cheshire and used instead of the asylum's well water.

Photo by author 2011 Richard Knight collection

Photo of Fairfield Hospital circa 1995 by author, piloted by Bill Bowker. The main asylum building is on the left, the new wing built in 1938 is on the top right and below that the grid of huts built for the London Chest Hospital in World War II.

A Royal Commission on 'Lunacy and Mental Disorders' examined the care of lunatics and the mentally disordered in 1925 and made the comparison with people who suffered from physical illnesses. In 1930 the Mental Treatment Act established that patients could be admitted to hospitals on a voluntary basis, they did not have to be detained under the law and they did not need to have the written consent of the Medical Superintendent in order to leave, but did have to give 3 days notice in case somebody thought that they should be detained. They also stopped being called lunatics, they were now just patients. The law took account of the milder degrees of disturbance experienced by patients and separate provision was made for them. A new wing was built at Three Counties for voluntary patients, which was called Fairfield Hospital, and opened in June 1939. The coming of the war led to it being handed over and being used by the Royal Free Hospital as part of the Emergency Medical Services, moving patients away from London and the risk of being bombed. On the aerial view of the hospital, taken about 1995, the wing can be seen on the top right with a curved hedge behind. Incidentally the grid of huts in the photo was built for the London Chest Hospital during World War II. It was taken over and used for elderly and longstay patients after the war and until the hospital closed. Hill End Asylum was used by St Bartholomew's Hospital during the war and treated casualties. The mentally ill patients were dispersed elsewhere, including to Three Counties Asylum.

Three Counties Asylum had its own fire service. This fireman's helmet shows the HBH initials of the three counties, Hertfordshire, Bedfordshire and Huntingdonshire.

Photo by author 2011 Richard Knight collection

I have not covered the treatments offered for the less severely ill, usually termed neuroses, or those who we should not regard as ill but merely experiencing mild anxiety and mood changes as the result of stress. For such problems the Victorian gentlefolk would retire to spas, the first opening at Stansteadbury in south east Herts in 1841. Later in the century Sir Edward Bulwer Lytton was known to take the waters at Malvern and an eminent physician advised people to go to the Italian Riviera to cure nervous disorders [5]. The poor would just put up with it or use the available drugs, alcohol or laudanum (opium).

By the end of the 19th century there emerged a new form of help, sometimes to relieve stress, sometimes to treat strange neurological problems such as paralysis of the limbs. Sigmund Freud started as a neurologist but gradually focussed on psychological problems and psychoanalysis was born. Whilst many may think that psychoanalysis and psychiatry are the same it is unusual for a psychiatrist to have undergone the rigorous and lengthy training that the former requires.

Freud's work on the 'neuroses' with psychoanalysis did not have a wide usage, but the recognition that people who were 'shell-shocked' in the First World War did need specialist psychological help, promoted the treatment of neurosis. In the Second World War the same concern led to the development of the application of psychoanalysis to be more widely available in the form of group therapy and therapeutic communities. More recently the identification of 'post traumatic stress disorder' led to other therapies being used successfully.

Whilst psychoanalysis became more influential it did not have a significant effect on the management of the severely mentally ill in England, unlike the USA. Other psychological treatments which were developed in the 1960s and '70s, such as behaviour therapy, cognitive behaviour therapy and family therapy, did have a more direct impact on the management of what we know as schizophrenia and bipolar or manic depressive disorder. Psychological therapies are now seen as important in a comprehensive care package for such conditions, as detailed in the National Institute of Clinical Excellence guidelines [6].

Idiocy, mental deficiency and learning disability.

The asylums had always provided for the so called 'idiots', the term was later used specifically for people who are now referred to as having severe learning disability. Those with lesser degrees were named as 'imbeciles' and the 'feeble' or 'weak minded'. From some of the surveys done in the 19th century it is apparent that this group of people were identified and offered ongoing support at home and were placed in the workhouses as well as forming a sizeable number in the asylums. The men particularly also added to the prison population.

The different needs or nature of this group were being recognized by the middle of the 19th century. The first institution to care for 'idiots' was Park House in Highgate, North London, opened in 1847. In 1859 Essex Hall was opened for 'idiots and imbeciles' for people from Essex, Norfolk, Suffolk and Cambridgeshire. In 1869 – 1870 the Metropolitan Asylum for Pauper Imbeciles was erected near Watford in south west Herts, later known as Leavesden Hospital (one of two asylums opened in 1870 by the Metropolitan Asylums Board).

At first this separation seems entirely benign, just trying to do the best for them. However this can also be seen as a type of quarantining [7]. The move to segregate the 'weak-minded' was initially linked to concerns about the men, their criminal behaviour and vagrancy, and to keep them off the streets. After the 1890s concern was more about the women having children who were left in the care of the Poor Law authorities, and the intention was to isolate them from the men. Both concerns were also linked to theories about the degeneration, that 'insanity' and 'idiocy' were inherited and led to worse problems in later generations. The 'logical' step was then to think about eugenics or selective breeding to create a better human race. This was not enforced in England but in Alberta, Canada, a sexual sterilization law existed between 1928 and 1972. This could be applied to anybody who had mental illness or deficiency [8]. Unfortunately immigrants to Alberta who were not conversant in English could fail the IQ test that was used to screen for mental deficiency, and as a result be sterilized under this legislation! The same type of thinking led to many of the atrocities of Hitler's Germany.

However the desire to provide separate accommodation and services for the mentally deficient was not necessarily so sinister. The Mental Deficiency Act of 1913 decreed that the Lunacy Commission should be replaced by the Board of Control, which was then responsible for the mentally ill and those with 'mental deficiency' or learning disabilities. The Act envisaged that institutions caring for the latter should be small and educationally orientated, rather than medical establishments.

One of the official visitors to TCA in 1894 had proposed some separation from the mental ill and was uneasy about the "*idiots mixed up with ordinary inmates*". The Visiting Committee who managed TCA proposed to use the adjoining Wilbury Farm for the mentally deficient but by 1921 had only achieved some separation of the two groups of patients within the asylum. Mentally deficient children were still being admitted to Three Counties until 1938 [9], when Bromham Colony, north of Bedford, was fully opened. Bromham had been taking in residents since 1931 and became a 'hospital' in 1950.

The Hill End Asylum serving the south, east and west

Three Counties Hospital Tokens. These could only be spent at and within the hospital. Many patients were paid this way if they worked on the farm or did domestic work. The only cash they had would have been given to them by a visiting friend or relative.
From the Bedford Museum collection, photograph by Rosalyn Knight. This and other artefacts can be found on the Three Counties Website http://www.threecountiesasylum.co.uk

of Hertfordshire also retained such patients until Cell Barnes Colony, later renamed 'Hospital', was built on an adjoining site and opened in 1933 [10]. This hospital provided the help for residents of the Hitchin area until it was closed in 1998. Services were then provided for a few years by Harperbury Hospital, near London Colney in south Herts, which started life as the Hangars Certified Institution in 1925 and became the Middlesex Colony from 1934 until 1949. In Kelly's 1937 directory Harperbury's purpose is described – *"The Colony is intended for mental defectives who are socially inadaptable in the community, or who are neglected or without visible means of support. Male defectives who are capable of being employed are provided with suitable agricultural occupations on the land, or at various industrial occupations in the Colony's workshops. Female defectives are suitably employed in the laundry, general kitchen or workrooms. Children who are capable of it are given various simple occupations"* [11].

The services for the 'mentally deficient', or 'handicapped', later referred to as having learning disabilities, continued to remain mostly separate from adult general psychiatry or mental health services. There was some overlap as there is no sharp division between the two populations, although an IQ test has been used in the past to make that artificial divide.

The new treatments

In the 1930s three treatments were introduced which promised improvements for those with the most severe mental disorders, insulin coma, leucotomy and electroconvulsive therapy.

Insulin coma therapy entailed giving patients insulin which reduced their blood sugar level to the point at which they became comatose. Insulin was discovered in 1922. By the following year staff at an American psychiatric hospital thought that insulin relieved depression in-patients who were given it to control diabetes. It was subsequently used for people who had lost their appetites and refused to eat and also in a small dose to relieve withdrawal symptoms in people who had been addicted to morphine, the addicted patients having been *"restless and agitated"* became *"tranquil and accessible"*. Manfred Sakel, who had discovered its usefulness for addicts, also noted that insulin made agitated patients more tranquil. He moved on and tried it for patients with schizophrenia, finding that insulin induced comas gave a 70% remission or reduction in symptoms in a trial with 50 patients [12].

It was hazardous, as insulin causes a low blood sugar level (hypoglycaemia), which if severe can cause coma and death. But it seemed a worthwhile risk as nothing else was available, and some patients did improve. It was the first treatment that seemed to have a good effect on schizophrenia. Nurses who were involved with the treatment have told me how it seemed to work and gave them a good relationship with the patients – the patients' lives depended on the careful observations and quick actions of their carers – and maybe that close relationship contributed to the improvements observed.

Another new treatment, electroconvulsive therapy (ECT), was introduced in the 1930s. This became widespread in the 1940s and is still in use today. This was first used because of the observation, later found to be wrong, that people with epilepsy who had convulsive fits did not develop schizophrenia. Fits were then induced in people who suffered from schizophrenia using an injection of cardiazol. The only noticeable improvement came in those who were also melancholic or depressed. It was then given just to depressed people and had a remarkably good effect.

The third new treatment was leucotomy, an operation to sever some of the connecting fibres in the brain. This was tried as it had been observed that some behavioural changes had occurred in chimpanzees whose frontal parts of the brain had been destroyed. Dr Moniz (a Nobel Prize winning Portuguese neurologist) heard about this at a conference and wondered if such an operation could relieve anxiety states in humans. He then arranged for a neurosurgeon to perform such operations on asylum patients, reporting that a third were cured, a third helped and a third unchanged. Edward Shorter in describing the treatment, notes that Moniz gave little detail to support such claims, suggesting that he was more driven to stake his place in history than follow scientific methods [13]. The new treatment was well advertised and thousands of patients in the USA were so treated. Unfortunately long term effects of unhelpful personality changes and epilepsy followed.

Leucotomies were done at TCH, starting in 1943. The managing committee negotiated with Mr W McKissock, a surgeon from King's College and St George's Hospitals in London, for him to perform 2-3 'pre-frontal leucotomies' at each visit to the hospital, for a fee of not less than 3 – 5 guineas [14]. By the next month he had done 3 operations, but he reported that it was too early to comment on the results. Soon after the committee dealt with a request from the

The London Chest Hospital (left) was evacuated to Three Counties Hospital during World War II. The "huts" remained into the 1990s, though the wooden cladding for some of them was upgraded to brick. They were laid out in a grid, A to F and 1 to 7. Some were combined to make larger wards. The author worked on A1, A2/3, B3 and C4 from 1981 – 88. Photo from Mike O'Donovan of himself and a friend. Three Counties Website

The "huts", circa 1985 . A therapeutic environment? Photo from author's collection

City Mental Hospital in Leicester asking if they could send patients to have the operation, but TCH said they could not manage this due to shortage of staff.

Each treatment may seem to some to be barbaric, but at the time there was no other effective treatment, and the alternative was for people to remain in hospital and suffer increasing disability because of the effects of the mental illness.

In 1948 insulin coma and ECT were being frequently used at Three Counties and seemed to have good effects. 'Modified insulin' was similar to insulin coma therapy but used lower doses and was safer. Arthur Monk [15] retrieved a summary of the results for 1948:-

	Male	female	total	discharged	relapsed
Insulin coma	20	26	46	29	1
Modified insulin therapy	37	79	116	55	9
ECT	99	190	289	168	17
Insulin and ECT	24	40	64	36	2
Total	180	335	515	288	29

The results appear to be moderately good, depending on how results were measured, but those details are not documented. It appeared to those using the methods that the results were encouraging, for over half of the total treated became fit for discharge. However no figures are given for those who did not receive the treatment and how they fared. So all we can really conclude from this is that the treatments were in frequent use.

All three treatments became less popular after the medications introduced in the 1950s gave good results and were much less hazardous.

The side effects of leucotomy led to that being virtually abandoned except for a small number of people who have had severe and disabling symptoms which are completely resistant to all other possible treatments. A much more refined and less damaging operation of bilateral stereotactic anterior capsulotomy is now done. In 2007 and 2008 there were two operations done in England, after careful screening including, as is mandatory, a review by the independent Mental Health Act Commission, since replaced by the Care Quality Commission. Both patients showed positive results from the surgery according to the Commission [16].

Insulin coma was abandoned almost overnight in 1958 when it was shown that it had no benefit over the less hazardous barbiturate narcosis therapy, which continued to be used until the 1990s.

ECT has continued to be used for people with severe depression, albeit reserved for those who do not improve with medication and are at high risk of suicide or self injury while waiting for medication to work. The use of ECT in mania and schizophrenia has been advocated but is rarely used. It was also helpful for some mothers with severe postnatal psychosis, particularly if, in a deluded state of mind, they believed it was right to harm themselves or their baby.

Making ECT machines in Letchworth

One of the Three Counties Hospital staff, Dr Robert Russell, saw a commercial opportunity in the late 1940s and began manufacturing ECT machines. He described making the first in his rooms at TCH having realised that the Ediswan machine being used was unreliable [17]. They were then produced by a company which otherwise made electric fires in a disused cinema in Baldock. His company, named Ectron, was incorporated in 1950 and the factory for the machines was set up in Letchworth, just east of Hitchin. The number of machines made is uncertain, but when I met Dr Russell in the early 1990s he estimated that at one time half of the ECT machines used in England had come from Ectron. The first machine, Ectron Mark 1, was produced in 1949 and by 1965 the serial number on a machine was 1016. Francis Russell, his son who worked in the company until it was sold in 2005, told me that original machines were used around the world for many years, and that the company would receive requests for spare parts for them from Pakistan long after they had ceased manufacturing them. Ectron expanded and bought out Theratronics, another manufacturer, to gain a monopoly in the British market.

Ectron tried modifications of the machines. There were various technical questions in applying the treatment that were researched and debated. The technique is to apply an electrical current to the skull in the region of the temples. The exact site to place the electrodes, the strength of the current and the length of time it was applied were all investigated. The rule of thumb was that the electrical impulse needed to be sufficient to induce a convulsion, similar to an epileptic fit. Dr Russell's simple formula for

ECT machines were initially very simple (above left), just some circuitry to reduce the voltage and current, and a switch.

Ectron Duopulse machine (right), showing the two paddles which were applied to each side of the head. The machine produced a constant current at 30 watts, and the stimulus was electronically timed. The numbing effects of electricity were known by the ancient Greeks from contact with the cramp-fish, or electrical torpedo. In the 18th century 'frictional electricity' machines were invented and were used all over the country by showmen. In 1787 John Birch described the beneficial effects of electricity applied to the head of a depressed man [18]. In the 1820s Joshua Ransom "had an electrical apparatus with which he used to shock the people of Hitchin when placed on a glass legged stool" [19].

Photos by author, machines from collection of Francis Russell

the timing with early machines, before the stimulus was electronically timed, was that it had to be applied long enough to spell out loud *"E-C-T-R-O-N"*.

Although Ectron continued to adapt and improve the machines the sophistication of their competitor's machines increased also. When, in the 1990s, the gold standard became the inclusion of electroencephalographs, which were able to detect and measure the production of fits by monitoring the electrical patterns of the brain, the use of Ectron machines at the mental health unit at the Lister Hospital ceased. The company still manufactures the 'Ectonustim' ECT machine and other 'electro-medical equipment'.

Useful medication and redundant asylums

The first medication which is still in current use is lithium which was introduced in the late 1940s'. It calmed people with schizophrenia and also with mania. It took another 20 years before its potential was widely recognized and it has remained a standard treatment for people with bipolar disorder, also known as manic depressive disorder. The first antipsychotic drug, chlorpromazine, evolved from antihistamine drugs that were being tried and tested in 1951. It was first used in France and was found to calm patients who were agitated, and later in North America to have a specific effect on people with schizophrenia in reducing hallucinations and delusions.

The first antidepressant identified, in 1957, was iproniazid. It was a monoamine oxidase inhibitor (MAOI), discovered when it was observed that a drug being tested on people suffering from tuberculosis, improved their mood. Imipramine evolved from research on antihistamines and was first used in 1958. This led over the next 30 years to the development of many popular antidepressant drugs with similar chemical structures, called tricyclics. After that the Prozac type antidepressants (specific serotonin reuptake inhibitors) emerged. All of these have been described as changing the neurotransmitters, or chemical connections between nerve cells, which control mood in the brain. Variations of these, said to inhibit or enhance various neurotransmitters, have since emerged.

Standard medicine bottle for Three Counties Hospital. Photo by author, courtesy of Rodney Langstaff

As both depression and schizophrenia were relatively common and cures would generate profits for the pharmaceutical industry, a large number of products have been developed and heavily marketed. The advantages of one over another seem to have been oversold as the adverse effects or poor results found in some trials of medication have been suppressed. Pharmaceutical companies have at times exaggerated the benefits, or suppressed poor results in trials, and also provided free gifts to doctors, all to influence their prescribing habits. However behind the sleaze the advantages of many such medications are enormous, or so it seems at present.

My problem when I have to take medication is that I forget to do so. With schizophrenia the evidence is that medication has to be taken long term and regularly, but people forget and may avoid taking it if it has any side effects. So when an injectable form was developed in 1960, the so called depot medication, people did not have to remember daily but had to remember once a month. Over time community psychiatric nurses were appointed and they monitored and gave the injections, reminding the patients and visiting them at home to ensure they received it. This was much more reliable and gave better results. It seemed then that the cure and care of people with severe mental illness would be simple, but that was not completely so.

It became apparent in the late 1950s that keeping patients in long stay wards of asylums often led to them developing handicaps because of that environment. Some of what had been taken to be the effects of the illness of schizophrenia were actually the effects of being warehoused in large wards with little stimulation and no sense of responsibility, with lack of motivation and inability to think for themselves. Studies showed that the lack of social stimulation led to what had been termed negative symptoms, social withdrawal and apathy [20]. Later it was realised that some of the 'wonder' drugs were being given in too large a dose and caused apathy and severe effects on muscle control. However, the overall picture was of patients improving and shaking off the worst of the psychotic symptoms which had prevented them living normal lives with their families, or at least out of the hospital.

In 1959 a new Mental Health Act replaced the Mental Treatment Act of 1930 and the Lunacy Act of 1890. The emphasis was now that patients would normally receive treatment as with anybody else with a 'physical' illness on an informal basis. If people did need to be admitted against their will it became a clinical and administrative procedure and not judicial, albeit with a clear appeal mechanism.

The Government foresaw that the asylums would vanish as the thousands of long term patients were cured and discharged. Enoch Powell, as Minister of Health, made a powerful speech in 1961 when he envisaged the landmarks of the asylums, the water towers, being demolished, but not, in his view, without much resistance from the staff whose livelihood was being threatened. A few asylums

The spy hole for "improved inspection" into a seclusion room, specially designed so that nurses could look to the side of the room. Seclusion was used for many years, originally replacing physical restraint, in special rooms within secure or general admission wards. The asylums sometimes had these rooms padded so that the agitated patient would be less likely to harm themselves by butting or hitting walls.
It is not clear who would read and follow up on the advert at the bottom of the plate "ALSO IMPROVED SANITARY LEAD GUTTERS"

Richard Knight collection Photo by author 2011

were closed quickly but scandals about the number of patients either ending up on the streets of London or being placed en masse in soulless seaside boarding houses led to the staff developing much more careful resettlement schemes.

In 1957 a Rehabilitation Unit was formed at Three Counties Hospital, renamed that year as Fairfield Hospital. This seemed to consist of a working group of physically able patients who could do road and footway maintenance around the hospital [21]. In 1976 Fairfield Hospital staff established a more recognizable rehabilitation team with a unit at the hospital (Boundary House) and a resettlement scheme, being a series of lodgings and group homes in Hitchin, Letchworth and the Bedfordshire towns and villages.

The first psychiatrist working mainly in the Hitchin area was appointed in 1963. He was Dr Bernard Mallett, who wrote about the services being provided at that time [22]. With the support of two junior doctors, who were specialising in psychiatry, and one 'houseman', who probably had no working experience in psychiatry or any other branch of medicine, he covered the North Herts (Local) Service. This was what had been the Hitchin Parish Union area of 27 parishes including Baldock, Letchworth and Stevenage, as well as Biggleswade, a total population then of 174,000 people. He was responsible for 430 in-patients (the other 800 patients at Fairfield being under the care of two other consultants) with 460 people being admitted to the wards each year (with a similar number being discharged). He and his team assessed 400 people newly referred from their general practitioners and had 1700 follow up clinic appointments to deal with each year. The idea of community based staff to visit and support people at home had not then taken off, but there were two 'mental welfare officers' based in Stevenage who dealt with patients needing to be detained under the Mental Health Act (1959).

New wards, new ways of working

The national agenda was for people to be looked after in specialised mental health units on the site of general hospitals, just as the first asylums from the 1750s were attached to the infirmaries dealing with the physically ill. By 1973 the acute in-patients, those needing admission for the first time or requiring short stay admissions, were accommodated in the newly built wing at the Lister Hospital. The 1975 White Paper 'Better Services for the Mentally Ill' advocated the replacement of mental hospitals with a range of community facilities.

Bernard Mallett was joined by another consultant to share the work, who did not stay long, and then by Dr Frank Lappin in 1974. Frank said that on his first day in post he discovered that he would be responsible for all of the North Herts patients still at Fairfield, about 200 in total. When I arrived in 1981 the community staff had grown to the magnificent number of seven, 4 community psychiatric nurses and 3 social workers. With 7 other medical staff we covered all of the adult and elderly psychiatric services. Over the next 10 years specialist teams for patients with drug related problems and for the elderly were formed.

The problem of the increasing numbers of elderly people with memory loss or dementia had caused strain on all of the services. The present and increasing problem was well noted in the publication 'The Rising Tide' in 1982 (produced

Male Dining Room (top) in the 1950s, now part of the health club facilities. Below the original Main Entrance with the outside of the Male Dining Room on right in the 1950s.

Postcards from Terry Knight collection

by The Health Advisory Service). More needed to stay in hospital as local old people's homes could not cope with them. The wards for older people with physical illnesses were admitting but were not able to discharge them, and their beds were full. The relatives of people with dementia found that they were left to cope and suffered stress when they could get no respite. The nurse who was in charge of a makeshift day hospital, where people could come for the day to give their relatives and friends respite, formed a relatives' support group with some of the longsuffering carers. This was an excellent pressure group that spoke up whenever the case for new staff or facilities was being made. By 1990 a new day hospital and assessment wards for the elderly had been planned but money ran out as too much had been spent on a flagship general hospital in London. Fortunately Glaxo plc, the pharmaceutical company, decided to build their large facility in Stevenage and asked if anybody wanted a million pounds to build a health facility. We had the plans and jumped at the chance, and it was built, adjoining the Mental Health Unit on the Lister Hospital site. The only drawback was that it really had to be called the Glaxo Unit, whereas it could have been called the Mallett Unit in recognition of all the work that Bernard had put into the planning.

Soon after joining the local service in 1981 I was involved in planning the development of services. The North Herts District, for which we were responsible, was the same area as the Hitchin Poor Law Union covered in 1835, including Stevenage and not Royston. A scheme which occupied the time of myself and one of the nursing officers was to try and relocate all of the 'North Herts' patients from Fairfield to the vacant North Herts Maternity Hospital in Bedford Road in Hitchin. This was quickly abandoned when the Safeway supermarket chain decided to buy it and build their store, now Waitrose.

The next step was to develop community mental health teams, a small group of doctors, nurses, social workers, psychologists, occupational therapists and office staff, based in the three main population centres of Hitchin, Letchworth and Stevenage. The negotiations for this were difficult as it required an agreement between Social Services and the North Herts Health Authority. That was eventually reached after a consultation entitled 'Tomorrow's Services'. One of the sticking points in the discussions, and there were a few despite the good will and good

The Mental Health Unit at Lister Hospital, Stevenage, built 1973. The ground floor on the left originally housed the ECT suite, adjacent to the crèche. Later uses of this area included a day hospital for the elderly, a fitness room and then the Crisis Team base.

Photo author's collection 1985

The 1988 consultation document for the development of local mental health teams, community mental health centres and support services in Hitchin, Letchworth and Stevenage. At that time the joint planning between health and social services was crucial. Ten years later the two were combined in the Herts Partnership NHS Trust for mental health (and other) services.

thinking on both sides, was that Social Services wanted the new 'community mental health centres' to be a new start, not to be in buildings that would have negative or unhappy associations for patients, or clients as they preferred to say. In the event, having explored various locations, there had to be an acceptance that we could not have a free choice and had to accept what was available. The Stevenage team ended up in the old police station at Southgate, the manager's office being an old police cell, the Letchworth team started on the site of the workhouse children's home in Briar Patch, and then moved to a vacated GP's surgery on Norton Way South (St Michael's House), and the Hitchin team moved into an office at the Union Workhouse site at Chalkdell, which had become Hitchin Hospital. Fortunately the ghosts of time past did not seem to have any bad effect on the teams or their patients.

As teams developed to assess and help people newly diagnosed as having mental illness, so Social Services also set up new 'Community Support Teams'. This was to provide more daytime activities and home visits, to help with the tasks of finding and running a home, claiming due benefits and managing the money. Working perhaps like the outdoor relief officers, almost 200 years before, community workers aimed to keep people independent and out of hospital.

Fairfield closes

The eventual demise of Fairfield came in 1999. Over the previous 10 years various schemes had been devised for replacing the old asylum. The long-stay wards in the main building or in the 'huts' were run down as patients were either helped to live independently or placed in small group living homes in Letchworth and other areas. Those that needed more help and supervision from the North Herts and Stevenage area moved to newly built accommodation at Hampden House and Gainsford House in Hitchin. Other accommodation for people who would need intensive support, but not admission to hospital, was provided in a rehabilitation unit and a housing association complex in Stevenage. Fairfield had always provided an intensive care ward for people who were too disturbed or difficult to manage on the open (unlocked) wards at the Lister Hospital unit.

The old and the new. The author at the abandoned hospital on the left, the foreground showing the base of the 'airing courts', where patients in Victorian days took their exercise. The new on the right - the asylum, now upgraded with smart residences in Fairfield Hall, exercise now taken in the gymnasium and pool of the health club. The surrounding grounds have been developed as Fairfield Park with 750 houses to-date.

Photo (left) by Priscilla Douglas 1998 and (right) by the author 2008

This ward was moved to a specially built unit in Luton, the Orchard Unit, since renamed the Robin Pinto Unit.

Elderly patients, many suffering from memory loss and inability to care for themselves as the result of dementia, were moved to long-stay units in Stevenage (Elizabeth and Victoria Court, near the Lister Hospital). Fairfield emptied and closed. Before it did so, the excellent history of the institution with many memories from patients and staff, 'A Place in the Country', was produced [3].

National Service Framework and PIGs

Having established what had been advocated in a Government White Paper in 1975, a comprehensive community mental health service, ideas moved on. A more focussed type of work with people suffering the most disruptive type of mental illness, the more severe degree of schizophrenia, was advocated. The National Service Framework for Mental Health was published in 1999 to improve standards in mental health care. This was wide ranging and included topics which had become more evident as awareness of mental health care has evolved, including insufficient involvement of users and carers and stigmatising public attitudes. The issues of early response to relapse and safe management of risk, were linked to the need for clear and well communicated care plans and a good access to in-patient care when necessary.

Assertive Outreach Teams were intended to provide for a small group of patients who suffer from schizophrenia and who are at high risk of relapsing or becoming ill again for a variety of reasons. These could be due either to a lack of response to medication, difficulties in taking the medication or experiencing stress, or using some of the 'recreational drugs' such as cannabis or cocaine which can bring on psychotic symptoms in some people. A small team offering intensive support helps patients deal with everyday stresses and tries to ensure that they take medication as and when required. The team for North Herts (and Stevenage) was set up in 1998 and has been based in Centenary House in Hitchin.

Other community teams needed for an improved service were suggested in a Policy Implementation Guideline (PIG) which was published in 2001, which advocated more intensive home-based work. Teams that had been tried in a few areas were now introduced nationally. A Crisis and Home Treatment Team to assess and help people over a short period of time was started locally. It was expected that those who had suddenly become unwell or were overwhelmed by events could be helped to avoid admission to hospital. This has largely seemed to work

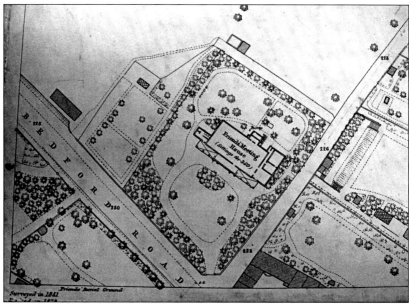

Centenary House, on the junction of Bedford Road and Grammar School Walk in Hitchin, was originally the Friends' (or Quakers') Meeting House from 1840 until 1956. It was later extended and became the Hitchin Rural District Council offices, the Hitchin Urban District Council occupying the Town Hall, then the Registry Office and from about 1975 the local social services office. It housed the Hitchin Mental Health Team from 1993, and the Assertive Outreach Team from 1998.
Plan of the Friends' Meeting House from survey of 1851 in Hitchin Museum

successfully, with a reduction of the number of in-patient places across the county.

Across the county an Early Intervention in Psychosis Team was employed to take on the care of people in their first episode of psychosis; working on the basis that the earlier the treatment is started and the better it is maintained, the better the recovery and the less are the long term effects. It was the same idea which drove Lord Shaftesbury and others in the 19th century to try and admit people into the asylum as soon as they became insane, as they believed that the early medical attention would lead to a better outcome. Early intervention now is intended to provide effective medication at the right dose, psychological help to manage stress and cope with symptoms, and personal support when life is difficult. That should help avoid hospital care in many cases and provide the best outcomes.

The fourth strand was the Enhanced Primary Care Team, to work more closely with GPs, to offer early help and avoid referral on to other more specialized teams. In 2007 this evolved into the IAPT (Improving Access to Psychological Therapies) programme, providing talking therapies and self-help to people with mild-to-moderate anxiety and depression. This follows various other initiatives of liaison and consultation with GPs over the previous three decades and the special funding of counsellors in GP surgeries. There has been a longstanding dilemma of how to offer the help to people with milder forms of emotional distress without taking resources away from the most severely ill, when there is a limit on both funds and trained staff.

Just as the Victorians sought, under the banner of utilitarianism, to centralize the services that they developed, there are signs of the current regimes doing the same. The role of the local community mental health teams (CMHTs), which once dealt with all of the patients in their patch of Hitchin or Letchworth or Stevenage communities, has been diminished as more specialized teams have developed, covering larger areas, in some cases county-wide. There has been an intention to move the three local CMHTs to an office base in Stevenage, thus reducing local access in the other two towns. The growth of community based, as opposed to hospital based services in the local area has led to staff numbers increasing from only 4 community nurses and 3 social workers in 1981, to over 80 community staff by 2010. This enormous change has clearly brought many benefits, and the task of finding the best way to use these valuable resources will undoubtedly bring further changes. The transformation to find the best model of care nationally for various geographical areas has still to be found, and is still being debated [23].

I had wondered whether the desire to centralize, to make efficiency savings, and to focus all of the expertise in one place would lead to a single asylum for the county to be reconstructed for in-patients. A single in-patient unit for the county, based at Harperbury Hospital, south of St Albans, is now being planned. The difference from the Victorian institutions is that most of the long-term care is now in units across the county. What will clearly be lost in such a change for short-term care is the proximity of the in-patient unit to people's homes, with the consequent linkage to their close family and community. Such changes can be made for financial as well as clinical reasons. Some specialized services have an economy of scale and providing good care in scattered small units can be difficult, but the social and psychological impact of being cared for far from home needs to be assessed. There have been dilemmas even in the current arrangements with local in-patient wards. Across the country in-patients' care is often passed to a specialist consultant who only works on the wards. When discharged from hospital the patient returns to their former consultant's care. This has been seen as fragmenting of what was once the continuity provided by one psychiatrist, who provided care for a patient in the community and while admitted to hospital [24]. That loss of continuity and sense of being cared for is likely to be further eroded.

Following the trends, making the best use of a limited budget, responding to the Government's rules on how to organize a service, which is not always based on good evidence, is a difficult task. What has emerged in the recent past is a stronger commitment to hearing and responding to the patients', or users', experience of what helps, and what does not.

Changing Times

The old asylums had some good features. Once they had farms and patients worked in them, gaining a sense of purpose and accomplishment. When it was felt that patients could be exploited by that, they were not allowed to work. Therapy programmes seemed to struggle to provide that same sense of fulfilment. The demolition of the asylums was good in many ways, but they were also havens and homes for many, and gave a sense of belonging. While many have benefited from the resettlement into local communities, some of the people who were discharged then wandered around the town centres, seemingly aimless and unoccupied. Fashions change, enthusiasm for change is often understandable, but is not always sustained.

Other fashions have surfaced over the past 50 years. One of the foremost psychiatrists in the 1960s was William Sargant, a charismatic man who ridiculed the psychological therapies (while paradoxically writing about the power of psychological forces in 'The Battle for the Mind, the first psychological book I read, at the age of 14.). He was by all accounts someone who used his own personality in the therapeutic encounter, probably to instil hope, but also to push people into accepting whatever was his latest cure. He believed totally in the usefulness of 'physical methods of treatment', ECT, narcosis, certain antidepressant drugs and combinations of the same. He encouraged the vigorous use of treatments when perhaps other professionals were content to do nothing.

The anti-psychiatry movement in the 1960s had a different view. R.D. Laing wrote the 'The Divided Self' (the most recent book I had read before I was interviewed for my first job in psychiatry), an exploration of what the individual with schizophrenia was experiencing. The momentum for this was helped by the studies which identified family factors such as the 'double bind' espoused by Gregory Bateson and others. These put the blame for developing schizophrenia on the parents, often the *"refrigerator mother"*, seemingly cold and unresponsive to her suffering child. The truth probably lay in therapists observing a family traumatized by the development of a shocking and inexplicable disorder in their child. Laing had a loose definition of schizophrenia and seemed to believe that it was not 'the patient' that was ill, but he/she was probably quite sane but living in an insane world to which he/she was making the most appropriate response. Laing was in many ways inspiring, but very odd. In making contact with one patient who was very unwell and naked, Laing took off his own clothes to enter that person's world. He was a trained psychoanalyst and did not seem to be working from the same base as other psychiatrists. He was maybe a poet or a prophet, inspiring in some ways, but not particularly helpful in the ordinary care of the mentally ill.

Some other way between the extremes of Sargant and Laing seems to be the pattern for most psychiatrists. Following Sargant's model has been called 'naive psychiatry', making the assumption that it is all about making the diagnosis, applying the treatment and expecting the cure [25]. These days 'naive psychiatry' involves accepting the diagnostic framework (as set out in the ICD and DSM manuals – see appendix 2), applying the standard treatments, if possible approved by the National Institute for Clinical Excellence (NICE), and hoping for the best. Psychological therapies and counselling have played an increasing part in that regime; not the classical psychoanalysis but various forms of stress management and cognitive behaviour therapy.

'Post-psychiatry' has been another strand of thinking, not rejecting the idea of schizophrenia as the anti-psychiatry movement did, but accepting it as a distressing and disruptive disorder to which there needs to be a different approach. In this the emphasis has been put on working with the problem through the eyes and experience of the sufferer. In 1999 Bracken and Thomas wrote *"there is an ever widening gulf between the unreal world of neuroscience research, and the lives that are lived under the shadow of the label of schizophrenia, lives dulled by drugs and blighted by stigma... (mental health services) must work with those who experience psychosis, and their carers and supporters, to define a more human way of talking about and describing the experience"* [26]. It has also tried to change the language, from hallucinations which psychiatrist identify and classify, to talking about the 'voice hearers' and how they experience the 'voices' and try to manage the problem for themselves. If the *"neuroscience research"* (sophisticated brain scans and better understanding of the neurochemical and neurophysiological mechanisms), does bring better understanding and treatments, then everybody will be happier. But people need personal care, and not to be seen just as a collection of symptoms, chemicals or as social misfits.

Another stimulus to change over the past 10 years has been the 'recovery' movement. This focuses on the help that people who have suffered from severe mental illness need. It is not good enough to just ensure that people take their medication, receive some therapy and have a roof over their heads. It is important to support them in various activities of daily life, to connect with spiritual aspects of life, to participate in normal recreational activities and to impart optimism.

Samuel Tuke and the Recovery Movement

In 'Enabling Recovery', published in 2005, the authors quoted Samuel Tuke, saying that mental health care, or as he called it *"moral treatment"*, was about *"kindness, compassion, respect and hope of recovery"* [27]. They suggested that *"in the latter half of the 20th century some of the principles of moral treatment were rediscovered, through deinstitutionalisation…which all played a part in the development of recovery as a clinical philosophy"*. They further say that *"traditional medical approaches attempt to relieve symptoms, but give insufficient consideration to what happens next"*.

Samuel Tuke wrote 'The Description of the Retreat' in 1813 and influenced the development of mental health care in England and abroad throughout the 19th century (see chapter 3). The moral treatment he described did not work as well as people hoped in the large and impersonal asylums. However as the asylums have closed there has been a recognition that the same 'moral treatment' does have a place in recovery of people from severe mental illness.

Samuel Tuke had connections in Hitchin. He was born and lived in York but went to school in Hitchin, to George Blaxland's School in Bancroft, which existed from 1799 until 1801. He called Hitchin his second home and liked to come and stay with a favourite aunt, Elizabeth Wheeler, who lived in the town.

One of his sons, Daniel Hack Tuke, was the eminent alienist who visited and reported on 'Mad Lucas', the famous hermit (see chapter 5). Another son was James Hack Tuke, who came to live in Hitchin in 1852. He joined the bank which came to be known as Sharples, Tuke, Lucas and Seebohm, which later merged with others to become Barclays. He had no personal involvement in the world of lunacy and asylums but instead became very involved with the problem of the Irish famines. The potato blight had led to the starvation of thousands of Irish peasants between 1845 and 1849. Many had migrated to escape what seemed inevitable death if they stayed. Some travelled to Canada or the USA, many dying on the journey or even after arrival as they had contracted typhus or other diseases in the overcrowded and insanitary ships. Many came to England, moving on from Liverpool to anywhere they could find somewhere to stay, some of my ancestors probably amongst them. Some arrived in York where Samuel Tuke made shelters for them to stay. James first saw the plight of the Irish there and began to do what he could to relieve the disaster which was occurring [28].

James Hack Tuke moved to Hitchin in 1852 and died in the town in 1896. He was a faithful Quaker and is buried in their graveyard, now the "new" Quaker or Friends' Meeting House at the top of Brand Street.

Photo by author 2011

After James moved to Hitchin his father visited him. Writing in 1852 Samuel said that he had *"a tarrance of*

(Left) I started to work at Centenary House in 2001 when I joined the Assertive Outreach Team. As I arrived at work and walked to the team's office I passed a framed and ancient notice giving the Friends' times of worship. Between 1852 and his death in 1857, Samuel Tuke, one of the most influential men in the world of 19th century mental health reform, walked down that same corridor to join in the Quakers' meetings on Sunday mornings when visiting his son and family in Hitchin. It seems equally likely that his son Daniel, one of the most distinguished Victorian psychiatrists, would have also been a visitor.

Photo by author 2009

(Below) Friends' Meeting House in 1866, built on the site of Mr Whiting's farm yard in 1839. It became the Rural District Council offices after 1956, on the junction of Grammar School Walk and Bedford Road.

Hitchin Museum [29]

FRIENDs MEETING HOUSE.

three weeks with my son James" [30]. As a faithful Quaker he would have attended the local Friends' Meeting House on Sundays when in town. From 1840 until 1956 the Friends' Meeting House was in the building now called Centenary House. It was later used as the Hitchin Rural District Council offices until North Herts District Council was formed in 1974, and by 1976 was occupied by social services. The Hitchin Community Mental Health Team moved in when their office at the old Chalkdell workhouse site was demolished in the early 1990s, followed by other teams over the next 10 years. So present users of the building can rightly claim to be walking in the footsteps of Samuel Tuke.

Samuel Tuke's legacy continues. 'Recovery' has become a buzzword for good practice in helping people with long term severe mental illness. Modern treatments do not necessarily remove all of the symptoms, and despite some improvement life does not necessarily get back to normal. 'Recovery' is in one sense not new, many sufferers and their carers have been seeking it for years, but it had not been highlighted as a goal of the mental health services. Roberts et al, after quoting Samuel Tuke, describe recovery as *"an open ended and cautiously optimistic process of developing a hopeful and personal path forward alongside whatever remains of the individual's illness"* [27].

I think Samuel Tuke would have approved of such an emphasis. He promoted a view of how to help people recover, describing how at that time, in 1813, medical treatment and the standard management of restraint and confinement had little to offer. The difference now is that there are effective treatments and useful qualified staff, but a kind, compassionate, respectful and hopeful support remains valuable, perhaps close to what William Drage in 1664 called *"comforting the heart and cherishing the spirit"*.

It is fitting to end on this note. The history of mental health care does have echoes in the history of Hitchin across the centuries, and that history retains relevance today.

Notes

1. Bedfordshire and Luton Archives and Records Service LF 31/18
2. Shorter, Edward. 'A History of Psychiatry'. John Wiley. 1997. p 194
3. Pettigrew, Judith. Reynolds, Rory. Rouse, Sandra. 'A Place in the Country'. South Bedfordshire Community Health Care Trust. 1998. p 102
4. Shorter, p 104 - 9
5. Shorter, p 120 - ?
6. http://www.nice.org.uk/
7. Saunders, Jane. 'Quarantining the weak-minded: psychiatric definitions of degeneracy and the late-Victorian Asylum'. In 'The Anatomy of Madness. Vol III. Ed Bynum et al. Routledge. 1988 p 273 - 296
8. www.thecanadianencyclopedia.com/
9. Pettigrew et al, p 80 & 101
10. www.highfieldparktrust.co.uk
11. www.hertfordshire-genealogy.co.uk
12. Shorter, p 208 – 14
13. Shorter, p 226
14. Bedfordshire and Luton Archives and Records Service. LF 1/31, p 178

15. Monk, A. 'Fairfield: A Brief History', p 49. The Reverend Arthur Monk, the hospital chaplain, produced a number of statistics in his 1960 publication at the centenary of the hospital, but apologetically stated that he had only 3 months to produce it when 12 months was needed. Nevertheless he accumulated much useful information.
16. www.cqc.org.uk/_db/_documents/MHAC_Biennial_Report 0709_final.pdf
17. Pettigrew et al, p 102
18. Hunter, Richard & Macalpine, Ida. '300 Years of Psychiatry. 1535 – 1860" Oxford University Press. 1963. p 534 – 536
19. Hitchin Museum. Lawson Thompson Scrapbook (LTS). 3a, p 165
20. Wing, J & Brown, G. 'Social treatment of chronic schizophrenia: a comparative survey of three mental hospitals'. Journal of Mental Science. 1961. 107, 847-861
21. Monk, p 61
22. Mallett, Bernard. 'Community Care of the Mentally Ill with a Note of Progress in North Hertfordshire'. Guy's Hospital Reports. Vol 114. no.3. 1965. p 193 – 207
23. Kingdon, David. 'Transforming mental health services'. British Journal of Psychiatry (2011) 199: 1-2
24. Burns, Tom. 'The dog that failed to bark'. The Psychiatrist 2010; 34: 361-363
25. Whitwell, David. 'Recovery Beyond Psychiatry'. Free Association Books. 2005
26. Bracken, Pat and Thomas, Phil. 'Let's scrap schizophrenia'. http://www.critpsynet.freeuk.com/Sept99.htm
27. Roberts, Glen et al, 'Enabling Recovery'. Gaskell. 2006
28. Woodham-Smith,Cecil. 'The Great Hunger: Ireland: 1845-1849'. Penguin. 1992
29. Lawson Thompson Scrapbook. Vol 1, p 19
30. Hine, Reginald. 'The History of Hitchin'. George Allen & Unwin. Vol II, p 221

The herb-mixer, or apothecary. A woodcut used in Hine's "Hitchin Worthies' 1932. Wellcome Libraray, London [M00000457]

Appendix 1: Notes on the Lunacy Laws and Mental Health Acts.

1714 Vagrancy Act. Distinction made between lunatics and others - the rogues, vagabonds, sturdy beggars and vagrants. Lunatics exempted from whipping. Local magistrates (not one alone) could apprehend vagrants who were *"furiously mad and dangerous"*, no doctor required to assess them, and could safely lock them up – ie. in a gaol or house of correction, and could be removed from that parish if not settled or resident there, while the lunacy should continue – ie. no set period, for detention, restraint and maintenance.

1744 Vagrancy Act. Repeated specifications of 1714 Act but included provision of a charge for 'curing' such persons.

1774 Act for Regulating Private Madhouses. No person to take in more than one lunatic for profit without a licence. Within and up to 7 miles outside London licensing and visiting to be carried out by 5 Commissioners from the Royal College of Physicians, to be appointed annually by the College. No Commissioner should be directly or indirectly concerned in the keeping of any licensed house. Outside Metropolitan area licensing to be carried out by justices at the (County) Quarter Sessions - two justices and one physician to be nominated to make visits and reports. Visits to be done between 8am and 5pm. The Commissioners could not refuse to grant licences even if they knew that neglect or abuse of patients was happening. The only penalty was if the Commissioners were refused entry and then licences could be withdrawn. The proprietors had to send notice of reception of patients within 3 days of their admission; a medical order required for private patients but not for paupers.

1808 Better Care and Maintenance of Lunatics, being Paupers or Criminals, in England Act (County Asylum Act). Justices could erect an asylum. Committee of visiting justices to be appointed at Quarter Sessions for erection and periodic inspection of the asylum. Justices empowered to raise a county rate to pay for building the asylum. Patients to be admitted as under the 1744 Vagrancy Act – if 'dangerous at large' by authority of 2 justices, or justices could issue warrants on application by Overseers of the Poor. Discharge was by the visiting committee of justices.

1811 amendment. Allowed justices to refuse admission if there was not enough space at the asylum.

1815 amendment. Overseers of the poor required to provide returns on all idiots and lunatics within their parishes to the justices on request, and to provide a medical certificate for each. Any 2 justices could discharge patients.

1819 'Small Act'. Specified wording for certificates required. Patients could be admitted to the asylum by justices alone, not requiring overseers.

1828 Lunatic & Paupers or Criminals Maintenance (County Asylum) Act. Visiting justices to send annual returns of admission discharges and deaths to the Secretary of State for the Home Department. The Secretary of State could send visitors to inspect any asylum.

1828 Treatment of Insane Persons (Madhouse) Act. Metropolitan Commissioners replaced the Royal College of Physicians for licensing and inspecting London's licensed houses. Visitors to visit 4 times a year, and could do so at night if malpractice had been alleged on oath, and could revoke or refuse to issue licences. Certificates more detailed – private patients needed certificates signed by two doctors. Paupers to be admitted on signature of two justices or the parish overseer and one medical practitioner. Each house should have regular medical attention. Proprietors to keep records which could be inspected by visitors.

1834 Poor Law Amendment Act. Prohibited detention of dangerous lunatics and idiots in a workhouse for more than 2 weeks – but never fully observed.

1845 Lunatics Act. Lunacy Commission replaced Metropolitan Commission, had oversight of all arrangements for lunatics, JPs appointed by Quarter Sessions continued to license county asylums. Visiting somehow shared between JPs and Metropolitan Commissioners. LC to monitor & establish standards for certificates. Act prohibited any doctor interested in or attending licensed house from signing certificate for admission to that house.

1845 County Asylums Act. Mandatory for all counties to have an asylum

1886 Idiots Act. Sought to emphasise difference between lunatics and idiots, and specified admission and discharge procedures, which were the same as for lunatics.

1888 Local Government Act. County Councils took over responsibility for asylums from the Quarter Sessions.

1890 Lunacy Act. (which also applied to 'idiots'). Regarded as being very legalistic.

Admissions either - 1. Reception Order —for non paupers requiring relative making statement to justice of the peace (JP), supported by 2 medical certificates. 2. Urgency Order — for private patients when needed in a hurry, relative's petition and one medical certificate only, to last for just 7 days. 3. Summary Reception Order — usual for paupers. Poor law officer or police notified JP who issued an order which with one medical certificate authorized admission. If the person was found wandering then a poor law relieving officer or policeman could detain him for up to three days without certification. 4. Admission by Inquisition for Chancery lunatics – ie. those whose circumstances had been taken to court because of concerns over the control and management of property and wealth, involving the court of Chancery, an order being sought for both the admission of the person and the administration of their estate. This had roots in the *Praerogativa Regis* of Edward II – the starting point of lunacy legislation (Kathleen Jones. 'A History of the Mental Health Services'.).

The orders were to last for 12 months in the first instance.

Visits by the Lunacy commission to public and private asylums, more to the latter as public asylums were also to be visited 2 monthly by 2 members of the management committee.

Discharge could be done in various ways depending on who was involved in requesting or petitioning for admission, but these could be barred by the medical officer.

1913 Mental Deficiency Act. This covered four defined classes - idiots, imbeciles, feeble-minded persons and moral defectives, their condition having been present since birth or an early age. The Board of Control replaced the Lunacy Commission. Local authorities (county councils) to set up mental deficiency committees to identify cases, provide and maintain institutions for them and care for them in the community. Local education committee had special responsibility for them.

1924 – 6. Royal Commission on Lunacy and Mental Disorder. Talked about the mentally ill and not lunatics, and compared them with the physically ill. Noted that paupers was term used for those in public asylums, whether they were paying for the treatment or not. Keynote change from detention to prevention and treatment. The idea of community care was raised and MACA praised. Local authorities encouraged to set up out-patient clinics. Mental hospital should have less than a thousand patients.

1927 Mental Deficiency Act. Definition expanded 'mental deficiency' to all those who suffered arrested or incomplete development of the mind before the age of 18. Occupation and training became statutory responsibility of local authorities.

1929 Local Government Act. Board of Guardians abolished and the Poor Law replaced by Public Assistance Committees in county councils; pauper became 'rate-aided person'.

1930 Mental Treatment Act. Made provision for voluntary treatment, as well as 'temporary' and 'certified' patients, though voluntary patients had to give 3 days' notice of intention to leave hospital; county councils to establish psychiatric out-patient clinics; 'asylum' to be replaced by 'mental hospital' and 'lunatic' by 'patient' or 'person of unsound mind'.

1959 Mental Health Act. Replaced all previous acts. Emergency, assessment and treatment orders could be used by duly approved psychiatrists, other doctors and social workers. Mental Health Tribunals became the appeal body to review detentions, consisting of medical, legal and lay members. Overall intention was to make mental illness like physical illness with predominantly informal admissions to hospitals, and for local councils to be responsible for social care of people who did not need inpatient psychiatric treatment.

1983 Mental Health Act. Introduced specific conditions for treatment of detained patients, approved social workers to take responsibility for admission procedures under section (formal detention), and the Mental Health Act Commission to monitor the operation of the Act and the standards of in-patient units.

2007 Mental Health Act. Introduced supervised community treatment so that patients at home could be required to take treatment and if they refuse they can be returned to hospital – all intending to help people continuing on their treatment and reduce the likelihood of relapsing and needing an admission to hospital.

Keys to the asylum. Three Counties Asylum had two main wings.
one for males and the other for females, with separate keys.
These keys from collection of Richard Knight, photo by author

Appendix 2: Diagnosis, making sense of the disordered mind

"When I use a word," Humpty Dumpty said in a rather scornful tone, *"it means just what I choose it to mean, - neither more nor less".* Quoted of course from 'Alice Through the Looking Glass', and by Andrew Sims who goes on to say *"Diagnosis is much more than a word plucked out of the air and pinned onto a hapless 'patient'. It conveys meaning about the antecedents of the present state, about other conditions which are similar and, most important of all, about what is likely to happen in the future and, therefore, what should be done about it"* [1].

Doctors have tried to make sense of the speech and behaviour of people over the past centuries. This is not an exact science. 'Melancholia' and 'mania' were the main diagnoses used in the 17th century. Doctors were trying to make sense of the conditions and apply appropriate treatments. Amongst other treatments warm baths were advocated for melancholics, who were under-active, and cold baths for those found to be manic, or over-active. The word mania remains in use but has been refined over the years, now meaning a disturbance of mood, observed as a happy, talkative and overactive state. The person loses inhibitions and can act inappropriately and irresponsibly. While this can be useful in small doses, it is antisocial and personally damaging if persistent. The person breaks out of usual restraints, does things they might otherwise be frightened of doing, but can be more creative and productive. They can also upset others while not realising so, spend money which they do not have, and put themselves in dangerous situations because they fail to recognize risk, or assume that they have extraordinary powers. 'Melancholia' has disappeared from usage as a diagnosis, now replaced by the various forms of depression, which are classified as 'affective' or 'mood' disorders. If someone experiences both mania and depression then this is called a bipolar disorder.

Schizophrenia may have been called mania, or lunacy, or phrensie or simply madness in the 18th century. In the 19th century it may also have been called monomania, moral insanity, dementia or even melancholia. Other diagnoses in use then were delirium tremens, as now, referring to people experiencing the withdrawal from high alcohol consumption, general paralysis of the insane, or syphilis affecting the brain, epilepsy, idiocy and imbecility.

In 1893 Emile Kraepelin used the term 'dementia praecox' for what he thought was a single disorder, and that name was replaced by 'schizophrenia' in the 1920s. As different features of this condition were recognized subtypes were named as hebephrenic, paranoid, catatonic and simple schizophrenia, each type having more of one symptom than another from a range of abnormal behaviours and experiences. Some people experienced hallucinations such as hearing voices, some developed delusions or false beliefs, such as believing that they had special powers or were being ruthlessly persecuted. Others had very mixed up thinking where words lost their usual meanings, new words were substituted, and understanding what other people were talking about became difficult. Some developed abnormal postures and movements and some just withdrew and said and did nothing. However there was so much cross-over between these types of behaviour that the classification made little sense, and did not help in guiding doctors as to the type of treatments that might be useful for the different types of disorder. In trying to make sense of how different people experienced this condition the symptoms were then divided into positive and negative. Positive symptoms being hallucinations or delusions, negative being lack of emotions, disruption of normal thinking, social withdrawal and apathy.

In the 1970s it was realised that when somebody in the United Kingdom talked about 'schizophrenia' they meant something different from what was meant by the term in the USA. Different ideas and perceptions had fed into what each community understood by the word. By then various studies had been done on what treatments had been found useful for people with this illness, but if the treatments were not being given for the same problem, then there could be no real comparison with treatments on the other side of the Atlantic [2]. Such unhelpful differences have been reduced by attempts to be clearer in describing the symptoms, or phenomenon, experienced when people are unwell. Certain criteria have been used, such as 'how long has this been happening', 'has there been any change of mood such as depression or mania preceding any changes in behaviour', and 'has the person used any mind-altering drugs recently'. The attempt to identify clearly what people experience and describe when they are unwell, has led to researchers using the same words when asking questions about those experiences. The research interviews have been standardized, and manuals used so that the wording of questions is identical. All of this has helped in the process of making the diagnosis, and ensuring that what is described in one place would be the same elsewhere.

Diagnostic classifications have been developed with clear definitions of what the words mean, and what different types of disorders are being described. The American system is called the Diagnostic Statistical Manual of the American Psychiatric Association, DSM for short, now in its 4th version. In England the International Classification of Diseases (ICD), now in its 10th edition, issued by the World Health Organisation, is more likely to be used. Each is revised to refine and improve its usefulness.

Notes

1. Sims, Andrew. 'Symptoms in the Mind'. W.B. Saunders. 2nd edition 1995
2. Leff, Julian. 'International Variations in the Diagnosis of Psychiatric Illness'. British Journal of Psychiatry. 1977 131: 329-338

Sources

My schooldays' history seemed to give me an idea that there were just facts to be learnt. Reading in the history of mental health reveals different ways of discovering, interpreting and understanding the *"facts"*. A thesis by Sarah York, 'Suicide, Lunacy and the Asylum in Nineteenth-Century England' http://etheses.bham.ac.uk/801/1/York10PhD.pdf, gives some guide to understanding these different ways, with 'whigs', 'radicals' and 'revisionists' all writing about the history of mental health, represented in the list below by respectively Kathleen Jones, Andrew Scull and Roy Porter.

Books

Anderson, Brian: 'Nearly a Century. History of Hill End Hosp, 1899 – 1995'. *Hertfordshire Archives and Local Studies Acc 3959 1996*

Arnold, Catherine: 'Bedlam: London and Its Mad'. *Simon & Schuster 2008*

Bell, Patricia Ed: 'Southill and the Whitbreads'. *S C Whitbread 1995*

Brundage, Anthony: 'The English Poor Laws, 1700 – 1930'. *Palgrave 2002*

Bulwer Lytton, Rosina: 'A Blighted Life: a True Story', Intro by Marie Mulvey Roberts. *Thoemmes Press 1994, reprint of 1880 edition*

Bynum, Porter and Shepherd, Ed: 'The Anatomy of Madness' Vol II & III. *Tavistock Publications 1985*

Cashman, Bernard: 'A Proper House; Bedford Lunatic Asylum 1812 – 1860'. *North Bedfordshire Health Authority 1992*

Dickson, Mora: 'Teacher Extraordinary'. *The Book Guild 1986*

Fennell, Phil: 'Treatment Without Consent - Law, psychiatry and the treatment of mentally disordered people since 1845'. *Routledge 1996*

Fulford, Roger: 'A Study in Opposition'. *Macmillan 1967*

Higgs, Michelle: 'Life in the Victorian and Edwardian Workhouse'. *The History Press 2009*

Hunter, Richard and Macalpine, Ida: '300 Years in Psychiatry 1535 – 1860'. *Oxford University Press 1963*

Hunter, Richard and Macalpine, Ida: 'George 3rd and the Mad Business'. *Pimlico 1991*

Hunter, Richard and Macalpine, Ida: 'Psychiatry for the Poor; 1851 Colney Hatch Asylum - Friern Hospital 1973'. *Dawsons of Pall Mall 1974*

Jones, Kathleen: 'A History of the Mental Health Services'. *Routledge Keagan & Paul 1972*

Jones, Kathleen: 'Lunacy Law and Conscience 1744 – 1845'. *Routledge Keagan & Paul 1955*

Mitchell, Leslie: 'Bulwer Lytton - The Rise and Fall of a Victorian Man of Letters'. *Hambleton and London 2003*

Monk, Revd. Arthur: 'Fairfield Hospital - A Brief History, 1860 – 1960'. *Fairfield Hospital 1960, reprint 1978*

Parry- Jones, William Llewellyn: 'Trade in Lunacy'. *Routledge Kegan and Paul 1972*

Pettigrew, Judith; Reynolds, Rory; Rouse Sandra: 'A Place in the Country ; Three Counties Asylum 1860 – 1998'. *South Bedfordshire Community Health Care Trust 1998*

Pinel, Philippe: 'Medico-Philosophical Treatise on Mental Alienation', 2nd edition 1809, Retranslated 2008. *Wiley–Blackwell 2008*

Porter, Roy: 'Madmen; A Social History of Madhouses, Mad-Doctors & Lunatics'. *Tempus, illustr edn 2004 (first published as 'Mind Forg'd Manacles', 1987)*

Porter, Roy: 'The Greatest Benefit to Mankind'. *Fontana Press 1999*

Porter, Roy: 'Madness - A Brief History'. *Oxford University Press 2002*

Preston, Jane: 'That Odd Rich Old Woman'. *Plush Publishing 1998*

Rapp, Dean: 'Samuel Whitbread 1764 - 1815 A Social and Political Study'. *Garland Publ 1987*

Roberts, Glen; Davenport, Sarah; Holloway, Frank; Tattan, Theresa; Ed: 'Enabling Recovery – the principles and practice of rehabilitation psychiatry'. *Gaskell 2006*

Scull, Andrew: 'Madhouses, mad-doctors and madmen - The social history of psychiatry in the Victorian era'. *Athlone Press 1981.*

Scull, Andrew: 'Masters of Bedlam'. *Princeton University Press 1996*

Scull, Andrew: 'The Most Solitary of Afflictions; Madness and Society in Britain 1700 – 1900'. *Yale University Press 1993*

Shorter, Edward: 'A History of Psychiatry'. *John Wiley 1997*

Sutherland, J: 'Victorian Fiction - Writers, Publishers, Readers'. *Palgrave Macmillan; 2nd Revised edition 2005*

Walker, Simon: 'The Witches of Hertfordshire'. *Tempus Publ 2004*

Whitmore, Richard: 'Mad Lucas'. *North Hertfordshire District Council 1983*

Whitwell, David: 'Recovery Beyond Psychiatry'. *Free Association Books 2005*

Amongst many other websites -

www.hertfordshire-genealogy.co.uk
www.oxforddnb.com, (Oxford Dictionary of National Biography. Oxford University Press)
www.studymore.org.uk
www.threecountiesasylum.co.uk
www.workhouses.org.uk

Websites are updated and do change. Those used in the book were correct at the time of publication, but may not remain so!

Archives

Bedfordshire and Luton Archives & Records Service, Borough Hall, Cauldwell Street, Bedford, MK42 9AP
Hertfordshire Archives and Local Studies, County Hall, Pegs Lane, Hertford, SG13 8EJ
Hitchin Museum, Paynes Park, Hitchin, SG5 1EH
Knebworth House, Knebworth, SG3 6PY
National Archives, Kew, Surrey, TW9 4DU
Royal College of Psychiatrists, http://bjp.rcpsych.org/

Index

Hitchin Historical Society

The Society aims to increase and spread knowledge of the history of Hitchin, and is a registered charity. We hold regular meetings on the fourth Thursday of most months and arrange visits to local buildings and institutions, many of which are not normally open to the general public. We also organize trips to places of historical interest further afield. Members receive a regular newsletter and magazine, the Hitchin Journal. The Society also produces high-quality publications on the history of the town based on research into the origins and development of buildings, organizations, crafts, trades and other aspects of historical interest.

The Hitchin apothecary, William Drage, wrote in 1664 on how to cure *"Womb Melancholly"*, presumably meaning depression in women, with the following words :-

long continuance of this Disease, whenas 'tis very hard (if at all cura-
ble) to be removed.

C U R E.

Bleeding is first to be instituted (after an orderly Dyet, as is prescribed in the General Chapter of Melancholy) by Bleeding, open the
Cubit-Vein first; then, if the *Menstrua* be stopt, open the Ankle-Vein
some days before they are to come down: If Blood be more hot and black
according to the *Galenical* Rule, we may more freely draw it out.

2. Preparation, and Alteration of the melancholy Humour, is to be
made, by Cordials and Specificals for Melancholy ; Borage, Buglofs,
Dodder of Time, Balm, Rosemary, Archangel, Woodroof, Violet-
Leaves, Vipers Buglofs, Fumitary, Featherfew, &c. boild in Whey
clarified, and drunk ; or Syrups of the Juyce of Apples , of Dodder
of Time, of Borage, and the like, or Julaps of those Syrups and White-
Wine, or Cordial distilled Waters are good for variety and change,
which sometimes greatly pleaseth the Sick.

3. Purge with such as properly purge Melancholy, and are made
friendly to the *Uterus,* by the mixing therewith Specificals to carry the
force of the Medicine to operate more specifically upon the *Uterus.*

If she be Costive, help that by often Clifters. Medicines in substance, as in Pills, do dry too much, therefore Potions, or purging Julaps are preferred ; Extract of black Hellebore, of *Lapis Lazuli,* &c.
are Medicinal.

Venery is very helpful for her, acted moderately and seasonably.

Emollient and moistening Bathes are good, both to moisten and tem-
per, and hinder thick and dry Evaporations, and appease watching; for
which, if it be immoderate, we must use somnoriferous Emulsions, Julaps
and Applications to her Head, Pomanders to smell to ; and in extremi-
ty of watching, *Laudanum* to two or three Grains, may be given.

Comforters of the Heart, and Cherishers of the Spirits, are continually to be given, and whatever may avert and turn away Melancholy,
and make her chearful.

From the collection of Dr Gerry Tidy